LORD ACTON

LORD ACTON

A STUDY IN CONSCIENCE
AND POLITICS

by

GERTRUDE HIMMELFARB

THE UNIVERSITY OF CHICAGO PRESS
CHICAGO . ILLINOIS

THE UNIVERSITY OF CHICAGO PRESS, CHICAGO 37
Routledge & Kegan Paul, Ltd., London, England
W. J. Gage & Co., Limited, Toronto 2B, Canada

CONTENTS

CONTENTS

INTRODUCTION

LORD ACTON was born three years before Queen Victoria
ascended the throne and died the year after her death.
The only England he knew, Victorian England, is now a
civilization lost beyond recovery. Yet it is only now, while
his background recedes ever further from sight, that Acton
himself is beginning to come, for the first time, clearly into
view. It appears that we are privileged to see and understand
him as his contemporaries never did. He is of this age, more
than of his. He is, indeed, one of our great contemporaries.

It took almost forty years for Acton to come into his own.
In the epoch of complacency before and after the First World
War, men had little liking for the kind of intense spiritual
probing that Acton demanded of them. Acton was a pessimist
and a moralist, a combination hardly likely to endear him to a
world that was at the same time expansively optimistic and
narrowly materialistic. When the spiritual climate changed,
however, Acton found his home. Men who have witnessed
the horrors of German Nazism and Soviet Communism have
little heart for optimism or materialism and much respect for
such hard truths as 'power tends to corrupt and absolute
power corrupts absolutely'. Acton's well-turned epigrams denouncing nationalism, racism, and statism give a new literary
flavour to editorial sermons and academic dissertations.
Liberals who have come to be sceptical of the virtues of a
secular, placid and optimistic Liberalism have discovered in
Acton a Liberalism, religious in temper, which is able to cope
with the facts of human sin and corruption. Historians who
once regarded salvation as the automatic and inevitable by-

product of historical progress now find themselves agreeing with Acton that salvation requires an exercise of moral will, that the historian must sometimes turn his back upon the course of history and resist the 'wave of the future'. Because Acton was never taken in by history, he can speak with authority when history runs amok.

In the early part of the century, it was not Acton's ideas that men thought of when they thought of him at all, but the intriguing details of his personality. After his death, there was the usual outpouring of gracious obituaries and memorials. When his work was published in volume form for the first time, posthumously, most of the reviews were uncritical and undiscerning. Scholars paid brief tribute to his learning and Catholics quarrelled spasmodically about his orthodoxy. His name flickered here and there through the copious pages of Victorian memoirs. There were reminiscences about his fabulous erudition, his bibliophilic triumphs, his conversational skill and pedagogic ineptitude. There was much wonder and admiration but little genuine sympathy or understanding. When his son thought to commission an official life of his father, he turned to the leading Catholic biographer of the time, Wilfrid Ward. But Ward, himself the son of one of Acton's great antagonists, sensibly declined the invitation, explaining that filial piety deprived him of the proper feeling for his subject. No life has been written, and no adequate biography or critical study.

The present study is not so much the biography of a life as the biography of a mind. To Acton, ideas were the moving forces of the world. Since he was himself an exponent of what has since become known as 'the history of ideas', it is appropriate that his biography take the form of an intellectual biography. Indeed, it is hardly possible to conceive of any other kind of biography of Acton, for the drama of his life was the drama of his ideas. His conflicts with the Church, his quarrel with Döllinger, his teaching of history, his sense of his own purpose and character—all of these were motivated and determined by his ideas.

The most common flaw of intellectual biographies is that they tend to 'over-intellectualize' their subjects. In the act of recording and elucidating an idea, there lurks the temptation to systematize and organize it, often beyond the intention of the original thinker. The temptation is particularly strong in the case of Acton (himself an unsystematic although profound thinker), and if indulged in can do great violence to his ideas. The best protection against this is to keep as close to the text as possible, and not to permit interpretation or generalization to wander too far from their source in his writings. If parts of this study read like exercises in textual analysis, it is because I have wished to render the ideas of Acton faithfully and precisely. If at other times I have seemed to carp about his evasions or inconsistencies, it is because I have tried to take those ideas seriously, as he himself would have liked us to take them.

Six years have passed since I first decided upon the subject of this work, and during that time I have incurred many obligations. To no one am I more indebted than to Professor Louis Gottschalk, who has always given generously of his encouragement and assistance, not in this undertaking alone but in all that I have done since my first graduate studies at the University of Chicago. I take this occasion, too, to thank the other members of the Department of History of the University, particularly Professors William T. Hutchinson, S. William Halperin and the late Frances Gillespie, for the award of the fellowship that made it possible for me to examine Acton's manuscripts in England and for the benefit of their counsel. To Professor Herbert Butterfield of Cambridge University I am grateful for stimulating talks about Acton, and to both Professor and Mrs. Butterfield for their kindness to me in Cambridge in 1946–7. I remember with delight an afternoon in London with Dr. G. P. Gooch, who favoured me with reminiscences about Acton, his former teacher. At the London School of Economics, Professor Friedrich Hayek gave me an account of his efforts to establish an international Acton Society to promote the ideals of liberty and morality; and at Oxford University Dr. A. L. Poole, President of St. John's College, graciously permitted me to examine the letters written by Acton to his father, R. L. Poole. Others who earned my gratitude by reading and criticizing this work include Professor Alan Simpson, Professor Yves Simon, Daniel Bell, my brother Milton Himmelfarb, and my husband Irving Kristol. The library staffs of Cambridge University (particularly of the Anderson Room, where the Acton manuscripts are kept), the British Museum, the University of Chicago, Columbia University, the University of Pennsylvania, and the New York Public Library have been helpful in providing me with the material for this work.

I

VARIETIES OF ARISTOCRACY

LORD ACTON was looked upon as something of a curiosity even in his own day. Those who met him did not know whether to be more impressed with his fabulous erudition or with his exalted social position and it was commonly said of him that he knew everyone worth knowing and had read everything worth reading. When he was not himself entertaining on his English or Bavarian estate, he was likely to be a guest at one of the great houses of England or the Continent; at the same time his friends estimated that he read, annotated and practically committed to memory an average of two octavo volumes a day. His authority was sought to mediate an obscure point regarding the authorship of a sixteenth-century document, to explain the intention and anticipate the decision of the Cabinet, to reveal the latest gossip about an approaching marriage. He knew personally most of the distinguished historians and philosophers of Europe and America, and his intimates were numbered among the ruling Whig families, the old Tory aristocracy and Continental royalty; the names would read like a roster of nineteenth-century celebrities, starting with Cardinal Newman and ending with Prime Minister Gladstone or the Empress Frederick. He was well known in the papal court and at Windsor Castle. One of the most famous English Catholic laymen of his generation, he blandly announced that his favourite theologian was the German Protestant, Richard Rothe. It was hinted that he had been entrusted with a secret and solitary mission to Bismarck at a critical period of Anglo-German diplomacy in the 1870's, and that he had ghost-written some of the most learned books of his contemporaries. At table with his family he chatted in English with his children, in German with his wife, in French with his sister-in-law, and in Italian with his mother-in-law. He was a handsome man; the poet Richard Lowell said of him, 'He is one of the few men I have ever met, the inside of whose head more than keeps the promise of the out—and in his case that is saying a great deal.'[1] Lady Monkswell was equally favourably impressed but wavered between the conviction that however mixed his racial origins, his appearance was all 'John Bull', and 'whatever his heart is his head is French'.[2]

From this profusion of virtues and accomplishments there emerges the pattern of tragedy. For all of his erudition, Acton never produced a single full-sized volume for publication, and we know him to-day by posthumous collections of his periodical pieces, correspondence and lectures. The intellectual task toward which his life was oriented, the History of Liberty, is to-day, at best, 'the greatest book that never was written'.[3] This historian, who would plunder the archives for the little fact that made the difference but would take nothing less than all of history for his province, ended his life as the editor of an often uninspired co-operative work, the *Cambridge Modern History*, and as a lecturer doomed to speak past his audience. His thousand boxes of notes and notebooks, containing enough material and ideas for dozens of volumes, he bequeathed to the Cambridge University Library, where he hoped an enterprising scholar, after his death, might compose the history of liberty he had failed to write. It is a sad testimonial to the tragedy of wasted labour, and a feeble commemoration of a brilliant mind, that this mass of notes has here been exploited not for a history of liberty but for an intellectual biography of Acton.

His talents were prodigious and his situation brilliant. If

---

[1] *Memoirs and Letters of Sir James Paget*, ed. Stephen Paget (London, 1901), p. 405.

[2] Mary Monkswell, *A Victorian Diarist*, ed. E. C. F. Collier (London, 1944), pp. 158 and 230.

[3] L. M. Phillipps, *Europe Unbound* (London, 1916), p. 147 n.

he failed, it was, paradoxically, because his will to perfection was so irresistible. Just as his exorbitant scholarly standards tended to frustrate his productivity, so his moral scruples made him suspect in his religious communion. A Liberal Catholic, he was too Liberal for the Catholics and too Catholic for the Liberals. He accepted Roman Catholicism as the universal Church and its dogmas as the true statements of tradition and authority, but he quarrelled bitterly with the history of the Church and with its contemporary politics. Dedicated to the idea that religion was the essence of history, he nevertheless devoted a major part of his efforts to a criticism of institutional religion. Nor could he identify himself with any of the dominant philosophies of his day or feel kinship with the great men of his generation; the secularism of Mill and Morley, the positivism of Comte and Buckle, and the sceptical Protestantism of Matthew Arnold were equally alien to him.

Neither Liberals nor Catholics could afford to take Acton entirely seriously. His absolute moral standards were admirable but impossible of fulfilment, and he must often have impressed them as a profoundly eccentric doctrinaire. The statesman or ecclesiast who decided on public policy, the official who executed it, and the spectator or historian who passively condoned it were all subject to his implacable judgment. He could converse with much grace and wit to a casual dinner partner, but when he sensed that his former professor and close friend, Ignaz von Döllinger, was not so ruthlessly moral as himself, he declared that the time had come 'for our conversations to cease, for this world'.[1] Situated almost at the centre of the intellectual, political and religious life of his time, and acquainted with its leading personalities, he had good reason to complain of his isolation: 'I am absolutely alone in my essential ethical position';[2] 'I never had any contemporaries.'[3]

Acton died in 1902. It took some forty years for men to rediscover him, to find in him a prophet for our times. Long

[1] Cambridge University Library, Add. MSS., 5403. See below, p. 153.
[2] ibid, p. 154.
[3] 3 June 1881, *Letters of Lord Acton to Mary Gladstone*, ed. Herbert Paul (1st ed.; London, 1905), p. 208.

before nationalism, racism and 'democratic despotism' had assumed their virulent forms, he had predicted that they would some day threaten our civilization. Half a century before the recent religious revival, he had warned of the sterility of a materialistic, relativistic secularism. And the 'history of ideas' that is finally becoming respectable in academic institutions might adopt as its charter Acton's inaugural lecture delivered in 1895 when he accepted the chair of Regius Professor of Modern History at Cambridge University. What distinguishes him from so many other 'prophets' laboriously resurrected from history is the fact that he was a prophet in his own time as well, which is a more impressive feat than merely prophesying for a later time. This is the meaning of his isolation and the significance of his idea of absolute morality. Other men can and must traffic in the compromises, concessions and expedients that make up political and social life; the prophet cannot. John Morley, an eminently reasonable and sensible man, who knew Acton well, used to say of him that he was a standing riddle. Yet it was Morley who also said: 'If the gods granted me the privilege of recalling to life for half an hour's conversation some of the great men of the past I have had the good fortune to know, I should say Acton.'[1]

Acton was the unique combination of high moralist and man of the world. The first was a product of education, the second a circumstance of birth.

The Actons were an old English family of country squires, who are recorded as having occupied the estate of Aldenham in Shropshire as far back as the beginning of the fourteenth century.[2] During the Civil War, a Richard Acton was removed by the House of Commons as Lord Mayor of London, and in compensation Charles I awarded him the baronetcy. The Tory

[1] John H. Morgan, *John, Viscount Morley* (London, 1924), pp. 89–90. Dr. G. P. Gooch, in a conversation I had with him in the spring of 1947, fondly recalled this remark.

[2] Acton, the suburb of London, has no relation to the Acton family. Its name is said to be derived from 'Oak town', in the days when a forest covered the area.

sympathies of the family thus entrenched, Sir Edward Acton's name appeared on the list of those who opposed granting the crown to William and Mary following the 'Glorious Revolution'.[1] Another Sir Richard Acton, of the next century, summarily dissolved the Tory-Anglican ties of his ancestors by embracing Roman Catholicism in the 1750's. Soon after he died, in 1791, the title and estate reverted to a younger, less austere branch of the family, also Catholic, which had settled in France and then in Italy. By securing the affections of the Queen of Naples, John Acton had managed to convert the role of adventurer into the rank of Prime Minister of Naples. Succeeding to the English baronetcy, Sir John continued to live abroad even after his marriage, effected by special papal dispensation, to his niece. His grandson and namesake John Edward Emerich Dalberg Acton, was born to his eldest son, Sir Ferdinand Richard Edward Acton, in Naples on 10 January 1834.

Acton's mother, Marie Pelline de Dalberg, came from an older and more illustrious family than the Actons. Legend had it that the ancestor of the Dalbergs was no less than a relation of Jesus Christ, who had become a Roman soldier and had settled at Herrnsheim on the Rhine to found the ancestral estate. If this tale is apocryphal, and if the heritage was not quite so exalted, it was sufficiently distinguished in a profane way. 'Ist kein Dalberg da?' was a well-known expression in Germany as late as the nineteenth century. In 1494 Emperor Maximilian I had granted the Dalbergs the honour of being the first to be knighted at the coronation, and until the dissolution of the Holy Roman Empire it had remained the custom, during the ceremonies conferring knighthood, to inquire whether a Dalberg was present so that he might receive the privilege first. In the late eighteenth and early nineteenth centuries the Dalbergs shared the uncertain fate of the Empire. Duke Emeric Josef, Acton's grandfather, represented, like his paternal grandfather, a cadet branch of the family. He became a nationalized French subject during the Napoleonic wars, served in the provisional Government of 1814, accompanied Talleyrand as plenipotentiary to the Congress of Vienna, and

[1] *The Somers Tracts* (4 vols.; London, 1750), 2d. series, IV, 127-30.

after the Restoration was made a Minister of State and peer of France. Herrnsheim, the sole property to survive war and confiscation, descended to his only child Marie.

Aldenham and Herrnsheim eventually passed to Acton and became his main residences. Yet he never played the conventional part of either the English country squire or the Continental aristocrat. Nor was the tradition of the political adventurer or careerist, exhibited in different ways in the lives of both grandparents, more congenial. His paternal grandfather had died in 1811, his maternal grandfather in 1833, a year before Acton's birth, so that Acton himself knew neither personally. If he concerned himself with public affairs, it was only sporadically, in response to special principles and ideas, rather than in obedience to party and position. The activities of his paternal grandparent, in particular, including a period as head of a reign of terror in Palermo, were repugnant to him, and in spite of financial stringency later in life he refused to accept money due to him from the Italian fortune.

The Catholic controversialist and the historian were prefigured in Acton's family tree, but again not in forms particularly agreeable to him. Karl Theodor von Dalberg, uncle of Emeric Josef, had been archbishop-elector of Mainz and arch-chancellor of the Holy Roman Empire. With the dissolution of the Empire, he became an ardent partisan of Napoleon and was appointed prince primate of the Confederation of the Rhine. Acton could not have felt much affection for the ancestor who favoured a national Church subordinate to the State, and whose subservience to Napoleon was so marked that the latter's defeat brought a serious and permanent decline in his own position. On his father's side there was a less distant and more sympathetic ecclesiast. His uncle, Charles Edward Januarius Acton, was proclaimed a cardinal in January 1842, when John Acton was just eight years old. But there is little reason to suppose that before his death in 1847 he had exercised any very important influence on Acton's early life. Certainly Acton did not often find himself in the good graces of Rome that his uncle habitually enjoyed. The historian, another bequest of the paternal line, was Edward Gibbon, who boasted in his memoirs of his relation to 'that

6

ancient and loyal family of Shropshire baronets'.[1] For his own part Acton was less inclined to boast of his relationship with the historian who brashly described the rise of Christianity as 'the triumph of barbarism and religion', and he must have counted himself fortunate that he personally had no Gibbon blood, the Gibbons having been related only to the older branch of the family.

Acton's father died at an early age, leaving a young widow and the three-year-old son who succeeded him as eighth baronet.[2] With Lady Acton's remarriage in 1840, the family circle acquired another illustrious name and a new social tradition in the person of Lord Leveson, later the second Earl Granville. The Leveson-Gowers had been influential in English politics for generations, and Leveson's father, the first Earl Granville, held the coveted position of ambassador in Paris from 1824 to 1841.

The Granvilles were as important in the Whig political aristocracy as the Actons were in the country squirearchy and the Dalbergs among the nobility on the Continent. By the beginning of the nineteenth century a social fusion of the three aristocratic traditions was taking place, a process that was particularly marked in Paris, the melting pot of all aristocracies with cosmopolitan pretensions. While the Granvilles occupied the Paris embassy, the Dalbergs had a prominent place in the circle centring around Talleyrand, and the Actons maintained a house in the Faubourg St. Honoré. During the Paris 'season', it was inevitable that the three families should find themselves at the same balls, dinner parties and soirées.[3]

Lord Leveson, the eldest son of the Granvilles, had been educated at Eton and Christ Church, Oxford, before entering

[1] *Memoirs of My Life and Writings*, ed. Lord Sheffield ('World's Classics'; London, 1907), p. 12. See D. M. Low, *Edward Gibbon* (London, 1937), p. 182, for an incident involving Edward Gibbon and an earlier John Acton.

[2] An account of the death of Richard Acton, as he was generally known, is in Augustus Craven, *Récit d'une soeur* (2 vols.; Paris, 1892), II, 66–7.

[3] See *The Letters of Harriet, Countess Granville*, ed. F. Leveson Gower, (2 vols.; London, 1894), I, 380, for a caustic account of a party given by the Dalbergs.

upon his political career. He was Under-Secretary for Foreign Affairs in Lord Melbourne's Whig Ministry when he became engaged to Lady Acton, who had been a widow for three years. Although the match was socially agreeable, the difference in religion—Leveson belonged to the Church of England —raised serious difficulties. At one point the engagement was actually broken when Lady Acton insisted that the children of the marriage be Catholic. The differences were reconciled, however, and Leveson's sister, Lady Georgiana Fullerton (later a convert to Catholicism and an industrious author of didactic novels) declared herself much taken with her brother's fiancée, particularly with her extreme seriousness in religious matters.[1]

After her marriage, Lady Leveson continued to practise the piety for which she was noted. Since there were no children of her second marriage, she was not confronted with the disagreeable task of raising her sons as Anglicans. She was distracted neither by her new relations nor by the elegant and splendid society of Paris, Rome, Naples and London. Lord Leveson's younger brother, who spent the Easter vacation of 1841 in Rome with the recently married couple, recalled, many years later, his impressions of the 'leading society' of the city—'it was of course reactionary and clerical'—and the rigours of the Lenten fast which he and his brother alleviated by secretly repairing to a restaurant.[2]

Neither then nor later was Acton tempted to engage in such escapades. He carried into adulthood the devoutness to which he had been accustomed by his mother in childhood. His religious sensibility, deriving from this time and atmosphere, had not the emotional and romantic daring of some of the converts, but neither was it simply the product of intellectual demonstration and conviction. It was a sober and serious acceptance of deeply rooted beliefs which had commanded his assent since his earliest days, so that whatever his later difficulties with the Church, he never faltered in his religious duties and practices.

[1] Augustus Craven, *Life of Lady Georgiana Fullerton*, tr. H. J. Coleridge (London, 1888), p. 106.

[2] F. Leveson Gower, *Bygone Years* (London, 1905), p. 34.

It is not surprising that Acton should have been so little moved by the fact of his stepfather's Anglicanism; Leveson himself was not excessively troubled by religious scruples. What was important to Leveson—and this he made available to Acton—was a social and political environment which defined his character, his career and his interests. Upon the death of his father, Leveson became the second Earl Granville and assumed his position in the Anglican-Whig hierarchy that ruled England, a hierarchy that prided itself on its enlightened broad-mindedness and liberality, while it rested secure in its privilege and power. Granville's liberality was no ideological or sentimental fancy. It came to him, together with the tradition of political power, as an adjunct of his inherited estate. What distinguished his Liberalism most sharply from Toryism was his sponsorship of free trade, and this his biographer explained in terms of the special character of the family property, which was regarded 'as a source of mining and manufacturing wealth rather than of agricultural enterprise'.[1]

That the Granvilles were Whigs rather than Tories, however, was less important than the fact that they were aristocrats and not commoners. On the issue of free trade Granville was allied with the Radicals, Cobden and Bright, but in all other respects there was little in common between the Whig leaders, descendants of the great families of England, and the new, belligerently middle-class element in Parliament. Granville, related to the Gowers, Howards and Cavendishes, could never be accused of sharing what Acton later contemptuously described as Cobden's 'essentially bourgeois way of looking at things'.[2]

Granville possessed the temperament that went with a long tradition of parliamentary rule. He was the archetype of the Victorian Whig diplomat: supple, suave, amiable, loyal to his party, eminently practical. Acton's temperament clearly owed little to his stepfather. There was a brief period, early in his school days, when he proudly modelled himself on Granville,

[1] E. Fitzmaurice, *Life of Granville George Leveson Gower, Second Earl Granville* (2 vols.; London, 1905), I, 38.

[2] Mountstuart E. Grant Duff, *Notes from a Diary*, 1851-72 (2 vols.; London, 1897), I, 285.

proclaiming his allegiance to Whiggism and to the stock-hero of the Whigs, Macaulay. But he was soon disabused of the merits of both the party and the historian. And although later still Granville and Acton sat together in the Liberal Party, they were worlds apart in their political attitudes. When Acton became an enthusiastic Liberal it was under the more high-spirited and high-minded—more doctrinaire, at any rate—tutelage of Gladstone.

II

APPRENTICESHIP IN CATHOLICISM

THE most conspicuous circumstance of Acton's career as of his birth was its cosmopolitanism. He was almost equally at home in England, Germany, France and Italy; they were the scenes of his domestic and social life, the arenas of intellectual and political combat. A web of Actons, Dalbergs and Granvilles carried him from his mother's London salon, long remembered as a meeting place of distinguished foreigners and Englishmen, to the Acton estate at Aldenham, the homes of other Actons in Rome and Naples, the Bavarian estates of the Dalbergs, and vacation residences in Paris and on the Riviera. By the time he was eight he could speak English and French fluently, Italian perhaps less well, and was learning German.

Yet the distinction of Acton was not his cosmopolitanism, which was only a natural product of his background, or the cultured ease and linguistic facility that went effortlessly with that background. Granville, too, like a score of other well-situated and well-favoured sons, was a cultured cosmopolitan; he too spoke French perfectly. But while Granville was a dilettante in intellectual matters, Acton earned a deserved reputation for erudition. And even his cosmopolitanism did not make of Granville more than a typical English Liberal, while his stepson's individuality defied conventional national and party labels. Acton's learning and culture, like his ideas, were neither casually acquired nor casually expended. The languages he assimilated from his multilingual, multinational family were deliberately refined by years of careful study, and were cultivated as scholarly tools rather than as social graces. It was this seriousness and dedication of purpose that characterized the whole of his life, that made of his library not the cultured gentleman's lounge but the crowded workshop of the professional historian.

In the same way it was Acton's formal education more than the accidents of birth that gave to religion the prominence it had in his life. Around the names of his three main teachers can be written a history of mid-nineteenth-century Catholicism. Monsignor Dupanloup, his first instructor, was involved in one of the most interesting experiments in recent Catholic history, the attempt of the 'Liberal Catholic' group in France to reconcile the Liberal State with the Catholic Church. Cardinal Wiseman, President of Oscott College during Acton's student days, spearheaded the opposition movement of Ultramontanism, which exalted the authority of the Church over the secular State and of the Pope over the Church. Acton's last teacher and the great inspiration of his early life was Professor Döllinger, who attacked Ultramontanism in the name of an autonomous science, philosophy and history. In France, England and Germany, Acton had the good fortune to be at the source of the most dramatic movements in nineteenth-century Catholic thought.

Not only did his instructors occupy strategic positions in the history of the time, but they also played crucial parts in Acton's later life. Thus Dupanloup made his appearance first as a Liberal Catholic from whom Acton sought moral support and sympathy, then as a renegade Liberal meriting only contempt, and finally, in death, as the unwitting cause of the unhappiest episode in Acton's life, his alienation from Döllinger.

Félix Dupanloup had long been a friend and confessor to both the Actons and Dalbergs. Acton recalled, later in life, that it was he who had assisted at the death of Acton's father in 1837, and that his mother was in the habit of visiting Paris for the dual purpose of attending her dressmaker and going to confession to the Abbé.[1] After a spectacular rise in the Church,

[1] Add. MSS., 4975. Dupanloup has also been identified as Lady Acton's confessor at the difficult time of her second marriage (Craven, *Lady Fullerton*, p. 105).

in the course of which he was charged with the religious education of the princes of the royal house and received acclaim
for the death-bed reconciliation of Talleyrand with the Church,
Dupanloup was made supervisor of the preparatory seminary
of Saint Nicolas du Chardonnet. By one of his innovations,
the admission of youths who did not intend to take orders,
Acton entered the school in 1842, attending a branch of it
which had been moved to Gentilly on the outskirts of Paris.[1]

Acton remained at Saint Nicolas only one year, so that
it is likely that this first experiment in education was more
interesting retrospectively than at the time. He must have
been intrigued, later in life, by the thought that Ernest Renan,
perhaps the greatest heretic of the century, had left the school
shortly before his own arrival. And he might have compared
notes with Renan on the almost eccentric humanism of Dupanloup, which resulted in the transformation of the evening
'spiritual reading', generally interpreted as a reading of famous
religious prose, into a discussion of some literary and social
problem, such as romanticism. Or he might have contrasted
their experiences of disillusionment—Renan's when Dupanloup failed the test of science, Acton's when he failed the test
of Liberalism.

In 1843 Acton was removed from Saint Nicolas and the
temptations of a 'pagan' literature—as some orthodox theologians described its humanistic studies—to attend the more
conventional English Catholic school of Oscott, not far from
Oxford. Since he was expected to go on to Cambridge, it was
considered desirable that his early schooling be acquired in
England, and family precedent pointed to Oscott[2].

---

[1] In *Acton: the Formative Years* (London, 1946), Monsignor Mathew
held it to be improbable that Acton had ever studied with Dupanloup at
Saint Nicolas: 'If Acton was ever taught by Dupanloup, he does not seem
to have referred to it' (p. 54). Add. MSS., 4975, contains some information
on the relationship between Dupanloup and Acton's family and the explicit statement, in Acton's own hand, 'In 1842 I was at school under
Dupanloup at Gentilly.' Again in Add. MSS., 4905, he noted: 'I had no
religious ideas of my own. Educated under Dupanloup and Wiseman.'

[2] For mention of another Acton at Oscott, see M. F. Roskell, *Memoirs
of Francis Kerril Amherst* (London, 1903), p. 87.

The Right Reverend Nicholas Wiseman, who was later, as Cardinal and Archbishop of Westminster, to assume the part of Acton's main antagonist, had been appointed president of Oscott three years before Acton's arrival. Only thirty-eight years of age, he had already served as Rector of the English College in Rome for twelve years, and he had enthusiastic plans for his work in England. He fervently believed that the conversion of the English to the Roman Church was at hand, and that it needed only a bold and aggressive Catholic priesthood to hasten the event. And since it appeared that the conversion of England would start in Oxford, only a short distance from Oscott, he was strategically located for his purpose.

The 'Oxford Movement', as the High Church, Anglo-Catholic tendency in Oxford became known, had started with the publication of the famous 'Tracts of the Times' in 1833, and had developed a theological armour and a devoted following that exceeded the happiest expectations of its friends and the worst fears of its enemies. To Wiseman, the Oxford Movement was cause for unconcealed satisfaction and unlimited hopes. When the district clergy and old Catholic families protested that it was not the neighbouring Oxford eccentrics but the education of the boys at the school that should preoccupy the president, Wiseman grandly replied: 'Among the providential agencies that seemed justly timed, and even necessary for it [the conversion of England], appeared to me the erection of this noble college, in the very heart of England. Often in my darkest days and hours, feeling as if alone in my hopes, have I walked in front of it, and casting my eyes towards it, exclaimed to myself, "No, it was not to educate a few boys that this was erected, but to be the rallying point of the yet silent but vast movement towards the Catholic Church, which has commenced and must prosper." I felt as assured of this as if the word of prophecy had spoken it.' [1]

There was something prophetic, or at least remarkably perceptive, in Wiseman's vision. Oscott, although perhaps not quite the providential agency for the conversion of England,

[1] Wilfrid Ward, *The Life and Times of Cardinal Wiseman* (2 vols.; London, 1897), I, 348.

was instrumental in fashioning the great 'Catholic Revival' of the century. It was from Oscott that emissaries were sent out to Oxford to establish amicable relations. And it was to Oscott that the Oxford converts came; several gave up coveted fellowships at the university to become teachers at the boys' school. The greatest coup of all was John Henry Newman, who was received into the Church at Oscott in October, 1845, and took up residence, with other converts, at the old college buildings, renamed Maryvale. To Acton and the boys, the arrival of the converts signified the end of a tug-of-war between Oxford and Rome from which Wiseman, knight-errant in the service of the Pope and the true religion, had emerged victorious. They were in no position to appreciate the spiritual and intellectual travail experienced by Newman and the others before submitting to the ministrations of the priests who confidently awaited them. Acton later recalled the ingenuous pride of Wiseman as it was communicated to the boys: 'We were conscious that he was a conspicuous, even a celebrated man, and that he had the best of the Oxford controversy. The converts used to appear amongst us, and he seemed to exhibit their scalps.'[1]

'We had a feeling', Acton wrote, recalling the excitement of those years, 'that Oscott, next to Pekin, was a centre of the world.'[2] It was, in fact, the centre of the British Catholic world during Acton's residence there. Before Wiseman's arrival, Catholicism in England had been a modest, retiring sect, aspiring to nothing so much as inoffensiveness. Wiseman changed all that. 'We are like the Jews returned to Jerusalem, or like the first family after the Flood—we have to reconstruct everything,' he announced.[3] At Oscott he found the materials for reconstruction. George Spencer, one of the instructors, was a passionate believer in the conversion of England, a subject upon which he expatiated to his pupils at every opportunity,[4] and which he introduced to the Catholic public in the form of an 'association of prayer' for conversion. Even more

[1] ibid.   [2] ibid., p. 349.
[3] Percy Fitzgerald, *Fifty Years of Catholic Life and Progress* (2 vols.; London, 1901), I, 57.
[4] Urban Young, *Life of Father Ignatius Spencer* (London, 1933), p. 104.

useful for Wiseman's purpose was Augustus Welby Pugin, the famous church architect and professor of ecclesiastical art and antiquities at Oscott. Pugin was fanatically devoted to the flamboyant and Gothic in architecture, the Gregorian in music, and the high Roman and papist position in Church and State. When he completed the splendid St. George's Church in London in 1848, the dedication ceremony was the most elaborate Catholic event since the Reformation; Wiseman preached the sermon and Acton, then fourteen years old, had the honour of acting as thurifer. English Catholicism was no longer an alien Church discreetly assimilating the external fashions of the national Church. Proudly and brazenly it flaunted its peculiarities and advertised itself as the universal Church. It would never forget, nor would it permit its enemies to forget, the abject and anguished confessions of inferiority with which some of the most esteemed Anglicans had made their submissions.

As an introduction to contemporary Catholicism—its personalities, aspirations and triumphs—Oscott was perfect. As an education in ideas, however, it was less satisfactory. Retrospectively, Acton accounted for this by the heterogeneity of the teaching staff. The staff then consisted of the Oxford converts (Bernard Smith, John Brande Morris and Sir Peter le Page Renouf), several earlier Cambridge converts (including Spencer and Henry Logan, the vice-president), George Errington, whom Wiseman had brought with him from Rome, local midland clergy, and some Irish Catholics of whom Acton remembered particularly Thomas Craven Flanagan, author of a manual of British and Irish history (who probably inspired Acton to undertake his first historical project, a 'compendium of the chief facts in history', as he described it at the time).[1] Too preoccupied with more grandiose affairs, Wiseman did not suffer his talents to be absorbed by the school, and it was Acton's impression that he failed to amalgamate the diverse elements or even inspire them in any one direction. The boys used to catch glimpses of him with distinguished visitors— English nobility, French royalty, famous statesmen and ecclesiasts, philosophers and theologians. At one time he invited to

[1] Acton to his mother [1846], *Selections from the Correspondence of the First Lord Acton*, ed. J. N. Figgis and R. V. Laurence (London, 1917), p. 1.

the school Vincenzo Gioberti, the spokesman for the principle
of the separation of Church and State, at another, Gioberti's
main philosophical antagonist, Antonio Rosmini. 'The point
is', Acton explained, 'that he [Wiseman] was an all-round
person, and we did not clearly see his drift.'[1] For Acton this
was an admission of Wiseman's failure. An education, he believed should provide principles of discrimination and judgment, leading ideas by which history and philosophy were made
meaningful. Wiseman was obviously indifferent to such ideas.

This was Acton's quarrel with Wiseman, first as president
of Oscott and later as Archbishop of Westminster. Even Wiseman's commitment to Ultramontanism was not so much to
the idea as to the interest it represented, the interest of the
Pope; all other ideas—scientific, philosophical and political—
were subjected to the test of that interest. To the mature Acton
this was the great intellectual betrayal.

In 1848 Acton left Oscott for two years of private tuition at
Edinburgh under Logan, formerly the vice-president of Oscott. Little is known of this educational venture, except that
it was hoped he would learn Greek. Dissatisfied with his progress, he left Edinburgh, he later told a friend, knowing no
more than 500 words of that language.[2]

Probably the real purpose of the Edinburgh interlude was
to mark time until he could be admitted to the university.
Both his father and his uncle, the Cardinal, had studied at
Magdalene College, Cambridge. The degree at that time—they
had entered in 1822—was denied to Catholics, but the administration of the college was tolerant and chapel attendance
was not required. Of the Cardinal's Cambridge education
Wiseman once observed that it was a strange preparation for
the Roman purple. Almost as strange a preparation for the
position of Regius Professor was the rejection by three col-
leges, Magdalene included, of Acton's application for admis-

[1] Wilfrid Ward, *Wiseman*, I, 353. See a letter of Acton to Richard
Simpson, for another, harsher comment on Oscott (Francis A. Gasquet,
ed., *Lord Acton and his Circle* [London, 1906], p. 157).
[2] Mountstuart E. Grant Duff, *Out of the Past* (2 vols.; London, 1903),
II, 190.

sion, although by that time Catholic disabilities had been removed. In his inaugural lecture forty-five years later, Acton could not resist remarking upon the irony of the situation.

It is tempting to speculate what might have happened to Acton had the university been more disposed to accept Catholics.[1] Cambridge was not an atmosphere in which absolutes were likely to thrive, and it was in the form of absolutes—moral, historical and political—that Acton's spirit was fashioned.

MUNICH

By June 1850, Acton was settled in Munich at the home of Professor Johann Ignaz von Döllinger, the distinguished priest, theologian and Church historian.[2] He was not registered at the university, possibly because his German was not adequate; instead he planned to receive private instruction from Döllinger, supplemented by occasional courses of lec-

[1] In a letter to Gladstone, several months after the inaugural lecture, Acton suggested that 'Papal Aggression' might have had something to do with his rejection (28 January 1896, *Correspondence*, p. 157). In this, Acton was wrong. 'Papal Aggression', as the restoration of the Catholic hierarchy in England was popularly called, was announced by Wiseman, in the pastoral letter that so offended the English, on 7 October 1850. Acton's applications had been submitted late in 1849 or early in 1850, and the college authorities must have made their decision well before June, when Acton arrived in Munich.

[2] The date of Acton's arrival in Munich is almost always given as 1848. The editors of his correspondence, Figgis and Laurence, were probably originally responsible for the error. In one of his first letters from Munich to his family, Acton mentioned Döllinger's attendance at the sessions of the Assembly, and assuming that the reference was to the Frankfort Assembly to which he had been a delegate, the editors dated the letter as 1848 (*Correspondence*, p. 6). The *Dictionary of National Biography* and almost all subsequent biographers perpetuated the error. Acton's personal notes (Add. MSS., 4905) and the biography of Döllinger by Johann Friedrich (*Ignaz von Döllinger* [3 vols.; Munich, 1901], III, 71) establish the fact of Acton's arrival at Munich in the summer of 1850, when Döllinger was occupied with the Bavarian Assembly of which he was a member. Professor Herbert Butterfield made this point in his review of David Mathew's biography of Acton (*English Historical Review* [LXI] 1946, 414). Because Mathew took the conventional date of 1848 as the beginning of the Munich period, he was hard pressed to explain the applications to Cambridge in 1849 or 1850.

tures at the university. Several circumstances combined to make Munich the obvious choice after Cambridge. Apart from the fact that it was the most famous centre of Catholic learning at the time, it was also the home of the Arco-Valleys, who were related to Acton by way of the Dalbergs and whose daughter Acton was later to marry. Count Arco-Valley, an old friend of Döllinger, made the arrangements for Acton's stay in Munich and was host to the boy during week-ends in the city and vacations at Tegernsee.

The most decisive fact of Acton's life was his apprenticeship under Döllinger. It was to take him almost thirty years to assert his independence of 'the Professor', and even after that he was persistently regarded by his professional colleagues as more than half German and intellectually, at least, the facsimile of Döllinger. The resemblance, however, stopped there, for no one would have ventured to compare them in appearance, temperament or background. Acton was extremely handsome, both as youth and adult, with delicate, regular features and a well-proportioned body. Döllinger resembled Newman physically, with a bony, wrinkled face and ungainly stance. 'His personal appearance', one of Acton's first letters from Munich read, 'is certainly not prepossessing. His forehead is not particularly large, and a somewhat malevolent grin seems constantly to reside about his wide, low mouth.'[1] The son of a university professor, he led the austere, almost ascetic life of the religious bourgeois, and since he had the reserved, dispassionate manner that often went with long years of historical study (he was fifty-one when Acton first met him), he repelled many by his apparent coldness. Bernhard von Meyer, Acton's German tutor, who had reason to dislike Döllinger on political and intellectual grounds, complained: 'Dry in his whole demeanour, cutting in his expressions, his whole person breathes an air of icy indifference.'[2] Yet it was just this dispassion that captivated Acton. To the sixteen-year-old boy accustomed to the more casual ways of Oscott and Edinburgh, Döllinger must have appeared the personification of the dedicated intellect. His abstemious personal habits and his enormous capacity

[1] Acton to Granville [1850], *Correspondence*, p. 7.
[2] Friedrich, III, 73.

for work earned Acton's respect, and the avidity with which he collected books endeared him to his admiring student, who promptly succumbed to the same insatiable passion. 'His library', Acton delightedly reported, 'is as dusty and as valuable as the most fastidious taste could desire',[1] and it was not long before he was urging his mother to grant him a special book allowance.

To a large extent, the history of Döllinger was the history of Acton, for the pupil entered upon the master's ideas, prejudices and even past experiences with all the sympathy of a young disciple.[2] When Acton arrived in Munich in 1850, Döllinger was not yet set apart from the rest of the Munich faculty. Like them, he enjoyed the comfortable sensation of being a conscientious scholar, a loyal subject of the king, and a devoted servant of the Pope. Politically and ecclesiastically the Munich group had no quarrel with the existing state of affairs. They were Monarchists and Ultramontanes, for whom the principle of absolute authority in the State was perfectly consistent with the ideas of absolute authority in the Church. In this they were the heirs of a long and respectable tradition dating back to St. Gregory and revived in France by Louis de Bonald and Joseph de Maistre. For the more recent Liberal and democratic theories emanating from France, from Lamennais, Montalembert and Lacordaire, the Munich theologians had little use. The university was, as Acton later described it, a 'headquarters of Catholic Conservatism'.[3] For a brief while in 1847, when the notorious Lola Montez was installed as the mistress of the king, the Catholics, Döllinger included, had

[1] Acton to Granville [1850], *Correspondence*, p. 8.

[2] For the history of Döllinger and of the Munich group one need almost not go outside of Acton's own writings and notes. After Döllinger's death in 1890, Acton re-read his books and the voluminous correspondence of a lifetime and prepared to write a biography of his former master. One long article appeared in the *English Historical Review* (V [1890], 700–44), but the biography, like so many other projects, was abandoned, perhaps because Johann Friedrich, one of Döllinger's more faithful disciples, had also undertaken to publish one, and perhaps because Acton could not write a truly sympathetic biography and did not wish to write a hostile one. A great mass of notes remain which help illuminate many otherwise obscure passages in Döllinger's life and in Acton's relations with him.

[3] Add. MSS., 4909.

withdrawn their support from the king. And during the revolution of 1848, Döllinger had served as delegate to the Frankfort Parliament, although unerringly he had taken his seat with the extreme Right. The only hints of Liberalism in his conduct were his approval of a resolution banning the Jesuit Order from Germany (a resolution which found favour among the most orthodox of Catholics), and a speech recommending a national Church with a national council and diocesan and provincial synods. In all essential respects, however, Döllinger kept faith with Conservatism and Ultramontanism, and by 1850, when Acton arrived in Munich, the brief flirtation with revolution was long forgotten.

Compared with the stagnant condition of Catholic theology and history elsewhere (the Catholic faculty at Tübingen was the only one to compete with it, but in theology alone), Munich seemed to be seething with intellectual excitement— or so the impressionable Acton saw it. It had, in fact, recently inaugurated what appeared to be a renaissance of German Catholicism. Earlier in the century, Protestant scholarship had leaped far ahead, with Niebuhr and Ranke in history, Baur and Strauss in Biblical criticism, and Schelling and Schleier- macher in the philosophy of religion. When the Catholics of Munich and Tübingen undertook to provide their own answers to such problems as the historical criticism of the Old and New Testament, the relation of philosophy to religion and religion to mythology, and the character of religious dog- mas and institutions, there developed among them, as Acton later realized, a sense of party loyalty and partisan purpose. 'At Munich', he noted, 'there was a party with tactics, de- clamation, rhetoric, questions of expediency, questions of policy, with impartial truth in the background.'[1] There is no suggestion of deliberate dishonesty or insincerity. The group quite sensibly worked in unison and husbanded its resources: 'Divine, jurist, historian, politician, poet, working together for an acknowledged end, all of them seriously con- vinced, [their] aims practical, with their religion in their lives and in their thoughts.'[2] While in France at this time Catholics were quarrelling about novel political solutions to the problem

[1] Add. MSS., 4905.　　　　　　[2] Add. MSS., 4913.

21

of State and Church, and in England they were lost in visions of an enormously aggrandized ecclesiastical structure, in Germany their most eminent men were consecrated to the task of making Catholicism intellectually and theologically respectable. The Munich circle accomplished its mission so well that it assumed the intellectual leadership of world Catholicism.[1]

It was to Döllinger, the most distinguished scholar in Munich, that Acton looked for a revelation of the truths of philosophy, religion and history. The professor was a 'book of reference' on every question put to him, the boy wrote to his parents.[2] Outside of the physical sciences there seemed to be no limit to his intellectual capacity; he was almost as much at home in the Greek and Roman classics and English and German literature, as in theology, philosophy and history. The studies in which he directed Acton exhibited the same range. He set him to read Tacitus and Plutarch, supervised him in modern history, gave him exercises in English literature and composition, and assigned to him an instructor in German. During his first few weeks in Munich, Acton told a friend many years later,[3] he read through the whole of the *Biographie Universelle*—some fifty-five volumes not including the supplements. (This last, however, may not have been upon Döllinger's instigation; it sounds more like an enterprising young man's idea of a suitable introduction to modern culture.) Somewhat later, Döllinger embarked him upon an intensive course of medieval studies.[4] This curriculum so delighted Acton that when after four years Granville proposed that he return to England to continue his education there, he pleaded

[1] *The Memoirs of the Count de Falloux* contains an enthusiastic account of a visit to Munich in 1838, but errs in referring to Acton's residence in Döllinger's home at that early date (ed. C. B. Pitman [2 vols.; London, 1888], I, 162).

[2] [1850], *Correspondence*, p. 7.

[3] Grant Duff, *Out of the Past*, II, 190.

[4] Justus Hashagen on 'Leo', *Encyclopaedia Britannica* (11th ed.), attributed to Acton the English translation of Leo's *Rectitudines singularum personarum*, which appeared in 1852. Aside from the fact that the translator's preface carries the initials B. W. (probably B. William), it is unlikely that Acton, however precocious a youth, should have completed this work at the age of eighteen. Heinrich Leo was, however, one of the historians Acton studied carefully under Döllinger.

with him, in a long, impassioned letter, to be permitted to remain in Munich. He was not studying as a 'dilettante' or 'literary epicure', he severely reminded his stepfather, and the scholarship of Munich could be reproduced nowhere else.[1]

Only many years later did Acton discover that Munich and Döllinger were far from perfect, that the Munich circle, although 'vigorous, able and learned', was 'not remarkable for originality, or freshness, or warmth, or play of mind'; they were too busy 'defending a settled cause' to start 'a voyage of discovery'.[2] Even Döllinger, Acton was shocked to realize, had, by 1850, not yet emancipated himself from the Romantic school, 'where history was honeycombed with imagination and conjecture',[3] and he recommended to his pupil works, such as Creuzer's *Mythology*, that were not entirely respectable in the best academic society even then. Döllinger, like his colleagues, tended to be too much interested in 'the exposure of Protestant perversions of history'[4] to cultivate a completely disinterested, objective history.

Yet whatever his deficiencies as an historian and however extravagant the young Acton's estimate of him, Döllinger had a genuine respect for history, and this historical-mindedness, more than anything else, distinguished him from the majority of the Munich faculty and gave promise of his future deviation. It was from Döllinger that Acton received the theory of development, the idea that Christianity was essentially a history rather than a doctrinal system or philosophy, that its dogmas were not fixed for all time but underwent change and development.[5] The test of dogmas, in this view, was not the logical consistency of a system, but historical evidence and fact. In this philosophy of history and theory of

[1] 6 May 1854, *Correspondence*, p. 24.   [2] Add. MSS., 4913.

[3] 'Döllinger's Historical Work', *History of Freedom*, ed. J. N. Figgis and R. V. Laurence (London, 1907), p. 405.

[4] Acton as quoted in Friedrich, III, 72.

[5] The theory of development is more popularly known in the form given it by Newman in his *Essay on the Development of Christian Doctrine* of 1845 (recently reissued, ed. Charles F. Harrold [New York, 1949]). Newman was unfamiliar with German theology, with the work of Drey, Möhler or Döllinger, and it appears that he arrived at the theory independently.

development were concealed revolutionary implications which would eventually carry Döllinger, and Acton, far beyond the sanguine orthodoxy of the first half of the century, for if history could be the instrument of apologetics, a more sophisticated history might be made the instrument of criticism. It was no accident that the historians in Munich eventually found themselves among the religious Liberals, while the canonists remained staunch Ultramontanes.

The critical years for both Döllinger and Acton were the 1850's. Acton had come to Munich prepared to sit at the feet of the great master and receive from him the eternal truths of history, God and man. Instead, master and pupil were subjected to a series of experiences that set them off on a new and difficult path of controversy. Acton in his teens and early twenties and Döllinger in his fifties served their novitiate in religious liberalism together.

Yet if it is false to suppose that Acton mechanically followed in the steps of his revered professor, it is certainly more ludicrous to think, as some did, that the professor was aping the prejudices of his young student. The emergence of Döllinger's Liberalism came as a great blow to the Ultramontanes who had worked with him so harmoniously in the 'thirties and 'forties, and they cast their nets wide in the hope of dredging up a satisfactory explanation of the change that had appeared in him, one that would reflect not upon their own inadequacy but upon Döllinger's. The theories ranged from the vulgar to the ridiculous. Later Rome was regaled with stories of Döllinger's frustrated ambitions, and it was said that only his failure to rise in the ecclesiastical hierarchy could account for his waywardness in rejecting papal infallibility.[1] Less malicious, and contradicting this explanation, was that which held that Döllinger was professor first and priest only secondarily, that he lacked genuine religious sentiments and was led astray by false facts and insidious philosophies.[2] Joseph Jörg, once

---

[1] 'Döllinger', *Catholic Encyclopedia*, V, 97.

[2] According to Georges Goyau (*L'Allemagne Religieuse: le Catholicisme* [4 vols.; Paris, 1905–9]), Döllinger refused the archbishopric of Salzburg because it would have interfered with his scholarly work.

Döllinger's secretary and a leading Ultramontane, circulated a special version of this theory. Döllinger's real interests and abilities, he maintained, were not in politics—ecclesiastical or State—but in his academic studies, so that he was at the mercy of others for his political convictions. One of those who imposed his will upon Döllinger, Jörg found, was Acton.

Since 1850, Jörg later wrote, the young Lord Acton was his lodger; a richly gifted young man, earnest beyond his years . . . he had been sent to Munich for further education. He had until then lived in the Russell-Gladstone circle and he brought with him a strange antipathy toward Cardinal Wiseman, the introduction of the Catholic hierarchy in England, and particularly toward the Jesuits. Between him and Döllinger there developed a father-son relationship; but one presently noticed that the influence of the young lord was predominant.[1]

Acton had accompanied Döllinger to the Catholic Assembly at Linz in 1850, Jörg casually remarked, as if to account for Döllinger's speech in support of a national Church at that assembly. What Jörg did not see fit to mention was that Döllinger had developed this theme at least as early as 1847 and that it had occupied a prominent place in his speeches of 1848. Bernhard von Meyer, who shared Jörg's Ultramontane views but who far surpassed him in vindictiveness, also insinuated that the 'young Lord' exercised an immoderate influence upon Döllinger. But it was upon Meyer rather than Döllinger that Acton's social position seems to have made much the greater impression.

Acton's own testimony is more reliable and reasonable. Döllinger was not converted by him; he was converted by Döllinger, by the events of the 'fifties and the spirit of Munich. He had arrived there, he later noted, 'a raw English schoolboy, primed to the brim with Whig politics.' 'It was not Whiggism only,' he recalled, 'but Macaulay in particular that I was so full of';[2] and it was Döllinger who purged him of his Whig-Macaulayite sympathies. The professor succeeded so well in this that Granville belatedly attempted to recall his stepson from Munich in order to remove him from the contaminating

[1] Jörg, 'Döllinger', *Historisch-Politische Blätter*, CV (1890), 246.
[2] Add. MSS., 4905 and 4907.

influence of German philosophy and politics. But the damage had already been done, and he could not be persuaded to leave. Between Acton and Granville there remained a chasm that was never closed, and was only bridged much later when Döllinger's influence began to wane. Far from Döllinger's being won over to Whiggism, it was Acton who was converted to Döllinger's brand of Catholicism.

The responsibility for Döllinger's 'apostasy', as the Ultramontanes would have it, must be borne by the Ultramontanes themselves. The first event that made Döllinger waver in his devotion to Rome was the proclamation in 1854 of the dogma of the Immaculate Conception of Mary. The dogma was objectionable to him on two grounds: because historically it had never enjoyed the status of a divinely revealed truth, as is witnessed by the fact that many respectable Christians, including Thomas Aquinas, had demurred to it; and because it had been decreed only on the authority of Pius and without the confirmation of an ecumenical council, which was a premature exercise of a right not conferred upon the Pope until 1870 and resisted by Döllinger at that time. There is no doubt that Acton, then twenty years old, was well versed in the polemics occasioned by the dogma and had allied himself on the side of Döllinger. When the dogma had first been proposed, the theology faculty of Munich, with Döllinger as its main spokesman, formally went on record against it, and while Acton was not admitted to the councils of war, he did act as a kind of courier for Döllinger, carrying his message abroad and reporting back on the state of Catholic opinion. After the promulgation of the decree, Döllinger submitted, silencing his conscience, he later self-reproachfully confessed to Acton, with the excuse that he had done all he could to obstruct it before its promulgation,[1] a plea that was often on the lips of those who later submitted to the dogma of Infallibility. In the 1870's both Döllinger and Acton were to look back upon the decree of Immaculate Conception as a long stride on the downward path to Infallibility.

While the papacy was engaged in making of Catholicism

[1] Excerpt of letter from Döllinger to Acton, 29 December 1872, Add. MSS., 4911.

a more exclusive, dogmatic religion, some German theologians were attempting to bring it into the mainstream of modern culture and philosophy. In 1835 the work of one of these theologians, Georg Hermes, had been condemned for leaning too heavily on the Kantian formulations of natural reason and rationalistic religion, and during the 1850's there was a rash of similar treatises dedicated to the reconciliation of philosophy, science and religion. During his stay in Munich, Acton witnessed the great controversies provoked by Anton von Günther and Jakob Frohschammer, the former asserting a dualism of science and religion with science competent to postulate and establish its own truths, the latter insisting upon the sovereignty of science over religion. Although Döllinger had subscribed to the condemnation of Hermes in the 1830's, he now came to the defence of Günther and Frohschammer. If Rome condemned them, he warned, it condemned Catholics to intellectual sterility. But the warning was in vain.

By the middle of the 1850's, the Munich group was divided into two distinct factions, with charges of heresy freely bandied about. It had become painfully clear to Döllinger and Acton that an independent philosophy and an independent science were held to be incompatible with the scholastic theology favoured by Rome. They were soon to discover that history and historical science were also regarded with suspicion. A journey to Rome in the spring of 1857, when Acton was twenty-three and more of a companion than a pupil, served them both as a simultaneous initiation into the finer points of the science of history and the art of Roman censorship.

According to Acton, Döllinger used to commemorate his first and only visit to Rome as an 'epoch of emancipation'.[1] Actually it was only a move in the long process of emancipation. The interesting thing is that it was taken without premeditation. He and Acton did not go to Rome (as might have been expected with the Günther and Frohschammer episodes rankling in their minds), to prove a thesis or confirm their prejudices. They went to investigate the manuscripts in the Vatican library on the subject of medieval heresies. Although

[1] Add. MSS., 4905; *History of Freedom*, p. 410.

Acton was refused access to the manuscripts and had to rely on Döllinger's account of them, the materials proved to be even better than they had expected, and Döllinger devoted almost all of his time to study. Nevertheless the atmosphere of the city, the mere physical presence of monuments and scenes recalling nobler times, the oppressive climate of political and moral lassitude, worked its way into his spirit, and Döllinger came away, Acton recalled, 'despondent, without confidence and without respect'. Acton hastened to add, in order not to overstate the case, that he was also 'without horror or indignation',[1] that the overwhelming impression was one of incapacity and inefficiency rather than of immorality. 'He did not come away charged with visions of scandal in the spiritual order, of suffering in the temporal, or of tyranny in either. He was never in contact with the sinister side of things.'[2]

Döllinger, and Acton too, may have been spared the more 'sinister' aspect of Rome, but they were introduced to many dispiriting features of it. Döllinger had two memorable experiences. One was his meeting with the secretary of the Inquisition, Modena, who casually confessed his ignorance of German and then explained that a German book could be placed on the Index if the denouncer translated a single objectionable passage from it. When Döllinger protested that the denouncer's translation, perhaps unfaithful and in any case torn out of context, might easily misrepresent a subtle philosophical treatise, Modena blandly replied, 'It is our rule.'[3] The second was his audience with the Pope with its elaborate ceremonial, the women prostrating themselves before the Pope and the impatient haughtiness of the Pope assuring his visitors that 'only when the world had learned to bow before the Apostolic Chair would the welfare of mankind be assured'.[4]

Acton, too, was received by the Pope and carried away an impression not much more agreeable than that of Döllinger. The one gratifying memory he retained from the audience was

[1] Add. MSS., 4903 and 4905.   [2] *History of Freedom*, p. 411.
[3] Friedrich, III, 181; Louise von Kobell, *Conversations of Dr. Döllinger* (London, 1892), pp. 122–3.
[4] Kobell, p. 138; Alfred Plummer, 'Recollections of Dr. Döllinger'. *Expositor* (4th ser.), I (1890), 222, n. 1.

a reference to his mother's piety. It is apparent, from a journal kept by him at the time,[1] that the Pope preferred to regard him as a young seigneur, the grandson of the Minister of Naples and scion of the house of Acton and Dalberg, rather than as the gifted protégé of one of the great historians of the Church. With the protégé sharing the suspicion directed against his master, it was natural that he would also share Döllinger's contempt for the Vatican. His journal echoed Döllinger's complaint that the officials of the Roman court were appallingly ignorant of the state of learning abroad, were hostile to German theology and philosophy, and were unable to appreciate the work of the best converts, including Newman. From his own experience, Acton concluded that the Roman hierarchy deliberately frustrated the work of foreign scholars. Nor was the Pope immune from his strictures. Pius IX, he noted, was the intellectual inferior of his predecessor, with no knowledge whatever of theological matters. 'Now nobody feels that the Pope will think less of him because he knows nothing at all.'[2]

The visit to Rome did more than document the case against the Vatican. A few years earlier, Ranke's lectures, delivered in Munich, had inspired them with a new respect for manuscript materials and the scientific spirit of modern history. Rome was the first occasion when Döllinger (and, vicariously, Acton) could apply at length the modern historical techniques and become adept in the use of the tools of research that would convert history into a formidable weapon of criticism. It is from this visit, followed by those to the libraries of Vienna and Venice in 1863 and 1864, that Acton dated the revolution in Döllinger's conception of history.

The Döllinger of the early 'fifties, Acton found many years later, had pinned his faith on the imminence of a new 'conversion of Rome', a conversion to a purer, more humane and enlightened religion. By 1857 that faith was beginning to wear thin, and it barely survived the trip to Rome. Döllinger's emancipation from 'conventional history', as Acton put it,[3] went side by side with his emancipation from conventional, which meant Ultramontane, Catholicism. And Döllinger's

[1] Add. MSS., 5751.   [2] ibid.   [3] *History of Freedom*, p. 422.

emancipation was Acton's. For the professor this was a period of disillusionment, in which the work and ideas of half a lifetime were rendered precarious and obsolete. For the student it was the beginning of a long career of protest and criticism.

The trip to Rome was only one of a series of journeys upon which Acton accompanied Döllinger. Once a year from 1850 to 1858 (with the possible exception of 1856), they set off on a tour of Switzerland, Italy, Austria or England, carefully planning their itinerary so that they might stop off to see old friends or meet new ones, attend a congress of Catholic theologians, or explore the contents of libraries and bookstores.[1] Döllinger introduced his protégé to the intellectual *élite* of the Continent, philosophers, theologians, historians and statesmen, thus contributing to Acton's later reputation as the man who knew everyone worth knowing. It was at this time too that Acton laid the foundation for his magnificent library; Döllinger advised him in his purchases of rare books, and upon the death of Professor Ernst von Lasaulx he acquired Lasaulx's fine library.

On a trip to England in 1851, they met Gladstone, Manning, Pusey and some of his Oxford associates (Mozley, Pollen, Church), Wiseman and Newman. Most interesting was the meeting with Newman. Acton had only fleeting recollections of him as he had appeared at Oscott, and this was his first real introduction to one of his most remarkable contemporaries.[2] He was prepared to respect Newman because Döllinger respected him, but he was disconcerted by the temperamental and philosophical difference that became apparent as soon as Newman and Döllinger met. They were, as Newman later ex-

[1] Add. MSS., 5645, contains the itinerary of the trips made from 1850 through 1854. This is supplemented by random references elsewhere among the manuscripts and Vol. III of Friedrich.

[2] Mathew's *Acton* erroneously places the date of their first acquaintance, and that by correspondence, at 1854 (p. 144). Wilfrid Ward's biography of Newman refers to their earlier meeting in 1851, but later contradicts this by suggesting that they did not meet until about 1857 (*The Life of John Henry Cardinal Newman* [2 vols.; London, 1912], I, 264 and 443). The meeting in May 1851 (probably 26 May) is also mentioned in Add. MSS., 5645.

plained, 'like a dog and a fish trying to make friends'.[1] Döl-linger was a theologian *qua* historian; Newman was a theo-logian *qua* philosopher. History, Newman obscurely feared, was on the side of the Protestants, and he preferred to rest the Catholic case not on the facts and evidence of objective, im-partial history, as Döllinger did, but on the facts and evidence of personal belief and conviction. Nevertheless they met once more in 1858, again with Acton as intermediary, and con-tinued to hold each other in high regard, at least until the Vatican Council drove the wedge of heresy between them. Acton, however, had not Döllinger's tolerance. For a time, to be sure, he remained on good terms with Newman, but long before the Vatican Council he had assigned to him the per-manent label of enemy.

In 1853 Acton wandered far afield from the European scene when he visited the United States with a relative, Lord Elles-mere, Chief British Commissioner to the New York Industrial Exhibition.[2] To the galaxy of famous names in Acton's orbit were now added those of Sir Charles Lyell, the English geologist, William Prescott, the American historian, the poets James Russell Lowell and Henry Wadsworth Longfellow, and the Catholic essayist and journalist Orestes Brownson. He attended the sessions of the Massachusetts State Convention in Boston[3] and was dissuaded from going south to collect infor-mation about slavery only by the reports of the fevers rampant there in the summer. A visit to Harvard University affirmed his faith in the intellectual superiority of Munich, and con-firmed his suspicions of the superficiality and coarseness of American society, where 'money is the great object of life', and 'nothing is studied for its own sake, but only as it will be useful in making a practical man'.[4] Unabashed by great names,

[1] Add. MSS., 4987; A. W. Hutton, 'Personal Reminiscences of Cardinal Newman', *Expositor* (4th ser.), II (1890), 228.
[2] The *Dictionary of National Biography* erroneously assigned this visit to 1855 (2d supplement, p. 8).
[3] Both the *Dictionary of National Biography* and the editors of Acton's correspondence speak of his presence at the constitutional debates at Philadelphia instead of those in Boston.
[4] 'Lord Acton's American Diaries', *Fortnightly Review*, CX (1921), 930–1.

he confessed to a poor impression of Longfellow, who had hoped to ingratiate himself by praising Lord Ellesmere's translation of *Faust* for its 'perfectly gentlemanlike tone'.[1] Brownson, on the other hand, despite his Ultramontanism, impressed Acton favourably, and they argued amiably about the theory of development, Brownson claiming it to be a dangerous error with heretical implications.

This meeting with Brownson had two curious epilogues. The first was the unexpected dispatch of one of Brownson's sons to Munich to study under Döllinger, on the strength of the enthusiastic recommendation of the young Acton and in spite of Brownson's own doubts about Döllinger's orthodoxy. The second epilogue features Acton as a kind of primitive international clearing-house for Catholic intellectuals. On his return to England, Acton spoke to Newman of Brownson's 'extraordinary force and originality, his rare, natural capacity, his heartiness, and the disadvantage of his isolation'.[2] As a result, Newman, who had previously been branded as an infidel by Brownson in an article bearing the episcopal imprimatur, invited the American to a professorship at the Catholic University in Dublin.

Three years after the American trip Acton visited Russia, this time as secretary to Lord Granville, who was representing Queen Victoria at the coronation of Tsar Alexander II. Acton kept the financial accounts and made himself generally useful and agreeable.[3] The visit is memorable largely because it is the first evidence of a characteristic which was later to become more pronounced: Acton's ability to inhabit simultaneously

[1] ibid., p. 934.

[2] Add. MSS., 4987. See also Add. MSS., 4975 and 5463 for other references to the Brownson-Newman episode, and Henry A. Brownson, *Orestes A. Brownson's Middle Life* (Detroit, 1899), pp. 471–8, for a long letter by Acton to Brownson, dated Munich, 13 May 1854, urging Brownson to accept Newman's offer.

[3] Among Acton's manuscripts is one notebook described on the fly-leaf, in Acton's hand, as the 'Order Book, British Embassy, Moscow, 19 August 1856' (Add. MSS., 4872). See also Lord Granville's account of the trip in Fitzmaurice, I, 183–217, and references to it in Charlotte Blennerhassett, 'The Late Lord Acton', *Edinburgh Review*, CXCVII (1903), 502.

the worlds of scholarship and society, to delight his aristocratic friends with his erudition and his academic colleagues
with his intimate knowledge of high society.

America and Russia were outposts of civilization to Acton
and most of his contemporaries, and trips there were in the
nature of curiosities. France, on the other hand, was, like
Germany, an adopted homeland, and part of almost every year
was spent in Paris and on the Riviera. In France, as in Germany, it was Döllinger's influence that predominated—which
made Acton complain that the large legacy of friends and rela-
tives in Paris bequeathed to him by the Dalbergs, Actons and
Granvilles consumed time that could better have been spent
with the philosophers and theologians to whom Döllinger
had introduced him.

The men in France with whom Döllinger, and Acton after
him, were now identified were the Liberal Catholics. French
Liberal Catholicism had matured since its earlier Radical and
democratic days when Lamennais, Lacordaire and Montalembert had argued the case for 'God and Liberty' before Pope
Gregory XVI—and had lost. Under Montalembert and Falloux, the group had settled down to a more respectable
existence. In return for significant concessions on the part of
the Government of Louis Napoleon, particularly a generous
Education Bill restoring to the clergy a strategic position in the
schools, the Liberal Catholic journal, *Le Correspondant*, gave its
qualified support to the régime. Only *L'Univers*, the arch-
Ultramontane organ of Louis Veuillot, remained intractable,
refusing to come to terms with the 'democrat' Napoleon or
with the secular State he represented.

In the course of the 1850's it had become increasingly
evident to Döllinger and Acton that the conflict between
L'Univers and *Le Correspondant* paralleled that between Roman
scholasticism on the one hand and German history and philosophy on the other. Acton had no doubts as to his own loyalties. From Paris in the spring of 1856, he wrote to his mother:
'The evening at Montalembert's was most agreeable; I saw
there all of the collaborators on the Correspondant, the men
with whom I am most in agreement, above all Prince A. de
Broglie and my old friend Eckstein, of all the scholars in Paris

the one who pleases me best.'[1] Veuillot, whom he met the next day, he immediately regarded as an enemy.

Lines once blurred and uncertain were becoming sharper, and the area of neutrality between Liberal Catholicism and Ultramontanism was shrinking almost to the vanishing point. It was increasingly difficult for men like Döllinger to live in peace with both sides, as they had once done. In the 1850's the features of the final struggle of 1870 were becoming visible, and by the end of the decade it was already possible to name the leading combatants and often even the rank and file of each camp. With the clarification and simplification of issues, national distinctions were relegated to the background, and it required only minor strategical adjustments for Acton to transport the Liberal Catholicism of Germany and France to the very different terrain of England.

[1] *Correspondence*, p. 18. The letter is undated, but internal evidence places it in 1856. Baron Eckstein, to whom Acton referred, was a Danish convert, a diplomat, historian and lifelong friend of Acton.

III

CONFLICTS WITH ROME

WHEN Acton returned to England in 1858, it was as a self-appointed missionary charged with the emancipation of Catholic England from the narrow, sectarian spirit to which he saw it enslaved. He was not the first to favour his country with attentions of this sort. The old Catholic community that had managed, in its modest, unpretentious way, to preserve its faith during centuries of oppression and persecution was at the mercy of now one and then another group of energetic reformers who precipitously descended upon it to examine, analyse, and find it wanting.

In 1840, Wiseman, taking stock of the Catholic community in England, had found a small minority divorced from the affairs of State and excluded from the respectable institutions of learning, a community spiritually impoverished, politically timid, and ignorant of its mission in the crusade for the conversion of the world. As a cure for its diffidence and indifference, he had prescribed a spiritual and temporal identification with Rome. During the next two decades of the 'forties and 'fifties, English Catholicism was reconstructed in his image. The Oxford movement, the restoration of the hierarchy, and Wiseman's appointment as Archbishop of Westminster restored to the Church much of its old colour and vigour. Two vociferous Oxford converts, William George Ward, a layman, and Henry Edward Manning, provost of Westminster, pledged themselves to the task of suppressing the traditional anti-Roman, anti-papal temper of English Catholicism.

During the 'fifties a rival party of reform began to emerge, which saw salvation not in the stiffnecked scholasticism and Romanism of the Ultramontanes but in the Liberal Catholicism that had been so successful on the Continent. Where the Ultramontanes called for war against the secular State, the Liberals summoned English Catholics to a domestic house-cleaning to sweep away the outmoded prejudices that cluttered up their minds and to make room for the scientific, philosophical and historical discoveries in which the modern world abounded. Curiously enough, the Oxford movement, which had furnished the Ultramontanes with some of their most colourful figures, had also fed the ranks and leadership of the Liberals, so that each party could, with justice, accuse the other of being a foreign importation, not indigenous to the English Catholic mentality. Acton, of course, was an 'old Catholic', and could boast as respectable a heritage as most, but even he appeared in England as an alien, a product of foreign scholarship, who proposed, with all the complacent assurance of the proselyte recently come into the truth, to enlighten those unfortunates still immersed in sin and darkness. Moreover, although English Liberal Catholicism was henceforth to be associated with his name, he had not initiated the movement. By 1858, when he entered upon the scene as editor of the *Rambler*, organ of the Liberal Catholics, the journal had had a stormy history of ten years.

The *Rambler* had started publication in January 1848. It had been first a weekly and then a monthly, and had enjoyed a succession of editors, but the occasional innovations on its masthead betokened no change in its policy, no suspension of hostilities between it and the Ultramontane journal, the *Dublin Review*. Its purpose remained the same: to broaden the perspective of Catholics and instruct them in the ways of modern thought. Opponents disputed both its right to act as instructor and the method and content of its instruction, but what was rarely denied, at least privately, was the need for instruction of some sort. Even the indomitable Ward is said to have admitted that an English Catholic meeting a Protestant in controversy was like a barbarian meeting a civilized man. But Ward, unlike Acton, preferred the barbarian believer to the civilized man flirting with scepticism. When Frederick Faber, a convert priest and ardent Ultramontane, told him, 'I walk down the street in my habit, and I feel that I dispel invincible ignorance wherever I go,' Ward replied: 'But do you make conversions? For if you do not, the dispelling of invincible ignorance is not a good, but an evil, for it makes those who were formerly in good faith henceforth responsible for their errors.'[1]

That the *Rambler* might dispel ignorance only to produce what Ward was certain was a greater evil became apparent almost immediately. It was a constant source of irritation to the Ultramontanes, goading them on the stagnant condition of Catholic intellectual life, or teasing them with theological and philosophical speculations that verged on the heterodox. When Acton joined the *Rambler* early in 1858, as part proprietor and editor, the magazine had already provoked Cardinal Wiseman to open rebuke and covert warnings. Acton ignored both. His first serious tactical error came in January and February, 1859, when the *Rambler* took it upon itself to criticize the behaviour of the Catholic bishops in regard to a recently appointed Royal Commission. In presuming to encroach upon the episcopal prerogative, the journal exposed itself to censure, and Wiseman was provided with a legitimate excuse for intervening. It seemed at first as if Richard Simpson was the only offending editor, but Wiseman made it clear that unless Acton also resigned, the journal would not escape censure. On condition that Newman became editor, Acton and Simpson agreed to retire. Newman, whose strategy it was to make the principles of Liberal Catholicism acceptable by making the language more diplomatic, realized, after putting out only two issues, that the Ultramontanes would not be so easily appeased. When one of his own articles, 'On Consulting the Faithful in Matters of Doctrine', was delated to the Congregation of the Index at Rome for implying the fallibility of the Church, he hastily resigned. The *Rambler* was then returned to its former proprietors, Acton and Simpson, who were now joined by John Moore Capes. Acton and T. F. Wetherell were

[1] Bernard Ward, *The Sequel to Catholic Emancipation* (2 vols.; London, 1915), II, 258.

joint editors, with Simpson, as he himself put it, in the position of 'an exceptionally privileged contributor'.[1]

After the excitement of the last years abroad, Acton found it hard to put up with the combination of intellectual medio-crity and petty irascibility that he met with in England. Five years earlier, shortly before his twentieth birthday, he had re-solved that in some way he would put his scholarship and German learning to the service of his Catholic countrymen.[2] But no sooner did he apply himself to this purpose than he discovered that his services were unwanted and his altruistic motives suspect. The narrowness of the English Catholics, he wrote Döllinger in 1858, far surpassed his most disagree-able expectations. The strangest rumours circulated: 'The popular view is that a multitude of converts have conspired together, half to become apostates, the rest to remain in the Church in the hope that, as ostensible Catholics, they might do more harm through the *Rambler*.'[3] Later he complained that there was no satisfaction in editing a review 'where I see that I enjoy so little confidence and will be surrounded by so much malicious intrigue, gossip and ignorance'.[4]

Yet his spirits were less depressed than might be supposed, and he was caught up in a task made more piquant by the many opportunities it provided for ridiculing and plaguing the Ultramontanes. If he was forced to take abuse from the *Dublin Review*, he gave as good in return. Ammunition could be smuggled in by the most devious routes. Thus an osten-sibly innocent review of a book on Catherine de Medici could contain the casual but most provocative statement that al-though St. Augustine was the greatest doctor of the West, 'we

[1] Gasquet, p. liii. From Gasquet's introduction in *Lord Acton and His Circle*, it would appear that Acton was not associated with the journal until this time, whereas Acton's very first letter in that volume clearly intimates that he became part-proprietor and editor (or joint editor with Simpson) in February 1858 (Acton to Simpson, 16 February 1858, Gasquet, p. 1).

[2] Acton to Döllinger, December 1854, E. L. Woodward, 'The Place of Lord Acton in the Liberal Movement of the Nineteenth Century', *Politica*, IV (1939), 252.

[3] Friedrich, III, 210.

[4] Woodward, *Politica*, p. 253.

need not conceal the fact that he was also the father of Jansenism';[1] recriminations and counter-recriminations followed immediately, as Acton from previous experience must have known they would. Notwithstanding its title, the *Rambler* was no random collection of reflections and speculations. Not every article had a polemical intent, to be sure, but every controversial one, and some that need not have been controversial, did have. Through a variety of subjects—history, theology, politics, scholarship—a consistent tone was maintained, and almost every issue clearly labelled it the organ of Liberal Catholicism. Partly this resulted from the fact that between editors and authors there was constant collaboration. Contributors were fortunately anonymous, for it would often have been hard to decide where the author stopped and the editor began. The prominence of the editor is not surprising. Acton, after all, was not interested in journalism *per se*; he would much have preferred the more abstract, academic research of the university. For him journalism was merely an instrument for a well-defined purpose—and the purposiveness of a *Rambler* article was all too often unmistakable. To the Ultramontane, even the most unobjectionable essay appeared to be subversive in the pages of the *Rambler*.

The journal's animadversions on authority and the Church might not have been so serious at any other time, but the brief period of Acton's editorship coincided with what seemed to be a concerted attack on all religion, and particularly on the most dogmatic of religions, Roman Catholicism. John Stuart Mill was then at his zenith, and he was inculcating to a generation of readers the principles of religious scepticism and political Liberalism; *On Liberty*, the classical statement of his philosophy, appeared in 1859. The same year saw the publication of Charles Darwin's *Origin of Species*, a frontal attack on the Biblical account of creation. The new critical spirit even penetrated Oxford, and the offensive against religion, as it seemed to the more orthodox, was carried into the next year with *Essays and Reviews*, which had among its contributors the most estimable Oxford dons. In 1862 the Anglican Bishop Colenso published the pathetic tale of his experiences with the

---

[1] *Rambler*, X (1858), 216.

Zulus, who had resisted his missionary efforts and had instead succeeded in making him doubt the authenticity of Biblical revelation. At this time, when Christianity was fighting for its life, the *Rambler* perversely chose to provide its enemies with weapons, and, what was more important, with food for scandal. So, at any rate, the Ultramontanes would have it.

For Acton the point at issue was very different. He refused to take responsibility for the intentions of others, or to be associated, by amalgam, with deists or atheists. His only responsibility was to the truth, and he could not permit himself to be led astray by those with too little faith to view the truth dispassionately. There was no reason, he wrote, for Catholics to cling blindly to every detail of the Old Testament and to resist stubbornly the findings of Biblical scholars. Protestants, perhaps, having no other authority than the Bible, were unhappily obliged to defend the literal text at any cost. But Catholicism had the advantage of authorities whose function it was to single out and interpret the passages of dogmatic relevance, and of a long tradition of doctrinal development which showed the way to the assimilation of new findings'.[1] Science, he warned, was hostile to Catholics only when they rejected it and permitted it to be usurped by their enemies.[2] It was a testimony of faith as well as of knowledge to resist the temptation to ignore the sciences or to pervert them. In a private journal of 1858, he noted: 'We must not pursue science for ends independent of science. It must be pursued for its own sake, and must lead to its own results'.[3]

What the Ultramontanes, and Ward in particular, feared was that the idea of a truth independent of religion would lead to the cultivation of intellectual excellence at the expense of moral and spiritual excellence. This Acton denied. When he said that science must make its way without worrying about its effect on religion, he did not mean that religion must make way for science, and he made every concession to the scientific spirit without making a single concession to Protestantism, deism or atheism. If the Positivists spelled science with a

[1] 'Danger of Physical Sciences', *Rambler*, new series, VI (1862), 526–34.
[2] 'The Catholic Press', *Rambler*, XI (1859), 73–90.
[3] Add. MSS., 5752.

capital 'S', he thought it fatuous of them to spell god with a small 'g'. He protested that it was not scientific to make the *a priori* assumption that miracles cannot occur and hence that the Gospel, like Homer, must be treated as a myth. The Protestant rationalists violated their own scientific tenets when they rejected, out of hand, the very possibility of miracles. Catholics, he said, were more genuinely faithful both to natural experience and to religious commitment when they 'admit the possibility of miracles at all times, and at all times judge of their likelihood according to the evidence'.[1] The difference between Ward and Acton was not that Ward accepted the dogmas and miracles of Catholicism and that Acton did not, but rather that Ward exercised no critical intelligence in regard to them. Ward would have liked nothing better, as he confessed, than to be presented with a new dogma every morning, and perhaps a miracle as well, while Acton wished to apply the methods of naturalism as far as they would go and to judge even miracles on the basis of evidence. An entry in one of Acton's early journals reads: 'Historians have not to point out everywhere the hand of Providence, but to find out all the natural causes of things—enough will always remain that cannot be explained'.[2] If reason, for Acton, was not the whole of religion, neither was it its antithesis; it was rather an essential element in a mature and sensitive faith.

The 'chastity' of mathematics[3] was Acton's ideal for political as for scientific inquiry: 'In politics as in science the Church need not seek her own ends. She will obtain them if she encourages the pursuit of the ends of science, which are truth, and of the State, which are liberty. We ought to learn from mathematics fidelity to the principle and the method of inquiry and of government.'[4] Yet Acton himself was aware that the problems of politics were too complicated to lend

---

[1] 'Döllinger's History of Christianity', *Rambler*, new series, IV (1861), 168.
[2] Add. MSS., 5751. In Add. MSS., 4911, this is recorded as Döllinger's opinion.
[3] Acton to Simpson, 19 January 1859, Gasquet, p. 57.
[4] Acton to Simpson, 12 November 1861, ibid., p. 222.

themselves to such a bald claim for independence. In one of his early contributions to the *Rambler*, an essay entitled 'Political Thoughts on the Church,'[1] he tried to formulate a practical theory of the relation of Church and State in such a way as to do justice both to the idea of a Christian society and the ideal of liberty, and he found that the task required some ingenuity.

His real battle here, as in most of his *Rambler* pieces, was against Ultramontanism; but in order not to leave himself exposed to the charge of heresy or infidelity, he had first to engage in a rear-guard action against the combined forces of secular Liberalism and religious quietism. Both of these philosophies, Acton argued, shared the same delusion: that there was an absolute dichotomy of Church and State. To suppose, as they did, that Christianity could or should have no effect upon politics was to confess its inferiority to all other religions which could boast of having imposed their images upon society. In fact, Acton pointed out, the most revolutionary aspect of Christianity had been not its doctrinal innovations but its new sense of public rights and duties. It was for this reason that the Romans tolerated all religions except the one which threatened to revolutionize the heathen State. That the early Christians were themselves unaware of the full scope of the revolution they had set in motion and naïvely protested their loyalty to the empire does not detract from the political sagacity of the Romans. By the Middle Ages, when Christianity finally came of age with its own distinctive political and social institutions, religion could no longer pretend to be indifferent to politics.

If religion and politics were not irrevocably divorced, however, neither were they identical. In their longing to witness the divine order incarnate in the world, the Ultramontanes made the vulgar error of seeking their model in the theocracy of the Jews or the Greek State of antiquity—the very antithesis, Acton objected, to the Christian ideal. In the Jewish as in the Greek world, political and religious obligations had been one, with the State absolute over both. Christianity introduced the novel conception of a conscience immune from

[1] *Rambler*, XI (1859), 30–49; reprinted in *History of Freedom*, pp. 188–211.

political interference, a sanctuary of liberty. The despotism of antiquity was repudiated in the injunction to render to Caesar the things that are Caesar's and to God the things that are God's. Since it was in the Middle Ages that Christ's precept came to political fruition, those States that were most profoundly affected by the medieval experiences were those that were now the freest. Thus England, in spite of its religious apostasy, was the most truly Catholic State, while countries that were ostensibly and formally Catholic were least Catholic in political spirit. In France, Spain, Italy and Bavaria, the Church subordinated itself to absolutism. 'The demand for a really Catholic system of government falls with the greatest weight of reproach on the Catholic States.'[1]

It was no 'party line' that Acton was propounding, which accounts for the fact that the essay was both more difficult and more disconcerting than might be expected. Here, as elsewhere, he was forced to skirt the obvious alternatives, not out of deliberate equivocation or even unintended ambiguity, but because his ideas refused to submit to the ordinary categories of politics. Liberty of religion or the Christian State? men would ask; and Acton would reply: both, for the unique character of the Christian State is liberty. Modern politics and science or medieval politics and scholasticism? And Acton answered: modern science but medieval politics, for scholasticism is the pursuit of sterile formulas, while what generally passes as modern political doctrines are only the absolutistic ideas of antiquity refurbished by the Reformation.

Men were divided into two camps—and the *Rambler* straddled both. The Ultramontanes, defending the idea of the Christian State, loudly proclaimed their contempt for the pagan State which they accused the Liberals of fostering. Yet in Acton's terms it was the Ultramontanes themselves who were giving currency to the pagan ideal of a Church and State in one, and whose solicitude for the temporal interests of Catholic countries made them violate the spiritual ideals of the Catholic Church. The secular Liberals, on the other hand, concerned with the liberty of the State and not at all with the liberty of the Church, came to despotism by a new road. The

[1] ibid., p. 210.

43

only Christian solution was that expressed by the Liberal Catholics in the phrase, 'a free Church in a free State'. Because Catholics could not safely look to the State for favours, their only protection lay in liberty and independence. And to have a free Church there had to be a free nation, for an absolutist State would not tolerate a genuinely independent Church. The Ultramontanes, with their affinity for absolutism, were as great a calamity to religion as the most authoritarian secularists. 'In the presence of anarchy they sought a remedy in despotism; they opposed modern unbelief with an exploded superstition, and strove to expel the new devil with the old one.'[1] The *Univers*, Acton complained, was 'the justification of all that Protestants reproach us with'.[2]

Protestantism, however, had its own cross to bear and its own conscience to appease. In the most distinguished essay of his youth, 'The Protestant Theory of Persecution',[3] Acton undertook to examine what was historically and politically the most urgent problem of religious liberty, that of religious toleration. The subject took him into a re-examination of Protestantism's claim to the paternity of Liberalism and toleration.

Protestantism, Acton found, was no more the progenitor of political freedom than was Catholicism. On the contrary, the modern absolutist State was created when Protestantism abolished the autonomy and privileges of the corporate bodies that formerly made up society. The only liberty recognized by the Protestants was the liberty of the individual; the only authority was the authority of the State. Thus the individual acquired the right to worship in whatever religion he wished, but his Church was deprived of the right to administer its own laws. By this means, the emancipation of the individual became a refined technique for ensuring his utter subjection, and the limited power previously exercised by the Church was replaced by the absolute power of the State.

It had seemed, in the first years of the Reformation, as if

---

[1] 'The Count de Montalembert', *Rambler*, X (1858), 423.
[2] Add. MSS., 5528.
[3] *Rambler*, new series, VI (1862), 318–51; reprinted in *Essays on Freedom and Power*, ed. Gertrude Himmelfarb (Boston, 1948), pp. 88–127.

religious freedom might be an integral feature of Protestant-ism, but this turned out to be no more than a shrewd exploita-tion of necessity. So long as the secular powers were joined in league against the Reformation, the Protestants had no choice but to claim the right of religious freedom: 'Every relig-ious party, however exclusive or servile its theory may be, if it is in contradiction with a system generally accepted and pro-tected by law, must necessarily, at its first appearance, assume the protection of the idea that the conscience is free. Before a new authority can be set up in the place of one that exists, there is an interval when the right of dissent must be proclaimed.'[1]

The situation was soon altered, however. When Zwinglian-ism, Anabaptism and the Peasant's War induced Luther to seek the support of the princes, he discovered that the sacrifice of the doctrine of liberty was no exorbitant payment for the security and power to be derived from the alliance with the State. It turned out, in fact, to be no sacrifice at all, for by a single judiciously constructed formula, he was able at the same time to deny the authority of Catholic princes and uphold that of Protestants: the civil power, he decreed, was responsible for the salvation of its subjects, salvation being defined in accordance with the confession of Augsburg. It was because Luther's doctrines were so conveniently subversive in Catholic countries and tyrannical in Protestant ones that Ranke could call him one of the greatest Conservatives that ever lived, while Luther's biographer, Karl Jürgens, could observe, more dis-criminatingly, that no one was at once so great an insurgent and so great a defender of order. 'Neither of these writers', Acton observed, 'understood that the same principle lies at the root both of revolution and of passive obedience, and that the difference is only in the temper of the person who applies it, and in the outward circumstances.'[2]

Theology completed the pattern of tyranny. In Lutheranism, the doctrine of justification by faith served to belittle good works, while in Calvinism the institution of the elect played havoc with the rights and liberties of those who had not been favoured with the visible token of salvation. Because it was absurd to suppose that kings could avoid occasional acts of

[1] *Freedom and Power*, pp. 91–2.   [2] ibid., p. 100.

injustice, Luther was careful to provide, not safeguards against their abuse of power, but the forgiveness of their sins. Thus armed with absolute power, rulers were charged with responsibility for the purity of the faith. Unregenerate men, who had neither moral virtue nor civil rights, had the choice of being converted or destroyed. This logic of persecution was so persuasive that even the lesser sects, the victims of Lutheranism, were taken in by it, and made the same absolute claims for their own religions that the Lutherans more effectively made for theirs.

Catholicism was also weighed down by a long history of persecution, but Acton thought it was neither as essential to the Catholic faith nor as deeply imbedded in the Catholic mentality as was Protestant intolerance. The early Catholic Church 'began with the principle of liberty, both as her claim and as her rule'.[1] When persecution came, it was based upon two ideas: the immorality of apostasy and the practical subversiveness of heresy, both of which were related to the medieval assumption of the religious unity of the empire. Catholics became persecutors for practical reasons—because heresy and apostasy were felt to undermine the moral sense upon which the political authority of the empire rested. For this reason, Jews, Mohammedans, heathens and even schismatics, who enjoyed personal freedom and the ownership of property, were denied political rights, rights that presupposed a conception of duty and morality to which they were presumably alien. This theory of persecution was available to Protestantism, and it would even have catered to their most sanguinary impulses, for it was capable of radical extension. Any departure from orthodoxy could have been—and sometimes was—stigmatized by the Catholics as blasphemy, and blasphemy was only a short step to immorality and immorality to the subversion of the civil order, the unity of society. Yet Protestants disdained this strategy. Instead of being content to defend persecution as a practical social expedient, they introduced the revolutionary idea that it could be justified by purely speculative reasons and could be directed against purely speculative errors. Catholic persecution may have been, indeed

[1] ibid., p. 126.

46

was, the more bloody, but Protestant persecution was the more soul-corrupting. The Protestant theory of persecution was a new, frightful aberration in the history of intolerance.

That modern Protestantism has abandoned persecution is not a symptom of repentance but a new adjustment to expediency. Failing to impose its will upon society, Protestantism had to resort to the claim of liberty. By the perverse dialectic of theory and history, the religious liberty of early Catholicism succumbed to the persecutions of the Inquisition, while the despotism of Protestantism gave way to a philosophy of religious Liberalism.

The English historian G. G. Coulton, who was a great admirer of Acton, was reluctant to admit 'The Protestant Theory of Persecution' into the corpus of Acton's work. Familiar with his later writings, Coulton refused to believe that Acton could have subscribed to sentiments that so often seemed to vindicate religious intolerance.[1] Yet it is difficult

---

[1] There has been some controversy about the authorship of this essay. In a footnote to a letter in *Lord Acton and His Circle*, Gasquet attributed it to Simpson (p. 258). The next year Figgis and Laurence, in a prefatory note to *The History of Freedom*, in which the essay was reprinted, affirmed that the essay was by Acton and that Gasquet had been in error. The dispute was revived many years later by Coulton in the *English Historical Review* (XLVI [1931], 460). Figgis and Laurence, he said, admitted the essay on the testimony of Wetherell, whose memory was not always reliable. Because the style did not impress him as 'Actonian', Coulton decided that Gasquet must have been right in ascribing it to Simpson. The whole controversy, however, appears to have been based upon a simple mistake. The words, 'your article', in Acton's letter to Simpson, which Gasquet assumed to refer to 'The Protestant Theory of Persecution', and which was his only reason for attributing that article to Simpson rather than to Acton, in fact referred to the essay, 'Moral Law and Political Legislation', which appeared in the same issue of the *Rambler*. Of this there is no doubt, for Acton's letter went on to discuss the exact problem posed in the essay on Moral Law (the misguided effort to apply the ascetic ideal to the sphere of public life), and concluded by suggesting as a title for that essay, 'Religion and Policy', which was only a variation of the title finally decided upon. It is easy to understand how Gasquet, perhaps unfamiliar with the latter essay, was misled into thinking that 'Religion and Policy' was an alternative title for 'The Protestant Theory'.

47

to think of anyone in England except Acton who would have been likely to quote so extensively from the German theologians, Döllinger, Möhler, Jarcke and Jörg, the latter two virtually unknown outside of Germany. Indeed the central theme of the essay—the distinction between Catholic and Protestant persecution, with its partiality for the Catholic brand—Acton had borrowed from Döllinger's *Church and Churches*, as his notes testify.[1]

'The Protestant Theory of Persecution' was no isolated specimen of Acton's views. His published work, and even more his private notebooks and journals of the time, consistently deplored but carefully refrained from repudiating persecution. Commenting on a review that had been submitted to the *Rambler*, he wrote: 'To say that persecution is wrong, nakedly, seems to me first of all untrue, but at the same time, it is in contradiction with solemn decrees, with Leo X's Bull against Luther, with a Breve of Benedict XIV of 1748, and with one of Pius VI of 1791.'[2] What he was, years later, to describe as the cardinal tenet of his Liberalism, the refusal to sanction murder, was in his youth a consideration of only secondary importance. At this time he could urge that the great injury perpetrated by the Inquisition was its contribution to political despotism and intellectual stagnation, and that the murder of 20,000 human beings was only one of the 'picturesque details' which excite the imaginations and passions of men, but obscure the real import of the institution.[3] He could even assign to the Inquisition the merit of being a 'true and effective guardian of the morality of the people' at a time when the medieval wars had reduced the Spaniards to barbarism.[4] Or he could describe persecution and tolerance as relative conditions, proper to different stages of civilization: 'At one period toleration would destroy society; at another, persecution is fatal to liberty.'[5] The ideas that Coulton found most disturbing in

[1] Add. MSS., 4903.
[2] Acton to Simpson, 13 December 1861, Gasquet, p. 243.
[3] Review of Karl von Hefele, *The Life of Cardinal Ximenes*, *Rambler*, new series, III (1860), 170.
[4] ibid.
[5] 'Smith's Irish History', *History of Freedom*, p. 252.

'The Protestant Theory' can be found in even harsher form elsewhere in Acton's early writings.

It is not really Acton's authorship that is at issue, but the essay itself. 'The Protestant Theory of Persecution' has the brilliance of an ingenious *tour de force*. The learning is impressive, the ideas are subtle, and the turns of thought are skilful; yet it is basically an exhibition of facility and virtuosity, sometimes lacking substance and often failing in conviction. This is not to suggest that Acton intended it as anything but a serious and honest contribution to the problem of religious intolerance. But he was in a difficult position, torn between a desire to yield to a Liberalism that threatened to sweep away everything before it, and a need to come to terms, at least on some points, with an orthodox reading of Church history that was fundamentally irreconcilable with Liberalism. The tortuous dialectic of the essay, intriguing the reader without necessarily commanding his assent, was a reflection of the tensions and pressures under which he worked.

As a speculative exercise the essay is beyond criticism. If Protestant and Catholic persecution were in fact distinguishable in the manner he suggested, the essay would have been profound as well as brilliant. The distinctions, however, seem to be more plausible than real. Authorities of Acton's own choosing—Henry C. Lea, for example, on the Inquisition—denied that even in theory Catholic persecution was limited to the practical and social; Catholics, like Protestants, were more exercised over the errors that corrupt a man's soul than those that corrupt society. In practice the distinction between Catholics and Protestants was even less tenable. The Spanish Inquisition, for example, was directed more against infidels—Jews and Moors—than against apostates. The case of Spain, in fact, exposes Acton at his weakest. On the theory that persecution for reasons of State was preferable to persecution for reasons of theology, he went so far as to suggest that while the Roman Inquisition of the Counter-Reformation could not be justified, the Spanish Inquisition, which was an instrument of the State, was in principle justified.[1] Yet one of his main

[1] Excerpt of a letter from Acton to Döllinger, 1 April 1862, Add. MSS., 4903.

E   49

objections to Protestantism was the fact that it had revived the
Church-State of antiquity, creating a single, undifferentiated
and absolute power. It would seem, from his own account,
that Catholic Spain had anticipated Protestantism in this matter.
His argument had come full circle, and his theoretical subtleties vanished when confronted with the crude, practical
workings of Catholic and Protestant intolerance. Many years
later he was to reduce the question of persecution—both
Catholic and Protestant—to a much simpler formula, in which
persecution was murder and all those implicated in it were
murderers. The fine distinctions he had sought in his youth
were later to horrify him, and he was to discover that with an
evil of such enormity, these distinctions were bad taste, bad
ethics and bad history.

Yet it is only in retrospect, in comparison with Acton's
later writings, that 'The Protestant Theory of Persecution'
seems unduly complacent. At the time it was published it was
intended as a tract against persecution in general, rather than
as an apology for Catholic persecution in particular. Whatever
practices and theories had governed the past, the obligation
of Catholics and Protestants in the present, he was certain, was
to promote liberty and tolerance, an obligation that the Catholic Church should be particularly glad to discharge: 'No longer
compelled to devise theories in justification of a system imposed on her by the exigencies of half-organized societies, she
is enabled to revert to a policy more suited to her nature and
to her most venerable traditions; and the principle of liberty
has already restored to her much of that which the principle of
unity took away'.[1]

The course of Acton's progress towards a more thoroughgoing Liberalism should not obscure the genuine elements of
Liberalism present in his early work. If 'The Protestant Theory'
fell short of his later work, it did so not as a programme for the
nineteenth century but as an analysis of the fifteenth or sixteenth—and even in this respect it was already far advanced.
Compared with the enthusiastic praise lavished upon the
Inquisition by the Italian Ultramontane journal *Civiltà Cattolica* ('A sublime spectacle of social perfection', a 'model of

[1] 'Smith's Irish History', *History of Freedom*, p. 255.

justice'),¹ or the opportunism of the French Ultramontane,
Louis Veuillot (to whom is attributed the remark, 'When you
(the Liberals) are the masters, we claim complete liberty for
ourselves because your principles require it, and when we are
the masters, we refuse it to you because it is contrary to our
principles'),² Acton's defence of the Inquisition was notably
grudging.

On the first page of a new copy-book, probably some time
in 1861, Acton noted: 'Every effort has been made to accommodate the Church to the degenerate nature of man, and these
attempts are [a] great part of her history.'³ Among the accom-
modations he had in mind were religious persecution and the
temporal power of the papacy. Not of the essence of the
Church, they were expedients that might be understood and
even justified in their historical contexts. The mischief of
Ultramontanism, he felt, was that it exulted in them and sought
to perpetuate them.

The temporal power of the papacy in Italy had been an issue
in international politics all during the pontificate of Pius IX,
and was becoming one of the main points of contention between Ultramontanism and liberal Catholicism. When Acton
and Döllinger visited Rome in 1857, they had already been
making cautious, tentative approaches to the Liberal position.
'The Church', Acton then noted in his journal, 'was 700 years
without a territory, and might be so again for 7,000 years.
As things now are it cannot be, but such a state of things
might be possible.'⁴ In the next few years, the possible seemed
more and more probable. When Acton finally took public
cognizance of 'The Roman Question' in the *Rambler*, in January
1860,⁵ the disruption of the Papal States was imminent and an
assembly in the Romagna had already called for annexation
to the kingdom of Sardinia.

'The Roman Question' was a study in the art of temporizing.

¹ Cited by Friedrich, III, 439.
² Emile de Laveleye, *Le Gouvernement dans la démocratie* (2 vols.; Paris,
1891), I, 187–8.
³ Add. MSS., 4860.   ⁴ Add. MSS., 5751.
⁵ *Rambler*, new series, II (1860), 137–54.

Acton could not summon much enthusiasm to the defence of the Pope, nor great vindictiveness to the trouncing of the Italian nationalists. He conceded to the nationalists the injustice of withholding from the subjects of the Pope, because of a supposed religious interest which they did not consider decisive, those political rights which are normally granted to all men: 'It is invidious to assert that the subjects of the Pope must be necessarily less free than those of other princes. Can any spiritual necessity be an excuse for so gross a political wrong?'[1] But he promptly redressed the balance. The revolutionists, he said, were not offended, as they might properly have been, by the 'human defect' of the temporal power, the maladministration of the Pope, but by the 'divine institution' of the papacy, the fact that the Church existed by divine sanction rather than on the sufferance of an omnipotent State. Against the revolutionary theory that all power was derived from the people and none from God, and that the State, presumably representing the general will, was absolute, Acton looked to the temporal power of the Pope as a counter-assertion of independence. Since the indispensable conditions of independence were property and sovereignty, these were the attributes of the power claimed by the Pope. The temporal power, then, although not of the nature and essence of the Church, was a necessary expedient forced upon her by a profane world. 'It is her protection against the State, and a monument of her imperfect victory over the ideas of the outer world. It is not so much an advantage as a necessity, not so much desirable as inevitable.'[2]

When 'The Roman Question' appeared, it met with the approval of few outside of the *Rambler*'s immediate circle. And even within the inner circle there was dissatisfaction. Wetherell (nominally joint-editor with Acton, but who had been prevented by other work from engaging actively in an editorial capacity) submitted his resignation, explaining that he could not go so far as Acton in support of the temporal power, and withdrew it only after he was assured that he had misunderstood the point of the article. The Ultramontanes, on the other hand, automatically distrusting everything issuing from the

---

[1] ibid., p. 140. [2] ibid., p. 149.

pen of Acton or the pages of the *Rambler*, took the article to be a weasel-mouthed attack on the temporal power. Partisanship ran high, and the minimal position Acton was trying to reach, based upon a weighing of lesser evils, gave offence now to one side, now to the other.

While working on the essay, Acton had written: 'I am afraid I am a partisan of sinking ships, and I know none more ostensibly sinking just now than St. Peter's.'[1] His arguments were unorthodox and he made concessions to the Italian nationalists, but he was privately convinced that this was the only honest and effective way to defend the temporal power. Gradually, however, the inherent vulgarity of politics won out over the subtleties of Acton's theories, and it appeared that the popular alternatives, secular Liberalism *versus* Ultramontanism, were in fact the only feasible alternatives. The Ultramontanes, who had always predicted that the radical spirit of free inquiry cultivated by the *Rambler* would jeopardize the entire structure of the papacy, seemed vindicated. During 1860 and 1861 the journal trod the downward path of Liberalism.

Of a Belgian statesman, an anti-clerical Catholic described as a double-barrelled gun with one barrel to shoot at his enemies and the other at his friends, Acton commented approvingly: '*Rambler, tout pur.*'[2] Until 1860 he had hoped to be above the battle, or, at worst, to wage an independent war with a private strategy and congenial subalterns. By 1861, however, for all practical purposes his forces had been merged with those of the Liberals; in the ideal of the 'united front' of a later day, they marched separately and fought together.

It was Döllinger, as usual, who called the turn. In April 1861 he delivered the Odeon lectures in Munich, later published in an expanded version under the title, *Church and Churches*, and marking a new stage in his divergence from Rome. The lectures drew out and extended the implications of what he and Acton had hinted at before: the temporal power, no necessary part of the Catholic system, should be abdicated graciously and voluntarily before the nationalists seized it by force. Döllinger had consulted with Acton before

[1] Acton to Simpson, 7 December 1859, Gasquet, p. 113.
[2] Acton to Simpson, July 1860, ibid., p. 145.

delivering the lectures and again while preparing them for the press, and barely was the book set in type before Acton started to write his account of it for the *Rambler*, a sixty-two page leading article for the November issue called 'Döllinger on the Temporal Power'.[1] He wrote to Simpson to warn him: 'I will do it very gently, but there are things in the book to make each particular hair to stand on end, so it will not be well to put overmuch in the other articles.'[2]

'Döllinger on the Temporal Power' was a condensation of *Church and Churches* and at the same time a defence of it against possible criticism. There was a certain artfulness in both the essay and the book, for although they were obviously meant as treatises on the temporal power and attacks on papal policy, they came to their subjects by way of a long historical and critical digression into the nature of Protestantism. The Ultramontane might have interpreted this, with some justice, as a design to placate him and draw his righteous anger from the more offensive passages. But it was also intended to bring the issue into a larger perspective, to keep in view the enemy outside the gates as well as within. Their criticisms of Rome, Acton and Döllinger had to make clear, implied no acceptance of the Protestant reading of history, and if the papal States were in need of reform, the history of Protestant despotism and dissolution provided no model for that reform. It was as Catholics interested in strengthening their Church that they undertook to chastise it, Catholics conscious of 'the almost triumphant security which belongs to a Church possessing an acknowledged authority, a definite organization, and a system brought down by tradition from the apostolic age.'[3]

Having set down these first principles of their faith, they could then proceed to the matter at hand, the rescue of the Church from the suicidal dependence upon the temporal power at a time when the temporal power was being snatched away from under it. In the interest of self-preservation, the temporal

---

[1] *Rambler*, new series, VI (1861), 1–62; reprinted in *History of Freedom*, pp. 301–74. In May, under 'Current Events', Acton had reported on the Odeon lectures, but since there had been no official text at the time, he took the occasion in his November article to regret his premature and hasty report.   [2] 25 September 1861, Gasquet, p. 198.

[3] *History of Freedom*, p. 343.

power had to be sharply distinguished from the essence of the Church. As a matter of plain historical fact, the Popes had not always had the temporal power, and when they had they would sometimes have been better off without it, for the good of both their spiritual and temporal obligations. A government of priests was likely to be the worst possible government, for priests, the bearers of grace and indulgence, found it hard to bend their will to an impartial, secular law.

The Pope, Döllinger and Acton concluded on an unexpectedly hopeful note, should withdraw from the anomalous position in which he had been placed. As a fitting place of refuge, they recommended Germany, where Catholicism had preserved in its greatest purity the Christian ideal of a Church unfettered by a secular bureaucracy and unfortified by the dubious authority of the police. Eventually a restoration of the papal sovereignty over some territory, perhaps much reduced in size and protected by international law, would be desirable, because in a Europe of absolute States the Pope could not be independent as a subject. But in the meantime the Pope would be nowhere less independent than in an Italy governed by a Piedmont despot and occupied by French troops. Should the restoration take place some time in the future, Acton warned, care should be taken that the Italians would not again be put in the dilemma of having to choose between the Pope and freedom. 'The Powers have clearly no right to restore the Pope for the sake of religion unless they restore freedom for the sake of the people.'[1] As for the Pope, the important thing to keep in mind was that it was not absolute power that he required to secure his independence; 'the not being governed, not the right of governing', was crucial, though to be sure, 'governing is the only way to avoid being governed'.[2]

HAZARDS OF RELIGIOUS JOURNALISM

The tempers that had already been exacerbated by the *Rambler's* haughty pronouncements on science and scholarship

[1] Acton to Simpson, 23 November 1861, Gasquet, p. 229.
[2] Acton to Simpson, 9 October 1861, ibid., p. 213.

and by its strictures on Church history came to the breaking point on the issue of the temporal power. Wilfrid Ward, the son of W. G. Ward, has described the hysteria with which this controversy was charged in the 'sixties, the whispered reports that X was 'not sound' on the temporal power, the feverish gossip which put a man 'for' or 'against' it.[1] The *Saturday Review* professed to be astonished at the violence of Catholic polemics: 'It is clear, from the extraordinary freedom with which names and persons are handled, and from the eagerness of bishops and dignitaries to enter into the lists, that an amount of pugnacity exists among Roman Catholics which by no means finds sufficient vent in its onslaught on Protestantism.'[2]

The *Dublin Review*, the voice of Ultramontanism, was not so much infuriated by the facts adduced by Döllinger and Acton, or even their conclusions, as by the spirit in which they were presented. To suppose that facts could be pitted against the expressed will of the Pope seemed to it presumptuous and arrogant. And to assume the dry, critical tone of the impartial scholar, at a time when 'the Father of Christendom is deserted by friends, beset by enemies, mocked, calumniated, abused',[3] was the final outrage. The *Rambler* stood convicted of a 'want of reverence for authority'.[4] In June 1861, Acton was given notice that the journal's position on the temporal power would not go unchallenged. Cardinal Antonelli, Secretary of State to the Pope, insisted that the *Rambler* come out unequivocally for the temporal power and against the Liberal Party, which was supporting the Italian nationalists. Apparently on instructions from Wiseman, Manning met with Acton to warn him of an impending censure from Rome and to recommend that he dissociate himself from the journal to avoid being implicated in it. Newman, when informed by Acton of these developments, agreed that Antonelli was exceeding his authority, but

[1] Ward, *Newman*, I, 526.
[2] *Saturday Review*, XIV (1862), 195.
[3] 'Döllinger and the Temporal Power of the Popes', *Dublin Review*, L (1861), 200.
[4] Wilfrid Ward, *William George Ward and the Catholic Revival* (London, 1893), p. 147.

urged him nevertheless to give up the journal and retire to Aldenham, where he might occupy himself with less ephemeral and more rewarding work than the editing of a periodical: 'Gibbon, in the beginning of his autobiography, refers to Aldenham—might it not become more classical (and somewhat dearer to a Catholic) than Lausanne? Gladstone, in the dedication of one of his early works to Lord Lyttelton, talks of his writing in the classical groves of Hagley; yet what is the history of Henry II to the "Opus Magnum" which might be identified with Aldenham?'[1]

But Acton would not be put off by these blandishments. He replied that the *Rambler* had consented to the exclusion of theology from its pages, and nothing remained over which the ecclesiastical authorities could properly claim jurisdiction. 'In political life', he reminded Newman,' we should not be deterred, I suppose, by the threat or fear of even excommunication, from doing what we should deem our duty.'[2]

Like many others, Newman considered Simpson rather than Acton to be the offending party. And there is no doubt but that Simpson's deadly wit took its toll among Ultramontanes whose pomposity was only equalled by ignorance. Yet, as Acton took pains to make clear, it was not the indiscretions of Simpson that brought down the ire of Ultramontanes, but the fundamental principles of Liberalism. If the contributors were outspoken and personal in their writing, they were accused of brazenness and irreverence; if they were dispassionate and objective they were accused of dissimulation and irreverence. Simpson once complained that when he touched on matters of theology he was reproved for going out of his province, and when he sedulously avoided them he was criticized for ignoring the supernatural and lapsing into infidelity. It was a 'losing game', Acton decided.[3] Newman at one time had suggested that in order to convince the bishops of the *Rambler's* orthodoxy, it ought to adopt a board of censors whose gravity and sense of responsibility would be unimpeachable. Besides him-

[1] 20 June 1861, Ward, *Newman*, I, 523.
[2] 2 July 1861, ibid., p. 527.
[3] Acton to Newman, 29 June 1860, ibid., p. 510.

self he had proposed Döllinger, Victor de Buck and Auguste Gratry, all priests. Acton replied by pointing out that Newman was the author of an article interpreted as heretical, Döllinger had written the note on the Jansenism of St. Augustine, de Buck had contributed a letter in which it was assumed that there was no dogmatic difference between the schismatics and the Church (which Acton prudently rejected), and Gratry had offered a paper on the difference between papism and Catholicism, of which he himself had said that if it should appear under his own name he would be obliged to leave the Oratory the same day. Given the facts of 'a hostile and illiterate episcopate, an ignorant clergy, a prejudiced and divided laity',[1] and faced with the prospect of imminent censure, the *Rambler* could only suspend publication.

In an ingenious but quite transparent move, Acton approached the editors of the *Dublin Review* with the proposal that the two journals merge, a proposal that was, of course, promptly declined. Having thus, to his own satisfaction at any rate, saddled the Ultramontanes with the onus of perpetuating Catholic factionalism, Acton proceeded with his plans to transform the *Rambler* into the more serious and scholarly quarterly, the *Home and Foreign Review*.

With the old staff and old ideas, the new title and format deceived no one, and the *Home and Foreign Review* inherited all the ill-will formerly directed against the *Rambler*. From its first issue, when it insisted upon speaking of Pope Paul III's 'son' rather than the conventional euphemism of 'nephew', until the last stormy issue just two years later, the journal carried on an incessant feud with the hierarchy. Immediately upon its appearance, Wiseman had censured both the *Rambler* and the *Review* for 'the absence for years of all reserve or reverence in its treatment of persons or of things deemed sacred, its grazing over the very edges of the most perilous abysses of error, and its habitual preferences of uncatholic to catholic instincts, tendencies and motives'.[2] The final crisis

[1] ibid.
[2] *Reply of his Eminence Cardinal Wiseman to an Address presented by the Clergy Secular and Regular of the Archdiocese of Westminster* (London, 1862), p. 27.

was precipitated once again by Döllinger. In a Catholic congress held in Munich in September 1863, Döllinger, attacking scholastic theology, had called for a bold, modern and independent philosophy to transcend the artificial barriers separating the Churches and effect a new religious union. Reporting on the congress in the *Review*, Acton enthusiastically seconded Döllinger's address.[1] By this act the journal became implicated in a papal brief, issued in December, censuring the views expressed in the speech.[2] With scholastic theology upheld as the true teaching of the Church, and the Roman congregations confirmed in their right to supervise science and scholarship, the *Home and Foreign Review* clearly stood condemned.

The last issue of the *Home and Foreign Review* appeared in April 1864. The article, 'Conflicts with Rome', which carried Acton's signature for the first time, reviewed the history of the journal and the decision to discontinue it:

'It would be wrong to abandon principles which have been well considered and are sincerely held, and it would also be wrong to assail the authority which contradicts them. The principles have not ceased to be true, nor the authority to be legitimate because the two are in contradiction. To submit the intellect and conscience without examining the reasonableness and justice of this decree, or to reject the authority on the ground of its having been abused, would equally be a sin, on one side against morals, on the other against faith. . . .

'Warned, therefore, by the language of the Brief, I will not provoke ecclesiastical authority to a more explicit repudiation of doctrines which are necessary to secure its influence upon the advance of modern science. I will not challenge a conflict which would only deceive the world into a belief that religion cannot be harmonized with all that is right and true in the progress of the present age. But I will sacrifice the existence of the *Review* to the defence of its principles, in order that I may combine the obedience which is due to legitimate ecclesiastical

[1] 'The Munich Congress', *Home and Foreign Review*, IV (1864), 209–44.
[2] The Brief was not published until March of the next year, which accounts for the fact that the laudatory report of Döllinger's address appeared in the *Review* in January 1864, and that not until April was the Brief discussed.

authority, with an equally conscientious maintenance of the rightful and necessary liberty of thought.'[1]

Later that year Matthew Arnold published his essay, 'The Function of Criticism at the Present Time', an eloquent plea for criticism that would also be creative, independent, honest, unencumbered by practical considerations or profane interests. There existed no criticism worthy of the name, he deplored, no free play of mind. As soon as a journal gave evidence of intellectual restlessness and imagination, it was made to feel its chains. 'We saw this the other day', Arnold wrote, 'in the extinction, so much to be regretted, of the *Home and Foreign Review*; perhaps in no organ of criticism in this country was there so much knowledge, so much play of mind; but these could not save it. *The Dublin Review* subordinates play of mind to the practical business of Roman Catholicism, and lives.'[2]

FORESHADOWINGS OF INFALLIBILITY

There was a pathetic bravado in the behaviour of the papacy at this time, a blustering display of confidence and intrepidity that was as bold as it was ill-founded. When Pius issued the decree of the Immaculate Conception of Mary, under whose special providence he regarded himself, he was sovereign in Rome only on the sufferance of the French emperor and French troops. When he boasted loudest of the immutability of his temporal power, that power was being irretrievably lost to him. And when, ten years to the day after the decree of Immaculate Conception, the papacy issued the most famous modern document of Ultramontane principles, the Syllabus of Errors, it followed by three months the publication of the convention between Napoleon III and King Victor Emmanuel by which Napoleon agreed to withdraw his support of the papal sovereignty.

The *Syllabus Errorum*, issued by Pius on 15 December 1864, and the Encyclical *Quanta Cura* which accompanied it, were an

---

[1] 'Conflicts with Rome', *History of Freedom*, pp. 487-8, 489.
[2] Arnold, *Essays Literary and Critical* (Everyman ed.; London, 1938), p. 13.

uncompromising repudiation of every distinctive principle of modern society. Like most organizational documents, these had a double function: to the Protestant, secular world, they served as an affirmation of Catholic principles; to dissident Catholics, preaching the gospel of 'a free Church in a free State', they were a warning and a threat. The Syllabus, a list of 'the principal errors of our time', is perhaps the most detailed indictment of Liberalism ever drawn up. Eighty propositions stood condemned as heresies. These ranged from beliefs that were flagrantly heretical—such as the denial of the existence of God—to those in which only the most extravagant Ultramontanes could find heresy. The casualties suffered by Acton were heavy. He discovered that it was now heretical to believe that: only dogmas of faith were binding on Catholic teachers and authors and that in all other matters they were free to follow the dictates of science, philosophy and history; scholasticism was inadequate in the modern age; the Church should renounce the temporal power and rely upon spiritual rather than coercive authority; it was an historical fact that the temporal power and other civil immunities enjoyed by the Church often originated with the civil authority, that Popes and ecumenical councils had been known to exceed the limits of their legitimate power, and that the papacy had not been entirely blameless in the disruption of the Church; the State had the right to supervise the education of the youth and to have a part in 'matters related to religion, morality and spiritual governments'; it was desirable that there should be a separation of Church and State, freedom of the Press and freedom of worship; and it was no longer necessary that the Catholic religion should be held as the exclusive religion of the State. The final heretical proposition reads like a statement of his faith: 'The Roman Pontiff can and ought to reconcile himself to, and agree with, progress, Liberalism, and modern civilization.'[1]

Confronted with this overwhelming challenge, many Catholics took refuge in hastily devised fictions. They decided that the Syllabus was really directed against other countries than their own, or they pretended that it contained no innovations.

[1] Philip Schaff, *The Creeds of Christendom* (3 vols.; New York, 1919), II, 233.

In desperation, some bishops (Dupanloup was among them) even tried to reduce the condemned propositions to absurdities and so make light of their condemnation. Acton was too strong-minded to resort to these stratagems. Catholics, he felt, should not be lulled into a false security. The Syllabus must be taken for what it was, an attack upon all of the most deeply cherished ideas of Liberalism, a defence of scholasticism, of absolute monarchy, and of the most objectionable principles of the Index and Inquisition.[1] It was an Ultramontane document, and the Ultramontanes had read it rightly.

What the Ultramontanes could not be trusted to decide, however, was the authority which the Syllabus and Encyclical could legitimately claim. Most Ultramontanes were agreed that although the Syllabus was not binding on all Catholics, the Encyclical was. Fortunately for Acton, the consensus of Church authorities supported the Liberal position that encyclicals were not of infallible authority and therefore not absolutely binding. From this he derived what comfort he could. In Italy, in the winter of 1864-5, he was asked to join other non-Italian Catholics in an address to the Pope. He drafted an address which conspicuously avoided reference to the Encyclical and Syllabus, but the others, regarding it as an insult to the Pope, rejected it. Acton withdrew from the committee, and when the document appeared, it was without his signature.

In the providential order of the world, as Acton once said of the institution of slavery, the Syllabus was an instrument for good as well as evil, for if it was designed to shackle the minds of Catholics, it sometimes had the perverse effect of liberating them. Although few were sufficiently disturbed to seek excommunication or voluntarily to leave the Church (Thomas Arnold, a convert, contributor to the *Rambler*, and brother of Matthew Arnold, was one of these), the Syllabus came as a shocking revelation of the extent to which Ultramontanism had permeated the Church and the depth of its hostility to modern culture. Now that Rome herself had spoken, it was no longer possible to maintain the benign deception that Veuillot, Ward and the editors of the *Civiltà*

[1] Add. MSS., 4903, 4905 and 5018.

Cattolica were indulging their private idiosyncrasies. Even Dupanloup, ever ready to reconcile papal pronouncements with his own easy version of Liberalism, was more troubled by the Syllabus than he pretended to be, and Newman quoted him as saying, 'If we can tide over the next ten years we are safe.'[1]

The next ten years, however, were not to be safely tided over, and things went from bad to worse for the Liberals. In Italy the Pope issued a Brief commending the exceedingly Ultramontane *Civiltà Cattolica*. In France *Le Monde*, successor to *L'Univers*, was generally taken to be the voice of official Catholicism. And in England Manning became Archbishop of Westminster in succession to Wiseman, who died in 1865.

Manning's appointment was a scandal in the opinion not only of Liberals but also of the old Catholic families, for it was the personal decision of the Pope in defiance of the expressed wish of the canons of the Chapter of Westminster. Among the laity Manning was distrusted because of the extreme narrowness of his views; within the ecclesiastical hierarchy he was feared because of the jealousy with which he guarded his prerogatives; and theologians and scholars dubbed him 'Monsignor Ignorante' in testimony to his imperfect grasp of Church ceremonials and doctrines. Compared with Manning, Wiseman had been a paragon of tolerance and understanding. But even Manning was not severe enough for the most zealous. Mgr. Talbot saw to it that Manning did not waver, and W. G. Ward, as self-appointed lay custodian of religious orthodoxy, kept Talbot in line. A regiment in full panoply was being pressed into service to defend the faith against the insidious attacks of Acton and his associates.

The only weapon available to the Liberal Catholics which had a chance of penetrating the armour of the Ultramontanes was the secular Press. Avowedly Catholic journals, like the *Rambler* and *Home and Foreign Review*, were too exposed to ecclesiastical censure; a non-religious journal, however, might be less vulnerable. Accordingly, in the autumn of 1866 plans were started for the issuance of a new weekly, the *Chronicle*, to be edited by Wetherell and financed by an intimate friend of

[1] Newman to Pusey, 17 November 1865, Ward, *Newman*, II, 101.

Acton, Sir Roland Blennerhassett, with the old staff of the *Home and Foreign Review* as contributors. The prospectus described it as being a religious journal only in the sense in which the *Saturday Review* was religious: it would assume the truth of Catholic dogma as the *Saturday Review* assumed the truth of Anglican, but it would not discuss it.

A statement of principles dedicated the *Chronicle* to good foreign and political reporting and an expert, cosmopolitan review of literature. In both departments Acton was a major contributor. He had spent the autumn of 1866 travelling on the Continent with his wife, Countess Marie, the daughter of Count Arco-Valley, whom he had married the previous year. In the winter the couple settled down in Rome, and during the brief duration of the *Chronicle*, from March 1867 to February 1868, Acton acted as its Roman correspondent. Aside from reports on Italy printed in the 'Current Events' columns of the journal, and about a hundred book reviews on a variety of historical subjects, he contributed many short essays, of which the predominant theme was the history and contemporary situation of the Church.

To many pious Catholics there seemed to be something perverse and hysterical in the way Acton attacked now one and now another feature of Church history and policy, and a collection of his periodical writings and correspondence might give even a sympathetic reader the impression of a professional 'muckraker' pouncing upon every incident that would serve to discredit his victim. Yet this was far from true. If his *Chronicle* writings are placed within the framework of contemporary events, it becomes evident that it was the provocative actions of the Pope and not Acton's own spontaneously aggressive impulses that gave birth to his criticisms.

Early in 1867 both Acton and Döllinger, within the space of a few months, published articles on the Inquisition, Acton in the form of an essay on Sarpi in the *Chronicle*,[1] and Döllinger in the form of a long historical account of the Roman Inquisition in the *Allgemeine Zeitung*. Both had been prompted by the same circumstance, the announcement that on the 1,800th anniversary of the martyrdom of the Apostles Peter and Paul,

[1] 'Fra Paolo Sarpi', *Chronicle*, I (1867), 14–17.

which was to be celebrated in Rome in June, Pedro de Arbués, the notorious Spanish Inquisitor murdered in 1485, would be canonized. The Inquisition, it appeared, was to be exhumed out of the dead past to be restored to life and glory.

In the article on Sarpi, Acton exposed some of the deceptions commonly practised by Catholics to conceal the wickedness of the Inquisition: de Maistre's theory that the Inquisition was an instrument of the State and not of the Church, Perrone's that few or no heretics suffered under the Roman Inquisition, and even Döllinger's that there were no victims after Bruno. It was time, Acton insisted, that men were made sensible of the extraordinary carelessness of the Church with human life. The Pope and his intimates had instigated and rewarded acts of deliberate murder, and these were the same men who were later canonized as saints—Charles Borromeo and Pius V. The fine distinctions of motives that had occupied Acton five years before in the 'Protestant Theory of Persecution' no longer seemed relevant or even true. Even before the Sarpi article he had come to the conclusion that Albigensianism, for example, had been suppressed not as an anti-social doctrine but as a purely theological heresy.[1] A notebook labelled 'Inquisition', dating probably to 1866 and 1867, reveals the distance he had travelled since 1862:

'Object of the Inquisition not to combat sin—for the sin was not judged by it unless accompanied by error. Nor even to put down error. For it punished untimely or unseemly remarks the same as blasphemy. Only unity. This became an outward, fictitious, hypocritical unity. The gravest sin was pardoned, but it was death to deny the donation of Constantine. So men learnt that outward submission must be given. All this to promote authority more than faith. When ideas were punished more severely than actions—for all this time the Church was softening the criminal law, and saving men from the consequences of crime:—and the Donation was put on a level with God's own law—men understood that authority went before sincerity.'[2]

[1] Review of H. Formby's *Pictorial Bible and Church History Stories*, Vol. III, in *Home and Foreign Review*, II (1863), 218.
[2] Add. MSS., 5536.

From a variety of texts Acton gleaned the one moral precept: means are not justified by their ends. Philip II of Spain was no hero for supposing that in the service of the Church any means were legitimate;[1] Popes skilled in diplomacy were not more admirable than those boasting only spiritual nobility;[2] corruption was no less evil because it was found in the Catholic Church;[3] and murder was no less murder because it was sanctioned by the Pope and had brigands as its victims.[4]

Although the *Chronicle* did not fall under the jurisdiction of Rome—perhaps partly because of this—it was liked no more than its predecessors, and Acton's credit with the hierarchy continued to deteriorate. The Pope himself seemed to regard his presence in Rome as a deliberate affront. When Newman's associate, Ambrose St. John, came to the Vatican in 1867, he discovered that the most damaging charge held against Newman was his connection with the *Rambler* eight years earlier. The Pope complained to St. John of those who were not Catholics 'in heart' and who were 'bringing in a semi-Catholicism'; the one name he mentioned was Acton's.[5]

The *Chronicle* suspended publication in February 1868, not, however, because of ecclesiastical censorship but because of political differences among the editors. In October 1869, Liberal Catholicism acquired another vehicle, this time the *North British Review*, originally, peculiarly enough an organ of the evangelical Scottish Free Kirk party. Again Wetherell was editor and Acton and Simpson were faithful contributors. In the first issue Acton had two long essays, one on the Vatican Council scheduled to convene in December, the other on an episode in Church history which had recently come into prominence, the Massacre of St. Bartholomew.

Again Acton did not go out of his way to find matter for controversy. The Massacre of St. Bartholomew happened, just then, to be the subject of a spate of volumes and articles

[1] Review of de Pidal's *Philippe II, Antonio Pérez, et la royaume d'Aragon*, in *Chronicle*, I (1867), 403.

[2] Review of Bergenroth's Introduction to Vol. II of *The Calendar of State Papers*, in *Chronicle*, I (1867), 588.

[3] 'Essays on Academical Literature', *Chronicle*, I (1867), 667.

[4] 'Current Events', *Chronicle*, I (1867), 27–8.

[5] Ambrose St. John to Newman, 4 May 1867, Ward, *Newman*, II, 167.

by Catholics purporting to revise the conventional theory according to which the massacre of thousands of French Huguenots on St. Bartholomew's day, 1572, had been premeditated and carried out by the Catholic party. In the *Chronicle* Acton had briefly reviewed a book on the Massacre,[1] and in the *North British Review* he examined at greater length the recent literature. He concluded that there was no evidence to absolve the Church of premeditated murder or the papal court of connivance. It was not only indisputable historical fact that told against the papacy, but the whole body of casuistry which made it an act of duty and mercy to kill a heretic so that he might be removed from sin. The Inquisition had prepared the way for the massacre by hardening the heart and corrupting the conscience of the Catholic world. Only when Catholics could no longer rely on force and had to take their case before public opinion did they seek to explain away what had once been boastfully acknowledged. 'The same motive which had justified the murder now prompted the lie', and a swarm of facts were invented to absolve the papacy from this monstrous crime.[2] To Döllinger at about this time, Acton wrote: 'The story is much more abominable than we all believed.'[3] His private notes, even more than his published articles, express the bitterness and repugnance with which he looked upon the practice of religious murder: 'S.B. [St. Bartholomew] is the greatest crime of modern times. It was committed on principles professed by Rome. It was approved, sanctioned, praised by the papacy. The Holy See went out of its way to signify to the world, by permanent and solemn acts, how entirely it admired a king who slaughtered his subjects treacherously, because they were Protestants. To proclaim for ever that because a man is a Protestant it is a pious [holy] deed to cut his throat in the night. . . .'[4]

The disputes over the Massacre of St. Bartholomew, the Inquisition and even the Syllabus of Errors were only skirmishes, local engagements in advance of the major battle to be

[1] 'The Massacre of St. Bartholomew', *Chronicle*, II (1868), 158–60.
[2] 'The Massacre of St. Bartholomew', *History of Freedom*, p. 148.
[3] Woodward, *Politica*, IV (1939), 256.
[4] Add. MSS., 5004. Ellipses in the original.

fought over the dogma of papal Infallibility. It had been a long and arduous campaign for Acton, but time was on his side. With maturity had come a fund of moral indignation, historical knowledge and a practical experience of politics that made him a formidable enemy of Rome and earned him the position of leader of the lay opposition during the Vatican Council.

IV

POLITICAL CONSERVATISM AND LIBERAL POLITICS

EDMUND BURKE: 'TEACHER OF MANKIND'

FROM his earliest association with the *Rambler*, Acton was engaged in cultivating two distinct interests and careers, one in religion, the other in politics. The two-fold programme he had set himself in 1858, of converting his co-religionists to a more valid Catholicism and introducing them to the true principles of political Conservatism, remained in effect through all the journalistic ventures of the 'sixties.

In politics as in religion, Acton was the pupil of Döllinger. It was Döllinger who had weaned him away from what he regarded as the facile Liberalism of Macaulay and had placed him on a diet of Burke, particularly Burke at his most conservative. 'My first literary impressions', Acton recalled in a note to Döllinger, 'were the recommendation of Bacon's Essays, Burke, Newman. . . . Macaulay was repugnant to you. Of Burke you loved particularly the Letters on a Regicide Peace—the literary starting point of Legitimism.'[1] As Macaulay was the hero of Granville, so Burke became the hero of his stepson, and this divergence of loyalties was far more significant than their common allegiance to the Liberal Party.

It was partly to reinstate Burke as the great sage of politics and to expel the upstart Macaulay that Acton undertook the editing of the *Rambler*. As his contribution to the political education of Catholics, he proposed an essay on the later

[1] Friedrich, III, 72.

Burke: 'In the writings of his last years (1792–97) whatever was Protestant or partial or revolutionary of 1688 in his political views disappeared, and what remained was a purely Catholic view of political principles and of history. I have much to say about this that nobody has ever said.'[1] The publication of a new biography of Burke was the occasion for Acton's first contribution to the *Rambler* and his first opportunity to recommend Burke as a 'teacher for Catholics'.[2] The real Burke, however, he warned, was not the brilliant party leader defending the American Revolution, but the profound philosopher who attacked the French Revolution. It was in this second period of his career that Burke emerged as the 'teacher of mankind'.[3]

What Acton particularly admired in the later Burke was his empirical philosophy of politics, his refusal to give way to the metaphysical abstractions, the *a priori* speculations, that had been insinuated into public life by the rationalists of the French Revolution. Facts, Burke had admonished, are a severe taskmaster. They prohibit the idle vanities of philosophy and the bureaucratic pretensions of a logical, all-embracing political science, a *summum bonum* of mankind available to the benevolent legislator or administrator. Against the revolutionist who would reform all of society in accord with a preconceived logical plan, they urge the Conservative wisdom of history and tradition, which have evolved institutions that stand the test of time if not of logic. It was the genius of the English political system to adhere to the facts of English history. 'The English constitution', Acton noted in 1858, 'was excellent until removed by foreign writers into the domain of theory, when in direct contradiction with its nature and origin it came to be admired as a common representative government'.[4] Correctly interpreted, it would have taught foreigners the wisdom of reflecting in their governments the history and character of their own countries, so that by resembling it least

---

[1] 16 February 1858, Gasquet, p. 4.
[2] ibid.
[3] Review of Thomas Macknight's *History of the Life and Times of Edmund Burke*, in *Rambler*, IX (1858), 273.
[4] Add. MSS., 5752.

in externals, their constitutions would have resembled it most in spirit. Continental Liberals might have learnt much from the English who, when they were obliged to resist oppression, harked back to their traditional laws, and when they had to appeal to rights, evoked their hereditary rather than natural rights. It was by the intensity of their Conservatism, not by the fanaticism of revolution, that the English purchased their freedom.[1]

The principle of Conservatism was history, the principle of revolution was sovereignty; the Conservative found law in history, the revolutionist found it in the will of the sovereign power. One of the great confusions of political thinking, Acton warned, was the curious fact that the Whig (or Liberal) Party had a double pedigree, tracing its descent on the one hand through Fox, Sidney and Milton to the Roundheads, and on the other through Burke to Somers and Selden, the parliamentarians in the reigns of the Stuarts. 'Between these two families there was more matter for civil war than between Cromwell and King Charles.'[2] Macaulay was a Whig of the Fox school, to whom nothing was sacred but the will of the people. Macaulay and Burke were separated by the same chasm that separated legitimate authority and popular sovereignty, for while a government in which the people were unrepresented was 'defective', one in which the law was not supreme was 'criminal'.[3]

Against what he described as the 'violent Liberalism'[4] of Macaulay, Acton urged not a programme of reaction, of opposition to all progress, but a slow evolution of institutions with changes arising from special historical situations rather than from the minds of presumptuous men. There was nothing admirable, he wrote, in the attempt to apply mechanically 'the dead letter of a written code to the great complications of

[1] Review of John George Phillimore's *History of England During the Reign of George III*, in *Home and Foreign Review*, III (1863), 713–15.
[2] Review of Frederick Arnold's *The Public Life of Lord Macaulay*, in *Home and Foreign Review*, II (1863), 258.
[3] Review of B. Carneri's *Demokratie, Nationalität und Napoleonismus*, in *Home and Foreign Review*, II (1863), 656.
[4] Review of Mark Napier's *Memorials and Letters . . . of Viscount Dundee*, in *Home and Foreign Review*, II (1863), 236.

politics.'[1] Law should, and normally did, follow the course of history, and the good jurist was he who knew how to distinguish between what was temporary and dispensable in it and what was essential. Acton deplored the 'immoral and subversive' habit of pitting the past against the future, assigning to one or the other exclusive validity.[2] The English were wise in refusing to be lured into the false dilemma of choosing between a sterile legalism and a series of arbitrary, violent innovations. They were wise to cherish the ancient principles of the constitution while contriving new forms by which to implement those principles.

The most revered principles of social organization and the most compatible with true liberty were aristocracy and monarchy, Acton argued, turning on its head the modern democratic theory that aristocracy and monarchy are the epitome of the arbitrary and illiberal. And not monarchy alone, but monarchy by the grace of God, by divine right, he declared to be the necessary condition for freedom. Freedom was secure, he reasoned, only when all authority was fixed and defined by law, inaccessible to arbitrary change, when there was a recognized 'divine, objective right, anterior to every human law, superior to every human will'.[3] The presence of an aristocracy in countries boasting a divine monarchy he adduced as proof of the legality and liberality of the government, for an aristocracy meant that others than the King had a share in power. The true government of brute force, he noted, was not monarchy but democracy:

'Government of one, or of a minority [is] not a government of force, but in spite of force, by virtue of some idea. The support makes up for inferiority of brute strength. This is aristocracy—which is not equivalent to simple strength.

'Democracy is government of the strongest, just as military despotism is. This is a bond of connection between the two. They are the brutal forms of government and as strength and authority go together, necessarily arbitrary.'[4]

---

[1] Review of A. Foucher de Careil's *Oeuvres de Leibnitz*, in *Home and Foreign Review*, I (1862), 544.

[2] ibid., p. 545.

[3] 'Foreign Affairs', *Rambler*, VI (1862), 555.   [4] Add. MSS., 5528.

The young Acton was truly the disciple of Burke—both in his metaphysics and his anti-metaphysics. He denounced the abstract, metaphysical reasoning of the French revolutionists, but almost in the same breath he supplied an alternative metaphysics of his own, with its special body of abstractions and eternal truths. Like Burke's, his theory of politics was empirical, while his theory of the State was metaphysical and even mystical. In almost the words of Burke he ascribed an ideal reality to the State that made it part of the divine order, as much of the primitive essence of a nation as its language, and uniting men together not by the natural and sensible bond of family but by a moral bond.[1] He had no more sympathy than Burke for the utilitarian conception of the State as a conglomeration of individuals assembled together to promote their common interests. If the end of society was happiness, as Macaulay's utilitarianism would have it, Acton saw the way open for a democratic sovereignty, the right of each generation to legislate for itself in defiance of law and tradition. On the same grounds that he distrusted utilitarianism, he also rejected the 'atheistical' theory that located the origin of the State and of civil rights in a social contract, for in that case, right would become 'a matter of convenience, subject to men, not above them'.[2]

Acton saw two great principles dividing the world and contending for mastery—antiquity and the Middle Ages—and his own allegiance was to the Middle Ages.[3] Antiquity exemplified the principle of absolute power, the State identical with the Church and the law subservient to men; the Middle Ages exemplified the principle of liberty, with Church and State distinct (although related) and authority subservient to law. The virtue of the Middle Ages was that it was an organic society, and it was organic because it was corporative—composed of distinct corporations and classes each enjoying social power in its own sphere and each represented, in its own way, in the organism that was the State. When modern society abolished the

[1] Review of James B. Robertson's *Lectures on Ancient and Modern History*, in *Rambler*, new series, II (1860), 397.
[2] Add. MSS., 5752.
[3] Add. MSS., 5528.

concept of the corporation, replacing the idea of moral persons with that of mere units, of equal and isolated individuals, it lost its organic character, and the State, instead of being the natural expression of its member parts, became an artificial body. No amount of constitutional pretences could alter the fact that the modern State was essentially arbitrary and absolute. 'The [modern] State', Acton wrote, 'is a mere machine; not fitted on to society like a glove, but rather compressing it like a thumbscrew; not growing out of society like its skin, but put upon it from without like a mould, into which society is forced to pour itself.'[1]

In the atomized society that seemed to be the ideal of modern States—Acton had in mind particularly the France of Napoleon III and the Italy of Cavour—he considered it a delusion to call for representative institutions that could, after all, in no way alter the fundamental fact of absolute sovereignty. When representative government was introduced into Germany, he argued, it came in together with military conscription and a more rigorous police system, and all were part of the same scheme to increase the power of the State and diminish the area of liberty.[2] In the organic State, on the other hand, representative institutions testified to the maturity of the country, and in the long run, although not at every stage of history, they were a 'test and token of freedom'.[3] In England, where a good part of the medieval heritage had been retained, the demand for electoral reform was proper, because 'a government which cannot be reformed does not merit to be preserved.'[4] But it should be reformed by a process of 'weighing instead of counting',[5] so that classes and interests, rather than single individuals, were represented.

By reviving the memory of Burke and the example of the Middle Ages, Acton must have hoped to drown out the persuasive voice of John Stuart Mill, who was preaching a

---

[1] 'Notes on the Present State of Austria', *Rambler*, new series, IV (1861), 199.
[2] Add. MSS., 5752.
[3] *Rambler*, IV, 199.
[4] Add. MSS., 5528.
[5] ibid.

typically modern gospel of freedom.[1] Mill's ideal was a community of free individuals willing to desert blind custom and tradition in order to follow the path of pure reason and happiness. Against this utopian variety of Liberalism, Acton urged the virtues of a practical, temporizing, expediential politics, a politics that would find freedom in a judicious mixture of authority, tradition and experience. It was a politics worthy of the title 'Conservatism' had that name not already been pre-empted by a political party.

AUSTRIA AND THE OLD RÉGIME; AMERICA AND THE NEW

The Austria of the 1860's provided a test case of Acton's views, for it boasted the Conservative attributes of tradition, aristocracy and monarchy. It was the country in which the old régime had made a last stand against the encroaching modern

[1] A long essay on Mill, published in the *Rambler* of November 1859 and March 1860, has been attributed to Acton by W. A. Shaw, *A Bibliography of the Historical Works of Dr. Creighton . . . Dr. Stubbs, Dr. S. R. Gardiner and the late Lord Acton* (London, 1903), p. 44, and by Herbert Paul, editor of *Letters of Lord Acton to Mary Gladstone*, pp. 29–30. The essay was, in fact, by Thomas Arnold, brother of Matthew Arnold and a convert to Catholicism. Among the Acton manuscripts in the Cambridge University Library is a letter to Newman, dated 7 June 1859, and signed 'T. Arnold', offering a paper on Mill's 'On Liberty'. Newman forwarded it to Acton (probably when Acton resumed the editorship of the journal), adding the note: 'I suspect Arnold would not write without pay. His name would be good. I declined his offer, as being too late' (Add. MSS., 4989). Too late for the issue then going to press, was probably Newman's meaning, for subsequently it was apparently decided to print it. In three letters of Acton to Simpson, dated 24, 28 and 30 August, he mentioned the article on Mill by Arnold (Gasquet, pp. 81, 83 and 85). Shaw and Paul were probably misled by the fact that the article was signed 'A', which, according to Paul, 'in his own review amounted to acknowledgment'. Paul also cited a letter of praise from Gladstone to Acton (8 May 1861, *Correspondence*, p. 158), which he took to refer to the Mill article, but which clearly had reference to 'Political Causes of the American Revolution'. (Mary [Gladstone] Drew repeated Paul's error in 'Acton and Gladstone', *Fortnightly Review*, CIX [1918], 840). That Paul was not too familiar with Acton's early work appears in his remark, wrong on two counts, that the essay on Mill was Acton's first contribution to the *Rambler*; by November 1859, Acton had been represented in the journal by a dozen articles and reviews.

democracies, and it was the old régime, moreover, in much of its original purity, with class distinctions, privileges and customs dating back to the late Middle Ages. 'The only real political *noblesse* on the Continent', Acton wrote, 'is the Austrian',[1] from which he concluded that since aristocracy was the necessary framework of liberty, the genuine Liberal, as distinguished from the vulgar variety, must look upon Austria with favour. And yet when he himself had occasion to comment on events in that country, a plaintive undertone was audible in his well modulated and respectful voice. Even in this early period, when he was at his most conservative and most indulgent, he had to confess regretfully that Austria did not fulfil her great promise. The aristocracy, he said, in wealth, influence, position and ability was almost the peer of England's;[2] the Concordat, concluded in 1855, was a noble concession to liberty;[3] the government was the most Catholic in spirit in all of Europe;[4] the reign of Francis Joseph was 'designed on the highest and most statesmanlike basis'.[5] But its much vaunted aristocracy was unfortunately separated by a wide chasm from the people, and the most encouraging contemporary development was not the strengthening of the aristocracy but the elevation of the middle class, 'the best preliminary to free institutions'.[6] The Concordat left Austria a mongrel State, 'half absolute, half free'.[7] The fact that the government was the most Catholic in spirit in all of Europe did not seem to prevent the Catholic Church of Austria from being one of the most demoralized in Europe.[8] And while the ideas of Francis Joseph were admirable, they were inevitably perverted in their execution, for there were few instruments able or willing to carry them out;[9] and even Francis Joseph did not truly appreciate the unique historical role of Austria,

[1] Acton to Simpson, 1862, Gasquet, p. 263.
[2] Add. MSS., 5528.
[3] 'Austrian Reforms', *Rambler*, new series, II (1860), 262-9.
[4] Add. MSS., 5528.
[5] ibid.
[6] ibid.
[7] Acton to Simpson, 7 October 1859, Gasquet, p. 94.
[8] *Rambler*, II, 262-9.
[9] ibid.

her ripeness for the representative institutions that a fully civilized, organic society required.[1]

The failure of Austria to exploit or even explore the unique potentialities of her history and situation was the result of the suicidal system of repression inaugurated after the Congress of Vienna. All States, Acton wrote, have their own particular fears and needs which invite tyranny. The young State welcomes tyranny as an incident in the concentration of its resources and power. Nations in their prime are apt to resent any hint of divided authority and subdue opposition with the over-bearing presumption of a power that knows itself to be irresistible. The old State, suspecting the artificiality and precariousness of its edifice, is oppressed by the feeling that the slightest motion or exertion, the least movement of religion or trade or literature, might topple it. Austria was a victim of this last form of insecurity and anxiety. 'Happy the people', Acton observed, 'whose existence as a State is not an absolute, inevitable necessity.'[2]

The pathos in Acton's account of the old régime was decidedly absent from his discussion of the 'new régime', the United States. Where Austria was a lost cause worthy of sympathy and compassion, the United States was the ominous wave of the future that had to be uncompromisingly resisted. The Southern States, desperately intent upon preventing the threatened deluge, commanded all of his respect. In May 1861, after the formal proclamation of secession and war, Acton published in the *Rambler* his essay on 'The Political Causes of the American Revolution'[3]—the 'revolution' being the Civil War. Only in its conscientious documentation did this article differ from most of the others appearing at this time, for apart from the Radicals of the *Fortnightly Review* (John Morley Leslie Stephen, George Lewes) and the Manchester contingent

[1] 'Notes on the Present State of Austria', *Rambler*, new series, IV (1861), 199.

[2] Review of Anton Springer's *Geschichte Oesterreichs seit dem Wiener Frieden*, in *Home and Foreign Review*, III (1863), 711.

[3] *Rambler*, new series, V (1861), 17–61; reprinted in *Freedom and Power*, pp. 196–250.

of Cobden and Bright, almost all of the articulate British public supported the South. Henry Adams, arriving in London in May with his father, the American Minister to Great Britain, thought they must have resembled a family of old Christian martyrs flung into an arena of lions. Acton would have regarded this as a most unseemly comparison; if the tribute of Christian martyrdom could be claimed by anyone, he would have preferred to reserve it for the Southerners who were being strangled by the monster of the North.

America was in the position of the young State for whom tyranny seemed to be an appropriate means of augmenting its power. Had this been all, Acton might have been obliged to favour it with some of the same indulgence he showed to the Austrian malady, the tyranny of old age. The full measure of the American evil, however, was its adherence to a political and social order, democracy, that made of tyranny a normal condition of life by subverting law to the popular will. Fortunately, Acton found, America was not a homogeneous community. There were within it contending parties and interests which might, if hard pressed, secede from the union rather than suffer extinction, and the majority, composed of many future, contingent minorities who secretly sympathized with its disaffected members, would fail to bring up enough force to prevent the secession. Therefore democracy, from being the strongest state on earth, would become the weakest, and its self-destruction was predicted as surely as its tyranny. America had already arrived at this critical point, having travelled the full circle of the democratic experience: the revolution; the abortive attempt to limit democracy in the form of the Conservative constitution; the rejection of States' Rights and the triumph of the democratic principle of centralized, popular government; and finally the defection and secession of the South. The collapse of the Union came about when the North added to the iniquities of democracy the fanatical intolerance of an idea, the idea of abolitionism.

The abolitionists played the role of devil's advocate for Acton, as the ideologists of the French Revolution did for Burke; they were the devotees of the *idée fixe*, who would overturn society rather than abandon their utopian ideals. The

78

abstract merit of the ideal in either case was not really the issue, although Acton was somewhat more tolerant of the arguments against slavery than Burke was of those against the Old Régime. What Acton most objected to was the way in which the abolitionist cause was promoted, the assumption that this ideal, or any other, could properly supersede the constitution and all the normal political obligations of men. The real enemies of the constitution were not the Southern slave owners who were forced to secede, but the rabid opponents of slavery who appealed from the constitution to an abstract law of nature, from the established institutions of a commonwealth to the popular will of an ephemeral majority. Burke might have composed this passage:

'It is as impossible to sympathize on religious grounds with the categorical prohibition of slavery as, on political grounds, with the opinions of the abolitionists. In this, as in all other things, they exhibit the same abstract, ideal absolutism, which is equally hostile with the Catholic and with the English spirit. Their democratic system poisons everything it touches. All constitutional questions are referred to the one fundamental principle of popular sovereignty, without consideration of policy or expediency.... The influence of these habits of abstract reasoning, to which we owe the revolution in Europe, is to make all things questions of principle and of abstract law. A principle is always appealed to in all cases, either of interest or necessity, and the consequence is, that a false and arbitrary political system produces a false and arbitrary code of ethics, and the theory of abolition is as erroneous as the theory of freedom.'[1]

Acton would have liked to confine the question of slavery within the boundaries of political expediency, but it inevitably escaped into the hinterland of the moral and religious conscience. And Acton's conscience in this matter at times seemed obdurate: 'Slavery [is] not hostile to Christianity in abstract, but always in the concrete, because the master is not necessarily a good Christian.'[2] Unlike absolutism, he felt, slavery was not immoral; it did not suspend the divine law in favour of a

[1] *Freedom and Power*, p. 246.   [2] Add. MSS., 5752.

human will, but only denied to the slave certain specified rights. It limited freedom, without limiting law. 'A slave may be exposed to great pains and great dangers; but if his position is so regulated by law that nothing actually immoral, such as the refusal of education or the severance of the marriage-tie, is permitted, he still, in a certain sphere, enjoys a restricted freedom.'[1] Just as the Christian subject is often called upon to obey an arbitrary monarch, so the slave must obey his master, for both are part of the 'divine economy'.[2] Indeed in some stages of history, slavery was not only morally permissible, it was prescribed as a necessary experience in discipline and probation, always provided, however, that the society administering the discipline was Christian.[3] In a specifically Christian sense, Acton recalled, freedom was a theological, not a social concept,[4] so that, in the words of another *Rambler* contributor, the 'freedom of the Lord' could be a bondman.[5] But if slavery was not an abstract evil, neither was it an abstract good, and Acton was prepared to admit that it had often retarded civilization and prosperity.[6] The burden of his argument was not that slavery was a Christian virtue and should be perpetuated, but rather that it should be eventually eliminated—eliminated, however, not as the abolitionists proposed, but as the Church had always laboured to reform mankind, 'by assimilating realities with ideals, and accommodating herself to times and circumstances'.[7]

When Matthew Arnold commended the *Home and Foreign Review* for its imaginative 'play of mind', he must have had in mind the religious controversies in which the journal entered with so much spirit and with such a hearty sense of principle.

[1] Review of Samuel Sugenheim's *Geschichte der Aufhebung der Leibeigenschaft und Hörigkeit in Europa*, in *Home and Foreign Review*, III (1863), 691–2.
[2] ibid., p. 692.
[3] Review of E. M. Hudson's *Second War of Independence*, in *Home and Foreign Review*, II (1863), 658.
[4] *Freedom and Power*, p. 247.
[5] 'The Negro Race and its Destiny', *Rambler*, new series, III (1860), 335.
[6] *Freedom and Power*, p. 247; *Home and Foreign Review*, II (1863), 658.
[7] *Freedom and Power*, p. 246.

In political matters, both the *Rambler* and its successor were worthy of Arnold's most caustic remarks on the suspicion of reason that seemed to paralyse English political thinking and threatened to make of the English constitution 'a colossal machine for the manufacture of Philistines'[1]. Acton's discussions of religious and scientific liberty had none of the Philistine's prejudice against 'enthusiasm'; when freedom of science was at stake, he could unabashedly assert: 'A true principle is more sacred than the most precious interest.'[2] In questions of politics, however, he thought it proper that interests should take precedence over principles. Perhaps he obscurely felt that the purely secular problems of politics were not deserving of the loftier moral commitments exacted by religious principles.

Acton's essay on the American Civil War was a political, not a moral tract, and it betrays an occasional hint of sophistry suggesting a lack of genuine feeling for the moral problems that agitated the abolitionists, an intimation of annoyance that these problems should have precipitated a war against the traditional and essentially congenial society of the Southern aristocracy. The Southern statesmen were gentlemen and scholars, while Lincoln was a rather comic political amateur, to be casually mentioned only once in the course of the fifty-odd pages of Acton's essay and not much more frequently in his notes (although there were extensive quotations from Calhoun, for example, in both).[3] It was only a greater delicacy of style that separated Acton from the editors of the cynical and urbane *Saturday Review*, who ridiculed Lincoln as a 'third-rate attorney' and mocked his 'confused grammar and blundering metaphors'.[4] Acton was not, certainly, as crass as the high Anglican Pusey who complained of the preposterousness of expending twenty million pounds for a mere opinion as to

[1] Arnold, p. 17.
[2] 'The Catholic Academy', *Rambler*, new series, V (1861), 294–5.
[3] The two-volume *Complete Works of Abraham Lincoln* (ed. J. G. Nicolay and J. Hay), in Acton's library was neither annotated nor marked by slips of paper, as were the works of the Southern statesmen, but this was probably because it was an edition of 1894, and Acton's interest in the Civil War waned somewhat after the 'sixties.
[4] *Saturday Review*, XII (1861), 624; ibid., XV (1863), 684.

the injustice of slavery, but he did consider it excessive to sacrifice a civilization for that opinion.

Gradually, however, as the moral issue assumed a larger dimension in Acton's thinking, some of the complacency with which he regarded slavery disappeared. In a lecture on 'The American Civil War', delivered in January 1866, he reproduced the essential thesis of his earlier *Rambler* essay, modified in one important respect—in its moral evaluation of slavery. There was, to be sure, no radical repudiation of his earlier view; he still believed that slavery, by stimulating the spirit of sacrifice and of charity, 'has been a mighty instrument not for evil only, but for good in the providential order of the world'.[1] But slavery as it existed in America, he was now convinced, was unquestionably immoral. The provisions of the servile law, by equating the slave with a sum of money and denying that he could enter into a valid contract, even the contract of marriage, deprived him of the basic rights of the human person. That some slaves endured great misery and others were humanely treated was unimportant compared with this essential deprivation. If slavery had been the only criterion for judgment of the Civil War, Acton's verdict would now have been that 'by one part of the nation it was wickedly defended, and by the other as wickedly removed'.[2]

As a practical concession, this was little enough, and in the lecture, as in his *Rambler* essay, his final decision was in favour of the South. But as a theoretical concession it was significant. To recognize the divorce between the moral and the political was the beginning of his emancipation from Burke and from the kind of philosophical empiricism which assumed that political morality was nothing more than political expediency. Even to suggest that the weight of morality might be on the other side from that of expediency was to open the way to the possibility that the former could overbalance the latter. It was, however, to take some years for that possibility to mature in Acton's thought. At this time, in spite of hints of theoretical deviations, he was still a practising Burkean.

[1] *Historical Essays and Studies*, ed. J. N. Figgis and R. V. Laurence (London, 1908), pp. 135–6.
[2] ibid., pp. 140–1.

The influence of Burke lingered longer in Acton's political thinking than in his religious. The lag is seen in the fact that the argument of 'The Protestant Theory of Persecution' of 1862 almost exactly parallels that of 'The American Civil War' of 1866. In the 'Protestant Theory' he had pronounced judgment against Protestantism, in spite of the fact that it was Catholicism that bore the burden of guilt for actual bloodshed and persecution. Similarly in the 'Civil War' he came out against the North in spite of the palpable immorality of Southern slavery. In both cases the moral issue was shunted aside, and political wisdom was permitted to override moral scruples. But whereas by 1866 his view of religious persecution had been radically simplified, so that nothing remained to detract from the moral infamy of persecution, his conception of slavery was still bogged down in extenuations and explanations. When he wrote to General Lee in November 1866, requesting information on the current situation in America and paying tribute to Lee's military skill, he concluded: 'Therefore I deemed that you were fighting the battles of our liberty, our progress, and our civilization; and I mourn for the stake which was lost at Richmond more deeply than I rejoice over that which was saved at Waterloo.'[1] Nowhere in the letter did he feel it necessary to introduce the disagreeable question of slavery.

NATIONALISM

All the sins of democracy—its penchant for abstractions, contempt for history and worship of the masses—Acton saw reflected in its most recent and unattractive offspring, nationalism. That nationalism was sired by democracy was the taunt of its enemies and the boast of its friends. In 1861, the same year John Stuart Mill published his *Considerations on Representative Government*[2] defending nationalism as a new phase in the progress of freedom, Acton published an article attacking it,

[1] D. S. Freeman, *Robert E. Lee* (4 vols.; New York, 1935), IV, 517.
[2] Mill, *Utilitarianism, Liberty and Representative Government* (Everyman ed.; London, 1910).

in the person of Cavour, as the modern betrayal of freedom.[1]
He confronted the evil again the following year in the first
number of the *Home and Foreign Review*.[2]

More abstract than any of his earlier articles, the essay on
'Nationality' was also more reflective and mellow. Sympatheti-
cally, Acton described the value of ideals in general, ideals
which inspired men to pursue remote and extravagant objects,
or which served to unite the disparate strivings of the masses
behind a single vision of the good and so brought about
changes that the few, for all of their wisdom, were incapable of
initiating. By its very nature, an ideal was neither entirely true
nor entirely feasible. But it took one excess to correct another,
an ideal to correct an evil.

Like Communism and democracy, Acton found, nationalism had the great virtue of keeping alive the consciousness of
wrong and the need for reform. But like them, it had over-
stated its case. The wrong was not so great as it imagined and
the need for reform not so urgent. The Old Régime, to be
sure, had not acknowledged the rights of nationality, but
neither had it violated them, for it had desired above all to
provoke no changes and excite no resentment, either on the
part of nations or of their sovereigns. By the partition of
Poland, which was the first act of aggression against an entire
nation, and the French Revolution, which transformed the
new sentiment of nationality into a political principle, the
revolution in Europe was installed.

The relations between nationalism and the Revolution, however, were less cordial than might have been expected. When
the democratic theory of self-government threatened to dis-

[1] 'Cavour', *Rambler*, new series, V (1861), 141–65; reprinted in *Historical
Essays*, pp. 174–203. Bishop Ullathorne, in an address to the clergy of
Birmingham warning them of the subversive philosophy of the *Rambler*
and *Home and Foreign Review*, took special objection to Acton's 'eulogy' of
Cavour (*A Letter on the Rambler and the Home and Foreign Review* [London,
1862], p. 36). The best thing Acton had to say of Cavour, and presumably
what Ullathorne took to be eulogistic, was that he was not 'consciously'
an enemy of religion (although he was objectively its enemy), and that
he was not so passionate or malicious as some of his associates.

[2] 'Nationality', *Home and Foreign Review*, I (1862), reprinted in *Freedom
and Power*, pp. 166–95.

solve society into its 'natural' social and geographical elements, nationalism came to unify society—and unify it not by rein- stating the traditional, historical unit of the State, but by establishing a new 'natural', physical and ethnological unit. Yet even this variety of nationalism proved to be unsatis- factory, for while it would have permitted the expansion of France to its 'natural' limits, it would also have confined it to those limits. At this point democracy was once again invoked, and it was discovered that the popular will could even prevail over nationalism, the popular will being interpreted as the will of France to embrace other nationalities or the will of other nationalities to be incorporated in France. This violation of nationalism sounded the death of the Revolution as the affirma- tion had once sounded its birth. And then, curiously enough, by a last ironic twist of history, nationalism, suppressed by the ungrateful victors at the Congress of Vienna, gave rise to new and more formidable revolutions.

Until the middle of the nineteenth century, nationalism had always appeared as the junior member in an alliance with liberty directed against oppression, with efficiency against mal- administration, or with religious freedom against persecution. In the time of Mazzini, nationalism finally came of age. Its theory was simple and unambiguous: the State, representing the general will, and the nation, representing a homogeneous people, should be co-extensive. This was nationalism in the democratic and revolutionary form it assumed on the Conti- nent, a nationalism that required a clean sweep of all the traditional liberties, rights and authorities. There was another theory of nationality, however, favoured by the English. According to this, nationality was an essential but not the supreme element in the State: the nation was only one of a multitude of corporations that went into the making of the free State, and the heterogeneity of nations within the State, like the variety of corporations, was the test and security of free- dom. And not only freedom but civilization itself depended upon national heterogeneity. A State reduced to a single nation would relapse into primitive barbarism as surely as if men were to renounce intercourse with each other. Those States were most perfect which, like the British and Austrian empires, included different races and nationalities without oppressing them: 'A State which is incompetent to satisfy different races condemns itself; a State which labours to neutralize, to absorb or to expel them, destroys its own vitality; a State which does not include them is destitute of the chief basis of self-government.'[1]

By its very excess, Acton predicted, the democratic theory of nationality would eventually be exhausted, for it would find itself, in a repetition of the French revolutionary experience, engaged in conflict with democracy itself. Democracy and Socialism, however misguided in their methods, at least had the admirable purpose of seeking an end to misery and starvation. Continental nationalism cared neither for liberty nor for well-being, and was both more absurd and more criminal than Socialism:

'Its course will be marked with material as well as moral ruin, in order that a new invention may prevail over the works of God and the interests of mankind. There is no principle of change, no phase of political speculation conceivable, more comprehensive, more subversive, or more arbitrary than this. It is a confutation of democracy, because it sets limits to the exercise of the popular will, and substitutes for it a higher principle. It prevents not only the division, but the extension of the State, and forbids to terminate war by conquest, and to obtain a security for peace. Thus, after surrendering the individual to the collective will, the revolutionary system makes the collective will subject to conditions which are independent of it, and rejects all law, only to be controlled by an accident.'[2]

The common denominator of all of Acton's early political judgments was the conception that to-day goes by the name of 'political pluralism'. Much of what strikes the modern reader as wilfully perverse and eccentric in his discussions of Austria, America or Italy is part of a consistent pattern of pluralist thought. It is as if he had steeled himself to approve of anything that might serve to divide society and prevent the levelling, unifying action of the State, however distasteful in

[1] *Freedom and Power*, p. 193.   [2] ibid., pp. 194–5.

itself the particular expedient might be. The traditions and idiosyncrasies of history, the diversity of classes, corporations, nationalities and races in society, the delicate balance of forces maintained by a constitution in which obsolete patterns of conduct and principles of organization were deliberately perpetuated—all were of use in resisting the ultimate evil, absolutism.

Even the idea of rights could be commandeered into service, if they were designed to withhold power from the State, rather than to exercise it over others. Unfortunately this was rarely the case, and the movements of liberation that played so prominent a part in his century—abolitionism, nationalism and democracy—he discovered to be less interested in liberating souls than in governing them. French democracy had not destroyed the absolute State; it had only altered the details of social and political control, and the principal effect of the revolution had been the abrogation of intermediate powers between the king and the people. Similarly the Northern States in the American union were not so much concerned with the emancipation of the slaves as in subjecting all of the South to the authority of the national government and reducing the entire population to a single, undifferentiated mass. In America as on the Continent, the ultimate ambition of self-styled liberals was the establishment of a democratic despotism. The idea in greatest disrepute among them was that of self-government. 'Foreign Liberalism demands, not freedom, but participation in power.'[1] And because power increases as the number of those who wield it increases, the most irresistible authority, the greatest tyranny, is that of a majority over a minority.'No despotism is more complete than that which is the aim of modern Liberals. . . . The Liberal doctrine subjects the desire of freedom to the desire of power, and the more it demands a share of power, the more it is averse to exemptions from it'.[2] It took a Conservative, Acton seemed to feel, to be truly a Liberal.

[1] 'Contemporary Events', *Rambler*, new series, II (1860), 265.
[2] ibid.

LIBERAL PARTY POLITICS

There were more obvious ways to act politically than through the intermediary of abstruse, scholarly journals. The floor of the House of Commons could have offered Acton a larger audience and more certain means of political influence, had he chosen to avail himself of it. But although he sat in Parliament, first in the House of Commons and then in the House of Lords, his important political pronouncements continued to be delivered in the pages of his journals. It was not as a political power that he fancied himself, but as an educator, unobtrusively functioning behind the scenes to shape an enlightened public opinion.

Had it not been for Lord Granville, Acton might never have embarked upon the more conventional form of political career. He had begun his political life, he once boasted,[1] at the precocious age of seven, as a juvenile canvasser for his stepfather at an undisputed election. In 1857 Granville reciprocated by seeking a candidacy for Acton in Clare, a Catholic county in Ireland. Acton agreed to stand for the election and even spoke, with conventional diffidence, of the honour of 'entering the noblest assembly in the world'.[2] But he haughtily laid down his conditions for the acceptance of the honour, and warned that Granville might be doing the Liberals a disservice by sponsoring his application: 'There is a sort of fastidiousness produced by long study which public life possibly tends to dissipate, but although the profession of anything like independence of party appears ridiculous, I am of opinion that to a Catholic a certain sort of independence is indispensable.'[3] Nor could he guarantee that the Irish Catholics would be entirely satisfied with him, for while religion would separate him from the Liberals, politics might separate him from the Irish. Granville must have taken this 'confession of faith', as Acton described it, with his customary imperturbability, for

[1] Mountstuart E. Grant Duff, *Notes from a Diary*, 1892–5 (2 vols.; London, 1904), II, 164.
[2] Acton to Granville [1857], *Correspondence*, p. 28.
[3] ibid.

he wrote his good friend, Lord Canning: 'I am trying to get Johnny Acton in for some place in Ireland. I am glad to find that, although he is only a moderate Whig, he is also a very moderate Catholic.'[1] By October he had forgotten that Acton had told him, 'I have an aversion and an incapacity for official life,'[2] and he cheerfully reported to Canning, 'He has, I am glad to say, a yearning for public life.'[3] Nothing came of the Clare opening, however, and Acton enjoyed a short-lived respite.

In the General Election of 1859, Granville obtained for Acton the Liberal nomination for the seat of Carlow, an Irish borough with a total population of 9,000, of whom only 236 met the eight-pound-household franchise requirement.[4] Eighty-five per cent. of this small electorate was Catholic, but there was a pronounced anti-Liberal sentiment, partly because the last Liberal representative had been associated with several financial scandals, and partly because the Catholic vote in both England and Ireland was turning to the Conservatives.

Neither confident of success nor eager for it, Acton devoted to his campaign the barest minimum of attention. From his sanctuary at Munich he wrote Simpson that Granville wanted him to try his chance in Ireland: 'I fear I shall be obliged to try it, "pour acquit de conscience", and because an election is cheaper than being sheriff, but I do not feel sanguine.'[5] He made not a single appearance at Carlow. Apart from a financial contribution to his agents, his efforts seem to have been confined to a single letter addressed to the local priest, consisting in equal proportions of platitudes about the superiority of general interests over party interests, judicious expressions of sympathy with the Irish tenant, and a genuine and even subtle

[1] 10 March 1857, Fitzmaurice, I, 227. The index to this work must be used with caution. There is a confusion of John Russell with John Acton, both of whom were 'Johnny' to Granville.
[2] Acton to Granville [1857], *Correspondence*, p. 28.
[3] 24 October 1857, Fitzmaurice, I, 262.
[4] The excellent article by James J. Auchmuty, 'Acton's Election as an Irish Member of Parliament', describes in detail the background and circumstances of the election based upon the reports in contemporary local newspapers and journals (*English Historical Review*, LXI [1946], 394–405).
[5] 5 April 1859, Gasquet, p. 67.

statement of personal principles. His explanation of why he was standing as a Liberal was unconventional enough: 'I am no partisan but I had rather reckon on Liberal principles than on the fears of the Tories. I am sure we cannot make friends of the Tories, and I do not think it wise to make enemies of the Liberals.'[1] With this moderate show of enthusiasm, he won a majority of only fourteen votes, but he had the distinction of being in one of the three Irish constituencies in which the Liberals showed a gain; for the first time since Emancipation, Ireland had gone Conservative. Although the results of the election were announced early in May, it was not until June that Acton finally arrived in Carlow to deliver a short and undistinguished speech of acceptance. On the 10th he cast his first vote in Parliament on the motion of confidence that turned out the Tory Derby Government and brought in Palmerston and Russell.

By this vote Acton also helped bring Gladstone into office. Even more than most of his contemporaries, Acton was later to worship Gladstone as the Grand Old Man of English politics, but at this time he was too much of a Catholic and too little of a Liberal to have any use for him. When the Pope had suggested to him, in 1857, that Gladstone, as a Puseyite, was perhaps friendlier to the Catholics than Palmerston or Granville, Acton had rejoined that in domestic affairs 'ambition made him useless', and in foreign affairs unsafe.[2] The events of 1859 did nothing to make him change his opinion. Like many of his contemporaries, he distrusted the sudden about-face executed by Gladstone, who had supported the Derby Government one day and had accepted office in the cabinet of its rivals a few days later. From his writings in the *Rambler* one would never have guessed that Acton was a member of the party which had made Gladstone Chancellor of Exchequer. In September 1859, he lashed out at Gladstone—curiously enough, not for once having been a Conservative, but for having turned Liberal. Gladstone, he wrote, had approached the state of mind described by Edmund Burke as 'a disposition to hope something from the variety and inconstancy of vil-

[1] Auchmuty, p. 401, quoting from the *Carlow Post*.
[2] Add. MSS., 5751.

lainy, rather than from the tiresome uniformity of fixed principle';[1] for the sake of popularity, he had sacrificed Conservative respectability, and his newly found bigotry and Radicalism had 'neither the merit of sincerity nor the excuse of blindness.'[2] Defending the asperity of these remarks, Acton later explained that he had not lost all hope in Gladstone, but all faith and almost all charity.

This was no momentary disaffection on Acton's part. Gladstone was considered an even more belligerent partisan of the Italian nationalists than most of the Liberals. To Acton this made him the associate of men who in the guise of 'patriot' combined the roles of conspirator and assassin[3]. Napoleon III was one of these disreputable associates, and Gladstone's admiration for the French Emperor, Acton found, was typical of those for whom villainy and success were infallible evidence of ability. Like many others he was repelled by Gladstone's tone of moral superiority and self-righteousness. 'He has not the instincts of a gentleman,' Acton noted, 'nothing handsome or chivalrous'.[4]

In these early years of the *Rambler*, Acton doubted the utility to Catholics of even a provisional alliance with the Liberals. 'We have got about as much as we shall get from them,' he suspected,[5] and recommended that Catholics decide between Liberal and Conservative candidates with reference to specific grievances. Between the parties as a whole he saw little to choose from. The most that could be said of them was that one was somewhat less to be feared than the other, and that together they represented the basis of true parliamentarianism; each derived its utility from the deficiencies of the other, and each kept the other within manageable bounds.[6] It was with good reason that he had warned his constituency not to expect

---

[1] 'Contemporary Events', *Rambler*, new series, I (1859), 407.
[2] ibid.
[3] 'National Defence', *Rambler*, new series, III (1860), 291.
[4] Add. MSS., 5528.
[5] Acton to Simpson, 16 February 1858, Gasquet, p. 4.
[6] This was the theme of an article by Simpson in 1859 on the 'Theory of Party' (*Rambler*, new series, I [1859], 332–52), with which Acton was so heartily in agreement that when he was attacked as its author, he did not disclaim it.

from him a slavish obedience to party: at one point in the debates on Italy, he and other Whig Catholics expressed their dissatisfaction with the policy of their party by rising in a body and leaving the House, which led Granville to comment in a letter to Canning, 'Johnny Acton has thrown us over.'[1]

Not until Acton's conversion to the Liberal position on Italy and his growing intimacy with Gladstone did his association with the Liberal Party become meaningful. The *Home and Foreign Review* was as militantly Liberal as the *Rambler* had been studiously neutral or even, on occasion, belligerently hostile. By 1863 Acton was taking issue with the constitutional historian, Thomas Erskine May, for suggesting that neither party possessed a monopoly of truth or virtue and that the English constitution depended upon the balance and conflict of both parties. 'Our political system', he now argued, in dramatic repudiation of his earlier view, 'is founded on definite principles, not on compact or compromise. Every compromise marks an imperfect realization of principle—a surrender of right to interest or force.'[2] Elsewhere he explained that Toryism was neither a necessary error nor a partial truth somehow essential to the functioning of the constitution; it could have no political principle or truth to contribute because it was destitute of political ideas, existing only to represent the interests of the Church and the landlord.[3]

It was one of the many ironies in Acton's life that when he was finally reconciled to the Liberal Party, his term in the House of Commons was more than half over. During his total of six years in the House he did little to endear himself to his constituency or to make himself known to the public. He seemed to consider it his duty to put himself forward always as a Catholic, perhaps because he felt that the Catholics required the services of the few spokesmen they had. And he confined his attention to the kind of practical grievances the *Rambler* had once specified as the proper domain of Catholic

[1] 4 August 1860, Fitzmaurice, I, 387.
[2] Review of Thomas E. May's *Constitutional History of England*, in *Home and Foreign Review*, III (1863), 717.
[3] Review of Thomas Macknight's *The Life of Viscount Bolingbroke*, in *Home and Foreign Review*, II (1863), 635.

members: he was on a committee to study the conditions of
Catholic prisoners, he put a question on the inspection of
Catholic schools, and he requested that the documents from
agents of the British government in Rome be made public.[1]
He was conscientious enough in his committee engagements
to complain that the House was occupying a good deal of his
time. 'If I could only get turned out of Parliament in an honest
way and settle down among my books,' he lamented to
Simpson as he outlined one of his favourite plans for the
publication of materials relating to the history of English
Catholicism.[2]

In 1865 he was accorded his wish to be turned out of
Parliament. He stood for Bridgnorth, the nearest town to
Aldenham, and although he was declared elected by a majority
of a single vote, he was unseated on a scrutiny the next year.
In 1868 he again stood for Bridgnorth without success. For all
of his curiosity about the most mundane questions of politics
—budgets, diplomacy, party tactics—the role of a Member of
Parliament was uncongenial, and he returned, with genuine
relief, to the life of a scholar and journalist. The editorial
policy of his journals was now more partisan than his own
behaviour in the House had once been. Both the *Chronicle* and
the *North British Review* were frankly Liberal, the *Chronicle*
going so far as to specify in its prospectus its adherence to the
Gladstonian school of Liberalism.

If there was any lingering ambition for parliamentary distinction, Acton was soon provided with a painless means of
satisfying it, one that did not require his currying favour with
a constituency. In August 1869, Gladstone, then Prime
Minister for the first time, submitted to Queen Victoria his
recommendations for the peerage. The list was distinguished
by the unprecedented appearance of a Jew (Nathaniel Roth-
schild, whose name, however, was later withdrawn) and two

[1] *Hansard's Parliamentary Debates*, 3rd series, CLXII (1861), 1652;
CLXVI (1862), 970; CLVIII (1860), 679–81. Add. MSS., 5528, contains
some notes entitled, 'Speech for Catholics', demanding redress for the
Catholic Irish, but there is nothing to indicate whether this was intended
as a campaign speech or an address to the House.
[2] 6 December 1860, Gasquet, pp. 155–6.

Roman Catholics, one of whom was Acton. Acton, he assured the Queen, 'is of the first order, and he is one of the most learned and accomplished, though one of the most modest and unassuming, men of the day'.[1] Granville also wrote to the Queen to allay her anxieties about the elevation of a Catholic to the peerage. His most telling argument was the fact that had Manning had any say in the matter, Acton would not be promoted.[2]

There may have been more behind the name of Manning than a calculated appeal to the Queen's prejudice. It is possible that Gladstone had in mind the rivalry between Acton and Manning when he drew up the list of peers, for no more opportune time could have been chosen to bestow this honour upon Acton. The Vatican Council was scheduled to meet in a few months, and the newly acquired title of 'Lord', as evidence of the good favour in which he was held by the party in power in England, was to be of considerable value in strengthening Acton's hand for the coming show of force at Rome.

[1] John Morley, *The Life of William Ewart Gladstone*, (3 vols.; New York, 1903), II, 430.
[2] Fitzmaurice, II, 17.

V

THE VATICAN COUNCIL

THE COUNCIL AND ITS AFTERMATH

THE question of papal Infallibility had a polemical history dating back to the Middle Ages and engaging, on both sides, respectable theologians and historians until the very eve of the Vatican Council. In opposing Infallibility, then, Acton was not, as his detractors pretended, indulging a private idiosyncrasy. He was following in the familiar tradition of one of his distinguished ancestors, Sir John Throckmorton, leader of the influential 'Catholic Committee' of the 1790's, who opened the campaign for the removal of Catholic disabilities by repudiating as a vicious slander the idea that papal Infallibility was a dogma of the Church. Acton could cite the testimony of ecclesiasts and lay historians, of official catechisms and manuals of theology published as late as 1860, to support his claim that Infallibility was a vulgar perversion of faith.

Pius IX, however, was not easily moved by historical evidence or theological arguments. He had produced a new dogma in 1854, had canonized more saints than all of the popes together for a century and a half, and had opened an offensive against the whole of modern civilization. Promises made by Catholics at the time of their emancipation in Great Britain could hardly prevail against the Pope's conviction that he was the inspired vehicle of the Holy Ghost and enjoyed the special benevolence of the Mother of God. The declaration of his Infallibility, foreshadowed in his very first encyclical of 1846 and eight years later in the dogma of Immaculate

Conception, was the logical culmination of the whole of his pontificate.

Long before the news was formally released, in 1867, it had been suspected that a general council would be convened and that papal Infallibility would be on the agenda. Historians and theologians sought instruction from the last general council held three centuries earlier, the Council of Trent, which had inaugurated the ill-famed, or defamed, Counter-Reformation. Acton, who had spent the winter of 1866-7 and the following autumn in the archives of Rome and Vienna examining the documents on the Council of Trent,[1] concluded that the next council could occupy itself to no better advantage than by abolishing many of the so-called Tridentine 'reforms', reforms that had perpetuated in the Church a spirit of intolerant absolutism and 'austere immorality'.[2] The strategy of the Ultramontanes, however, he knew, would be exactly the opposite: 'To proclaim the Pope infallible was their compendious security against hostile States and Churches, against human liberty and authority, against disintegrating tolerance and rationalizing science, against error and sin.'[3] In the *Chronicle*, Acton had denounced the Ultramontane compulsion to create new dogmas and add to the burdens of pious Catholics.[4] On the eve of the council he sounded these warnings again in the pages of the *North British Review*.

His essay, 'The Pope and the Council',[5] published in October 1869, was a summary of a book of that title which had appeared in Germany (and had immediately been translated into English) under the pseudonym of Janus who was commonly identified as Döllinger.[6] The work of Janus was the

[1] Add. MSS., 4979.

[2] 'The Vatican Council', *North British Review*, LIII (1871); reprinted in *Freedom and Power*, pp. 300-1.

[3] ibid., p. 302.

[4] 'The Next General Council', *Chronicle*, I (1867), 368-70.

[5] *North British Review*, CI (1869), 127-35.

[6] Part of the volume was an expansion of articles which had been published in March in the *Allgemeine Zeitung* of Augsburg. Friends of Döllinger at Munich agreed that Döllinger wrote the articles and that the book was composed by his colleague, Johannes Huber, under his supervision. (See Friedrich, III, 484-8; Eberhard Zirngiebl, *Johannes Huber*

most comprehensive historical documentation of the Liberal opposition to Infallibility and the most important treatise on the subject published at the time. The argument of Janus rested on the distinction between the ancient idea of the primacy of Peter and the modern papacy, that 'disfiguring, sickly, and choking excrescence on the organization of the Church'.[1] How the papacy lost its early innocence, degenerating into an absolute power, is the long and disreputable story of forgeries and fabrications, of which the Donation of Constantine in the eighth century and the Isidorian Decretals in the ninth were only the more flagrant episodes. Usurping the rights of the episcopacy and of the general councils, the papacy was finally driven to the principles and methods of the Inquisition to enforce its spurious claims, and to the theory of infallibility to elevate it beyond all human control. Janus piled high the sordid details of inventions and distorted texts, of Popes involved in contradiction and heresy, of historians falsifying history and theologians perverting theology.

Yet Acton found even Janus too mild for his tastes. The book presented so many new facts that he feared it might seem to supply the proponents of Infallibility with a refuge from the imputation of bad faith. Indeed Janus himself, in a sudden accession of generosity, allowed that contemporary advocates of Infallibility might be sincere. To Acton this was unthinkable. In the present stage of learning, he insisted, it was idle to pretend ignorance of the wilful falsehood and fraud upon which the theory of infallibility was based. Moreover the papal despotism was maintained by the same insidious arts with which it was first won. 'A man is not honest who accepts all the Papal decisions in questions of morality, for they have

[Gotha, 1881], p. 150). (According to one report, the publisher of the volume spoke of Döllinger as the author [Ferdinand Gregorovius, *Roman Journals*, ed. F. Althaus, tr. G. W. Hamilton (London, 1911), p. 338].) Acton may have provided Döllinger with some of the historical material (without knowing to what purpose it was to be put), but otherwise he was not involved either in the publication of the articles or of the volume, although the latter, at least in part, is often attributed to him (e.g., G. G. Coulton, *Papal Infallibility* [London, 1932], pp. 13 and 207).

[1] Janus, *The Pope and the Council*, authorized trans. (London, 1869), p. xix.

often been distinctly immoral; or who approves the conduct of the Popes in engrossing power, for it was stained with perfidy and falsehood; or who is ready to alter his convictions at their command, for his conscience is guided by no principle.'[1] Nor was Janus rigorous enough in other respects. No provision was made for the theory of development, a defect that led Acton to doubt the reputed authorship of Döllinger, in whose writing the theory played such a prominent part.[2] More serious was the reluctance of Janus to face up to the enormity of the evil of Trent or to such awkward questions as what doctrinal authority the Church could still be said to possess in the event that Infallibility was proclaimed.

Perhaps to satisfy Acton's criticism, and certainly to correct a gaping flaw in his reasoning which his opponents were quick to exploit, Döllinger published a pamphlet taking account of the theory of development.[3] The infallibilists, who had always been suspicious of the theory, had recently discovered that by interpreting it as a *carte blanche* for innovation, it might be used to justify a multitude of sins. Döllinger had to restore the original meaning of development, which was not the negation of tradition, but was rather the progressive fulfilment of a tradition working itself out by internal necessity. Janus, Acton's essay, and Döllinger's pamphlet contained the main counts in the indictment against Infallibility as the case stood just before the opening of the council. No amount of 'coaxing'

---

[1] 'The Pope and the Council', *North British Review*, CI (1869), 133.

[2] No one except Acton seems to have questioned Döllinger's authorship of the *Allgemeine Zeitung* articles, and Döllinger himself, when publicly identified as their author and challenged to deny it, did not do so. In July Acton maintained that Döllinger had not written them (Acton to Wetherell, 30 July 1869, Gasquet, p. 356), but he must have altered his opinion in September when he, Dupanloup and Döllinger met at Herrnsheim to discuss the impending council, and when the articles must have been mentioned. His remarks in the *North British Review* in October about the identity of Janus were probably intended as a warning that the whole work should not be ascribed to Döllinger, for in a letter written the next month he admitted that Döllinger was the 'inspiring mind' behind it (Acton to Gladstone, 24 November 1869, *Correspondence*, p. 86).

[3] 'Considerations for the Bishops of the Council Respecting the Question of Papal Infallibility', in *Declarations and Letters on the Vatican Decrees*, ed. F. H. Reusch (Edinburgh, 1891).

of the documents, to use Renan's famous phrase, could make of the Ultramontane defence—the book *Anti-Janus* by Joseph von Hergenröther[1]—more than a feeble essay in apologetics. Nor did Rome's prompt consignment of the work of Janus to the Index enhance the Ultramontane reputation for intellectual integrity or fearlessness.

Döllinger, the most outstanding German theologian of his generation, was not one of the many theologians invited by the Pope to assist at the preparations for the council. But two of his disciples were in Rome: Friedrich, who came as theologian to the Cardinal Prince Hohenlohe, papal chamberlain, Liberal Catholic and brother of the Prime Minister of Bavaria; and Acton, occupying no official position but strategically located because of his influential family connections and his inaccessibility to Vatican pressure.

Acton and Friedrich supplied Döllinger with the material for what became the most remarkable literary achievement of the council and one of the greatest scandals in Rome, the famous Quirinus letters.[2] From December 1869 until July 1870, through the whole course of the council, letters over the pseudonym of Quirinus appeared regularly in the *Allgemeine Zeitung*, revealing the most intimate backstairs secrets of Rome: unpublished or restricted documents, details of private interviews, secret machinations and intrigues, and the speculations, hopes and fears that ran through the council. The papal court tried vainly to uncover the identity of the ubiquitous author of 'Die Römische Briefe über das Konzil', the name under which they appeared in the *Zeitung*. Prominent Liberal Catholics were ordered to leave Rome; when it was once reported, erroneously, that Acton had been expelled, the New York *Nation* issued an indignant protest. But in spite of censorship exercised against suspects and oaths of secrecy imposed upon the bishops, the letters of Quirinus continued to appear with the same uncannily accurate information.

That Döllinger put the letters in their final shape for the

[1] Trans. J. B. Robertson (Dublin, 1870).
[2] Quirinus, *Letters from Rome on the Council*, authorized trans. (London, 1870).

99

Zeitung was not seriously doubted (except for one period when it was falsely rumoured that Huber had taken over this task). The only real question was the identity of his informants, and here too the facts have finally been established, although writers on the Vatican Council sometimes persist in assuming that they are still open to speculation. Friedrich, it appears, dispatched to Döllinger a series of letters from Rome and also part of his diary (which was later published and with Quirinus remains one of the best sources on the council). Acton forwarded, by way of the Bavarian Embassy, much material that Friedrich could not obtain, and when Friedrich returned to Germany in May, Acton bore the brunt of the work alone. After he, in turn, had left Rome, early in June, his cousin Count Arco, took over for the remaining six weeks of the council.[1] Döllinger often printed these communications exactly as he received them, so that whole passages from Acton's letters were printed verbatim over the pseudonym of Quirinus.[2]

Because the Quirinus letters convict the council of deliberate fraud and deception, apologists for Infallibility, under the pretence of neutrality, have tried to pass them off as violently partisan and, therefore, untrustworthy. Yet no one has succeeded in seriously disputing them, and those who have, with much effort, contrived to challenge some minor point in the narrative, have in the process unwittingly confirmed the burden of it.[3] The fact is that the violence often taken to be

---

[1] Johann Friedrich, 'Römische Briefe über das Konzil', *Revue internationale de théologie*, XI (1903), 621–8; Charlotte Blennerhassett, 'Acton', *Biographisches Jahrbuch und deutscher Nekrolog*, VII [1902], 19; Johann Friedrich von Schulte, *Lebenserinnerungen* (Giessen, 1908), I, 269.

[2] Friedrich and later Woodward, both of whom had access to the original manuscripts of Acton's letters, remarked upon this.

[3] This is the effect of a work intended to support the infallibilist position: Cuthbert Butler, *The Vatican Council* (2 vols.; London, 1930). A more recent example of the uncritical, off-hand rejection of Acton and Quirinus is Lillian Parker Wallace, *The Papacy and European Diplomacy* (Chapel Hill, 1948), in which the name of Acton is linked with the adjective, 'violent' (pp. 52, 67, and twice on 87), although no pretence is made of analysing his essays and letters or of refuting a single one of his charges. The partiality of the author is exposed by her obvious preference for Manning, who is never, in her pages, 'violent', but only 'ardent' as he 'pursued his unwavering course' (pp. 88 and 91).

characteristic of Quirinus was really a characteristic of the council itself. Even Pius found three distinct periods in the council, of which the first, the preparatory, was satanic, the second, the assemblies, human, and only the third, the decrees, divine. To Quirinus the entire council alternated between long periods of the satanic and brief intermissions of the human.

Much publicity had attended the summoning of bishops and theologians to Rome for the preliminary work of organization, but it remained for Quirinus to reveal the less publicized facts that as far as possible only those well disposed to Infallibility had been invited, and that not until protests by leading German Catholics was the University of Munich, the most celebrated (and Liberal) Catholic academy, represented at all. The Roman penchant for mystery first concealed from the theologians the real purpose for which they had been convened, and then bound them by the seal of secrecy of the Holy Office (the Inquisition). By these and many similar devices it was made certain that the regulations drawn up for the conduct of the council would redound to the Pope's favour. Thus it was decided that decrees would be issued in the name of the Pope instead of the council, a procedure not invoked even by the Council of Trent. Nor were the bishops to have the right to originate motions; this function was reserved to two commissions from which the 'minority', as the Liberal opposition became known, was carefully excluded, so that on the most important, the Commission on Faith, the 200 Liberal bishops had not a single representative. These rules of procedure were so much to the liking of the papal party that it was also decided to prohibit discussion or amendment of them at the council itself, which provoked Acton to remark that the Pope left the council with nothing but 'the function of approving'.[1]

In addition, the minority was grossly under-represented numerically at the council. Wherever it happened to be strong—Germany, the Austrian Empire, France and America —the number of bishops relative to the Catholic population was infinitesimal compared with the proportion in Italy and Spain, the main infallibilist countries. Typically in Acton's vein are the passages in Quirinus describing the preponder-

[1] Acton to Gladstone, 1 January 1870, *Correspondence*, p. 89.

ance of Latins at the council: the 700,000 inhabitants of the Roman States were represented by sixty-two bishops constituting half or two-thirds of every commission, while 1,700,000 Polish Catholics were represented by the Bishop of Breslau, who was not chosen for a single commission; four (out of sixty-two) Neapolitan and Sicilian bishops could, and did, out-vote the archbishops of Cologne, Cambray and Paris, representing a total of 4,700,000 Catholics. In ecclesiastical statistics, it appeared that twenty learned Germans counted for less than one untutored Italian. 'The predilection for the Infallibilist theory', Quirinus deduced, 'is in precise proportion to the ignorance of its advocates.'[1]

With the organization of the council weighted in advance against the minority, the additional impediments placed in the way of free discussion and consultation seemed supererogatory: debates conducted in Latin condemning nine-tenths of the prelates to silence and most of the others to confusion, wretched acoustics in the lavishly fitted and spectacularly high assembly hall, the refusal to permit bishops to examine the stenographic reports of even their own speeches, the prohibition of meetings of twenty or more bishops outside of the council, the strict censorship of literature (which meant that minority documents had to be printed in Naples or Vienna and smuggled in illegally), and the time-honoured custom of the Roman postal office of opening letters suspected of heresy or error. And if all these precautions should by chance fail, it was made a mortal sin to communicate anything that took place in the council, 'so that any bishop who should, for instance, show a theologian, whose advice he sought, a passage from the Schema under discussion, or repeat an expression used in one of the speeches, incurred lasting damnation!'[2]

When the opposition persisted in spite of these difficulties, other expedients, described by Quirinus, were attempted. Debate was cut short, minority speakers were interrupted, a few violent scenes were staged, and rules of order were liberally interpreted to favour the infallibilists. Toward the end of the council all pretence of sober and free discussion was abandoned, and the final text of the constitution was rushed

[1] Quirinus, p. 143. [2] ibid., p. 164.

through without any debate at all. Outside of the assembly hall, other more or less subtle mechanisms operated to undermine the spirit and destroy the force of the minority. There were the enticements of the well-stocked papal preserves—the titles, benedictions and dispensations which the Pope could issue or withhold at will. There were fifteen vacant cardinals' hats dangled over many more vacillating heads. The exercise of papal influence ranged from the most obvious appeal to clerical vanity, as in the case of a uniquely decorated stole bestowed upon one gratified bishop, to the genuine sentiments of affection felt for the Pope and the desire to compensate him for the disrespect of the world. Pius himself had thrown off the sham of neutrality early in the proceedings of the council, affirming his personal conviction of his Infallibility, issuing papal briefs commending the efforts of the majority bishops, and openly chastising and even censuring members of the minority. An aged Chaldean patriarch, having delivered a speech against infallibility, was roundly abused by the Pope and forced to resign his office, while another cardinal, the Archbishop of Bologne, guilty of the same offence, was confined to the isolation of his room and ordered to prepare a formal retraction. In most cases there was no need to exercise such overt pressure. Many Italian bishops and others from distant lands were not allowed to forget that it was the papal court that supplied them with food, lodging and travelling expenses.

If everything else failed, there remained one final threat, the idea that resistance to the Pope was blasphemy against the Holy Ghost, and that the members of the minority, as Manning assured them, were guilty of heresy even before the official promulgation of the dogma. Those who were worried because they could see nothing in the tradition of the Church to support the dogma of Infallibility were supposed to have been soothed by Pius' bland assurance, 'The tradition is myself,'[1] and by his frank admissions of divine inspiration. The assembly hall with the miserable acoustics was not so ill-chosen after all, it was later discovered, for the rays of the sun were seen to fall exactly on the place occupied by the papal throne from which Pius would announce his Infallibility. That

[1] ibid., p. 713.

the throne was not accidentally put in that position was suspected by those familiar with the Pope's attachment to the mystical symbol of the sun. On his own order a portrait had been painted of him, in which, in Quirinus' description, 'he stands in glorified attitude on a throne proclaiming his favourite dogma of the Immaculate Conception, while the Divine Trinity and the Holy Virgin look down from Heaven well pleased upon him, and from the Cross, borne in the arms of an angel, flashes a bright ray on his countenance.'[1]

In the guise of Quirinus, Acton helped expose the elaborate apparatus of temptation, exhortation and coercion which bore down upon the bishops at the council; at the same time in his own name, he occupied himself with a completely different strategy—the organization of protests from the major powers of Europe. The Bavarian minister, Prince von Hohenlohe, was the first officially to propose that the governments communicate to the Vatican their views on those questions raised at the council affecting the civil allegiance of Catholics. Acton used his influence with Gladstone, then Prime Minister, to rally support to Hohenlohe's scheme and to impede the work of the Ultramontanes. He persuaded Gladstone to release a letter expressing English displeasure with the idea of papal infallibility, thus giving the lie to Manning who had been assiduously cultivating the impression that he, as a good friend of the Prime Minister, could attest England's indifference. And he alerted Gladstone to the successive acts of hostility by which 'the papal absolutism' declared war against 'the rights of the Church, of the State, and of the Intellect'.[2] 'We have to meet', he wrote, 'an organized conspiracy to establish a power which would be the most formidable enemy of liberty as well as of science throughout the world.'[3] He described the proposals for ecclesiastical reform that would transfer a large body of civil law to the jurisdiction of the Church, which meant to the arbitrary will of the Pope, and the revival of old excommunications and censures which would reintroduce the criminal practices of the Inquisition and the deposing power. Without the intercession of the governments, he warned, the new 'papal

[1] ibid., p. 224.   [2] 1 January 1870, *Correspondence*, p. 91.   [3] ibid.

aggression' was certain to succeed. On 1 March, the English representative at the Vatican, Odo Russell, telegraphed the Foreign Office in London: 'Lord Acton is anxious the French Government should know that further loss of time will be fatal to the Bishops of the Opposition.'[1]

Just as Acton sought the intervention of Europe, so the majority bishops feared it, and through their own diplomatic channels played upon the cautious instinct of statesmen who feared involvement. Their chain of communications led from Manning through Odo Russell to Lord Clarendon, the Foreign Secretary. While Manning was publicly execrating the minority bishops for divulging information, he and three other infallibilists, absolved of the oath of secrecy by the Pope, were issuing their own private accounts of the proceedings. For many years Manning was to rail against the intrigues of Acton while keeping a discreet silence in regard to his own intrigues. He once complained to Gladstone that 'the shadow of Lord Acton beween you and the Catholics of Great Britain would do what I could never undo', to which Gladstone sharply retorted that he wished the general body of English Catholics compared to Acton, adding, in obvious criticism of Manning's own devious behaviour: 'For though I have noticed a great circumspection among his gifts, I have never seen anything that bore the slightest resemblance to a fraudulent reserve.'[2] As it turned out, Manning proved to be the more successful intriguer. When the Bavarian proposal for intervention was considered by the Cabinet, Lord Clarendon, the Foreign Secretary, supported oddly enough by Granville, prevailed against Gladstone. Acton had played his last trump card and had lost.[3]

In this matter, as in others, Acton had been the spearhead of the Liberal opposition. Odo Russell, a political opponent, paid tribute to the energies and talents that made him indispensable to the minority: 'Without his knowledge of language and of

[1] Shane Leslie, *Henry Edward Manning* (London, 1921), p. 223.
[2] ibid., pp. 231-2.
[3] When E. S. Purcell's *Life of Cardinal Manning* (2 vols., London), was published in 1896, Acton insisted that too much had been made of his correspondence with Gladstone, and that he recalled writing only two letters to him during the course of the council. Acton's memory was clearly at fault, for the *Correspondence* alone includes twelve letters.

theology the theologians of the various nations could not have understood each other, and without his virtues they could not have accepted and followed the lead of a layman so much younger than any of the Fathers of the Church.'[1] The Roman hierarchy, less generous in its judgments, saw in Acton only a contumacious courting of heresy. The Pope, for whom Acton's behaviour was not only religious apostasy but also, and perhaps more importantly, a personal affront, took no pains to conceal his displeasure. He even went so far as to deny his blessing to Acton's children, after which Acton fled in anguish to Russell's home to spend a sleepless night. Feeling ran so high against Acton that for a time he feared assassination at the hands of the Jesuits, which makes it possible to credit the rumour that he sometimes thought it prudent to move about Rome in disguise.

Weary of the long, ineffectual struggle and oppressed by the terrible heat of a Roman summer, Acton finally left Rome early in June, admitting defeat. For five more weeks the deliberations of the council dragged on, with the minority capable only of some delaying actions. On 13 July, the preliminary voting occurred. The 764 bishops in attendance in January had dwindled to 680 or 690, and of those eighty-eight voted *non-placet*, sixty-two *placet juxta modum*, and eighty or ninety abstained although they were present in Rome.[2] The opposition resolved to leave Rome in a body rather than yield to the dogma immediately, and in the public session of the 18th, when the dogma was solemnly promulgated, only two bishops remained to pronounce the words *non-placet* and then to make their submission.

The historian, William Lecky, visiting Rome in 1870, spoke of the justice of a much quoted saying, 'The bishops entered the council shepherds, they came out of it sheep.'[3] For the first time in the history of the Church, the Pope was accredited with

[1] Leslie, p. 220.
[2] These are the correct figures. Quirinus made the error of deducting the eighty or ninety abstentions from the 600 bishops who voted rather than from the 680 or 690 present in Rome at the time.
[3] Elizabeth Lecky, *A Memoir of the Right Honourable William Edward Hartpole Lecky* (London, 1909), p. 78.

supreme personal and immediate authority reaching to every individual communicant over the heads of all mediating officials, an authority extending not only to matters of faith and morality but also to Church governance and discipline. It was explicitly forbidden to appeal from a papal judgment to an ecumenical council, so that the last stronghold of the bishops was destroyed together with the whole structure of jurisdictional autonomy. Not satisfied with having scored a triumph over the bishops, the council, in the words of Manning's famous boast, had also 'triumphed over history'.[1] The decree proclaimed, as a divinely revealed dogma, the Infallibility of the Pope when he spoke *ex cathedra*, and solemnly pronounced anathema upon anyone who denied this Infallibility.

In the autopsy conducted by Acton several months after the close of the council, he discovered that the blows inflicted by Rome had been painful but not actually fatal to the minority, that the real cause of death was a prolonged act of suicide. The bishops, even those of the minority, had so long cultivated the habit of blind obedience, that they had become constitutionally incapable of effective opposition. 'They petitioned,' Acton said, 'they did not resist.'[2] Each time they were tempted to reject a decree, they decided instead to save their strength for the main battle, but by the time that battle had arrived, they had dissipated both their strength and their will-power. When in March they acquiesced to a decree proscribing opinions not actually heretical, Rome discovered that there was no principle they would not betray rather than defy the Pope in his wrath. No compromise was regarded as too costly, no subterfuge too ignoble.

Before this insidious infirmity of purpose, even the hatred of infallibility succumbed. Many minority bishops persuaded themselves that they did not doubt the dogma itself but only the opportuneness of its definition. With the 'Inopportunists', as they were known, Acton had no patience. To grant the truth of the dogma even obliquely, he insisted, was to grant

[1] Quirinus, p. 69.
[2] 'The Vatican Council', *North British Review*, LIII (1870), reprinted in *Freedom and Power*, p. 333.

everything. Nor did he think it possible to chance upon a compromise formula that would propitiate the majority and yet not offend the more rigorous members of the minority. No definition of papal Infallibility that the majority would consider worth having could be accepted by those for whom the only possible innovation was one that reduced the papal power. Acton's notes reflected his growing distrust of the minority itself:

'Take them all in all, the opposition are not better men than the others. They are better in one important item, but in that they are not entirely guided by the supreme motive of truth, but often of utility. It may be a calculation of what will serve religion, and in that case the majority are just as respectable as the minority. Their motive is equally good.

'The blunders and ignorance of many of the opposition show that it was not based on any firm foundation of certainty. Then, all the mitigated, conditional forms of resistance are virtually a surrender of principle.[1]

'Pius called us Jansenists. He meant not in point of grace, but of authority. He alluded to the silence respectueux, and meant to indicate the ceremonious practice by which men veiled their displeasure and disrespect.'[2]

The minority surrendered its last effective weapon when it tacitly admitted the ecumenicity of the council. That the council was not genuinely ecumenical Acton suspected as soon as it became clear that a mere majority rather than the customary unanimity would be sufficient to carry the dogma. Even the notorious Council of Trent had recognized that no decision of faith could be issued without substantial physical and moral unanimity. (Trent, surprisingly, proved to be freer than the Vatican Council, which was why the Pope had forbidden the bishops access to the Vatican documents relating to the procedure at Trent, and furiously dismissed the keeper of the Vatican archives when it became known that copies of the procedure had been circulated by Acton, among others.) Acton alone pressed the point of ecumenicity, and it was he who intro-

[1] Add. MSS., 5542.   [2] Add. MSS., 4992.

duced into a protest drawn up by the French minority bishops the paragraph stating that 'the claim to make dogmas in spite of the opposition of the minority endangers the authority, liberty, and ecumenicity of the Council'.[1] He had wanted to go further, to declare bluntly that until this claim was repudiated, the minority would not admit for discussion the topic of Infallibility. But the bishops of the opposition balked at this. Another attempt was made in June to issue a statement on the question of ecumenicity, but again it was rejected. 'They never used their strongest argument,' Acton noted, 'that they would not accept a dogma without unanimous consent. It might have failed, but it was deluding the Pope into the belief that they would yield, to avoid so carefully saying that they would not'.[2]

The last opportunity for defiance came at the solemn session on the 18th. It was proposed by the hardier of the minority bishops that they attend, repeat their votes of *non-placet*, and refuse their signatures to the decrees. 'They exhorted their brethren', Acton wrote, 'to set a conspicuous example of courage and fidelity, as the Catholic world would not remain true to the faith if the bishops were believed to have faltered.'[3] But they were irresolute to the last and left Rome without taking formal action. The Pope did not permit them the doubtful dignity of retreat, and called upon each to submit to the decrees. Acton had earlier observed that 'the only invincible opponent is the man who is prepared, in extremity, to defy excommunication, that is, who is as sure of the fallibility of the Pope as of revealed truth'.[4] And the minority bishops were not of this invincible cast. One after the other they yielded, some, like the theologian Auguste Gratry, explaining that the dogma was not so objectionable as he had feared because it claimed only official and not personal Infallibility, others submitting purely for the sake of obedience to avoid excommunication. There was no intervention of the Holy Ghost, as Manning predicted, but only a slow, painful process of soul-searching.

[1] Acton to Gladstone, 10 March 1870, *Correspondence*, p. 107.
[2] Add. MSS., 5542.   [3] *Freedom and Power*, p. 355.
[4] Acton to Gladstone, 1 January 1870, *Correspondence*, p. 96.

Acton was not at this time called upon to subscribe to the dogma. As a layman responsible neither for the salvation of souls nor the instruction of youth, he enjoyed a temporary immunity, which permitted him the luxury of acting as the moral censor of those who had already submitted or were contemplating submission. In September 1870, he published, over his own name, an open letter to an anonymous German bishop,[1] intended as a call of conscience to all the bishops of the minority. The letter opened with a testimonial to the ideals represented by the minority, and continued, for thirteen pages, to recapitulate the evidence from which the minority had concluded that the council was a 'conspiracy against divine truth and law' and the dogma a 'soul-destroying error'[2]— evidence so conclusive that one bishop insisted he would rather die than accept Infallibility, and another predicted the suicide of the Church. Yet in spite of their own testimony, some bishops had proclaimed the decrees to their dioceses with no mention of the errors and sins of which they were fabricated or the insufficient authority upon which they were issued. They had neither retracted their earlier views nor refuted them. As a result their followers were left without spiritual or religious guidance. Acton concluded his letter:

'It depends upon them [the bishops] whether the defence of the ancient Church organization would be held within lawful bounds and for the purpose of its preservation, or whether Catholic science would be forced into a conflict which would then be turned against the bearers of ecclesiastical authority itself.

'I believe you will not forget your words and you will not disown your work; for I place my trust in those bishops— there were Germans among them—who in the last hour of the Council exhorted their colleagues, "that one must persevere to the end and give the world an example of courage and constancy which it so greatly needs" '.[3]

Acton was apparently suggesting, although somewhat

[1] *Sendschreiben an einen deutschen Bischof des vaticanischen Concils* (Nördlängen, 1870).
[2] ibid., p. 16.　　　　　[3] ibid., pp. 18–19.

cryptically, that if the minority bishops persisted in their refusal to accept the decrees, their flock could do so in clear
conscience, confident that they were not flouting legitimate
authority. If the bishops surrendered their principles, however, those who continued to hold to the truth would be driven
into conflict with the episcopacy and so into schism. The first
alternative, he argued, was intellectually more honest and
spiritually less perilous.

The ultimate question that must have been plaguing Acton,
as it certainly did the minority bishops, he did not explicitly
raise. Should the bishops stand firm in their refusal to submit
even at the risk of excommunication? Had the letter been written in July or even August, Acton might conceivably have
been entertaining the naïve hope that Rome, faced with a
united and hostile episcopacy, would yield, either recalling
the council (which had never been officially terminated) to
alter the terms of Infallibility, or, more probably, simply
permitting the decrees to lapse into oblivion. But by September that hope had been certainly exploded. Resistance clearly
meant excommunication. Knowing that, Acton nevertheless
counselled resistance, perhaps because the excommunication
of a number of prominent bishops would be irrefutable proof
of lack of unanimity and therefore of the unecumenicity of the
council. As a last resort, Acton probably had in mind the for-
mation of a national Church independent of Rome but under
the direction of Catholic bishops. This would have the double
virtue of preserving 'the ancient Church organization . . .
within lawful bounds' and of reconciling 'Catholic science'
with 'the bearers of ecclesiastical authority'.[1]

A long essay by Acton, entitled 'The Vatican Council' and
published in the October issue of the *North British Review*, followed the same pattern of forthrightness in describing the
council and circumspection in alluding to the future. One of
the most satisfactory contemporary accounts of the council, it
remains to-day probably the best interpretive study. Systema-
tically and soberly Acton described the errors and frauds of
which Infallibility was compounded. Concluding his narrative
with the departure of the minority and the formal promulga-

[1] See p. 155.

tion of the decrees, he declared, for the first time, that the minority's decision to leave Rome was an abdication of principle only on the part of some, that for others it was an act of conscience and wisdom. Those, he pointed out, who were most firmly persuaded of the evil of Infallibility were most confident that the decrees would eventually dissolve of their own accord. They preferred, therefore, to rely on the 'guiding, healing hand of God'[1] rather than to precipitate a schism. They hoped to deliver the Church from the decrees by teaching Catholics to reject a council 'neither legitimate in constitution, free in action, nor unanimous in doctrine', and at the same time to 'observe moderation in contesting an authority over which great catastrophes impend'.[2]

Most of the bishops, however, saw no practical way of rejecting the council without rejecting the Church, and reluctantly submitted to the decrees. Appalled by the submission of one after another of the staunchest members of the minority, Acton wrote to some of them inquiring into their motives and reasons. The reply of Kenrick, Archbishop of St. Louis, typified the prevalent state of mind. Like Acton, Kenrick had hoped that a considerable part of the minority would join him in refusing to accept the decrees, thus depriving Infallibility of the seal of unanimity and ecumenical authority. The submission of most of the bishops, however, put the remaining few in the untenable position of seeming to defy the clearly established authority of the Church. This, Kenrick said, he had never intended to do. 'I could not defend the Council or its action but I always professed that the acceptance of either by the Church would supply its deficiency.'[3] His submission, he insisted, was an act of pure obedience and did not signify a change of heart. The decrees themselves were no less objectionable than they had been before, no less objectionable, for

[1] 'Vatican Council', *Freedom and Power*, p. 356.
[2] ibid.
[3] Johann Friedrich von Schulte, *Der Altkatholicismus* (Giessen, 1887), p. 267. In Add. MSS., 4905, Acton transcribed parts of Kenrick's reply without identifying them as such; as a result, in the introduction to *Freedom and Power* (p. xxvi), I mistakenly assumed the note to be an original expression of Acton's views. The wording is, of course, Kenrick's, although the view was one that Acton eventually adopted.

that matter, than many other practices and episodes in the history of the Church. Fortunately, he added, his functions were almost exclusively administrative, so that he would not have to teach or expound the doctrine of Infallibility.

The day before Kenrick sent off his letter to Acton justifying his submission, Döllinger wrote to Mgr. von Scherr, Archbishop of Munich, justifying his refusal to submit. Starting at almost exactly the same position as Kenrick, Döllinger had arrived at exactly the opposite conclusion. The decree offended him as a Christian, for it violated Christ's injunction against establishing the kingdom of this world; as a theologian, for it was in contradiction with the whole tradition of the Church; as an historian, for it flouted the warnings of history against universal sovereignty; and as a citizen, for it threatened to subvert the civic order and create a fatal discord between State and Church. Less than three weeks after dispatching this letter, Döllinger was excommunicated.

Acton appeared to be treading hard upon the heels of Döllinger. He translated into German his essay on the Vatican Council, which Rome, correctly interpreting it as a gesture of rebellion, promptly put on the Index. And his next public act seemed to be a public declaration of war. On 30 May, Döllinger and other recalcitrant priests and laymen issued their first statement following their excommunication, and Acton's name was fifth in the list of signatures appended to it. This 'Munich Declaration of Whitsuntide, 1871,'[1] rejecting the decrees illegally promulgated at Rome and reaffirming the dogmas of the ancient Catholic faith, was the declaration of independence that presaged the creation of the Old Catholic Church.

The sequel to the publication of this document, however, revealed Acton in a less belligerent mood than might have been expected. Sir Roland Blennerhassett, the Liberal Catholic and good friend of Acton who had been in Rome with him during the council and whose name appeared beside his on the document, wrote a letter to the London *Times* repudiating his own and Acton's signature. Neither signature was 'authentic',

[1] First published in the *Rheinischer Merkur* and reprinted in von Schulte, pp. 16–22.

he said, his own name, which appeared as 'Sir Blenner-Hassett' (Acton's as 'Lord Acton-Dalberg'), having been affixed to the document without his consent. In the course of the controversy that followed, two other signatories of the declaration elicited the facts that Blennerhassett had attended the final sessions of the Munich Conference at which the declaration had been drafted and had not then objected to the inclusion of his name, and that Acton, although not himself present at the final sitting, had been vouched for by Döllinger who was in his confidence.[1] Blennerhassett himself later admitted that he had not meant to divorce himself from the principles enunciated in the declaration but only from the assembly itself, which was a German one and in which he and Acton had no right to participate. Others, he added, who interpreted his letter rightly, were scandalized that he had done nothing more than repudiate that particular document.

Less scandalizing, perhaps, but more disturbing, was Acton's unusual reticence during this public exchange of letters. It is certain that, like Blennerhassett, he agreed completely with the purport of the declaration. But it is also apparent, from the fact that he studiously refrained from commenting on Blennerhassett's letter to *The Times*, that he was uncomfortable about the publication of the declaration, and perhaps for reasons other than those of Blennerhassett. Later this episode was to emerge as a turning point in Acton's relations with Rome.

---

[1] The secretary of the Munich Conference, Professor Berchtold, replied in a letter to the *Allgemeine Zeitung*, which was reprinted, together with a comment by von Schulte, in *Der Altkatholicismus*, p. 339. Acton's copy of this volume in the Cambridge University Library is scored at several points in the text of the declaration, but there are no query or exclamation marks to indicate disagreement either with the declaration itself or with the explanations of Berchtold and von Schulte.

F. E. Lally, one of Acton's biographers, claimed that the inclusion of Acton's name was 'wholly arbitrary and unwarranted', that Acton was neither 'present at the deliberations at von Moy's' nor 'in any way interested in them' (*As Lord Acton says* [Newport (R. I.), 1942], p. 107). None of these statements is accurate. Acton did attend the deliberations (although not the final one), was vitally interested in them, and the inclusion of his name was neither arbitrary nor unwarranted.

Events had carried Acton far beyond the single-minded indignation he had felt during the council or the desperate hopes he had entertained afterwards. In the summer of 1870 it had been possible to think that an adamant minority might force Rome to yield and, for those bishops at any rate, permit the decrees to remain a dead letter. Later that year, when he published his open letter and his essay and when it had become clear that Rome would exact submission or impose excommunication, he could fall back on the hope that the excommunicated bishops would lead a legitimate movement of resistance and reformation. This final hope was dispelled in April 1871, with the submission of the last two bishops. Deprived of episcopal leadership, the opposition forfeited its claim to ecclesiastical legitimacy. For a few more weeks Acton was drawn along by the momentum of the past year and a half during which he had incessantly preached the virtue of resistance. He attended the Whitsuntide meetings and tacitly, if not explicitly, permitted his name to appear on the declaration. But that he had begun to doubt the propriety of the Old Catholic movement, as it became known, is evident in his failure to repudiate the letter of Blennerhassett and, more decisively, in his absence from the Old Catholic Congress which met in Munich in September and to which Englishmen and laymen had been explicitly invited.

As the Old Catholic movement took form and matured in the next few years, Acton's instinctive distaste for schismatic groups came to the surface. Spurred on by ideological and organizational incentives, the Old Catholics left orthodox Roman Catholicism far behind, first when they invited the Jansenist Archbishop of Utrecht to consecrate the first bishop of the Old Catholic Church of Germany and so laid the basis for a new hierarchy, and later when they abolished compulsory celibacy of the clergy and auricular confession. Even Döllinger complained of the sectarian quality of the movement, and Acton had less reason than Döllinger to be in the unhappy position of a schismatic. He had not been excommunicated or even called upon to submit to the decrees, and as long as Rome did not trouble him, he could remain in the Church with a clear conscience. In this he had the approval of Döllinger, for whom excommunication had been personally a 'deliverance', but who nevertheless, as Acton put it, 'held very strongly that nobody should voluntarily sever himself from the Roman communion'.[1] When Eugène Michaud, a French Liberal theologian, left the Church of his own accord, without first having been excommunicated, Acton criticized him for 'renouncing communion with us who wish to remain in communion with Rome'.[2] Michaud's action implied that there had been nothing heretical in the Church before July 1870, which Acton contrasted to his own view that the decisive objection to the decrees was the fact that they sanctioned and revived old evils in the Church. 'I think very much worse', he wrote, 'of the Vor Juli Kirche than he does, and better of the Nachjuli Kirche.'[3]

He even picked a quarrel with Gladstone, who once chanced to use the term 'Ultramontanism' to describe the post-July Church. There were assuredly Ultramontane principles and practices in the Church, Acton argued, but Ultramontanism as a complete religious and moral system was so outrageous that no conscientious or intelligent man could possibly subscribe to it. Most of those who went by the label of Ultramontane made it a habit to deny, conceal or try to explain away the evils that had been perpetrated in the name of Ultramontanism, and they accepted the papacy only with private reservations and interpretations. It was impossible to exaggerate the depravity of Ultramontanism, but it was easy to exaggerate the depravity of Ultramontanes.

If Acton retreated from the position he had taken at the time of the council, it was only a tactical retreat. His distinctions between good and evil were as sharp and absolute as before, and he still discerned behind the mask of the inopportunist Dupanloup the unprepossessing countenance of the infallibilist Veuillot. Papal Infallibility still meant immorality and impiety—murder, lying and treachery. What he came to realize, however, since the harassed days of the council, was that the Vatican decrees neither brought these evils into existence nor made of them a consistent system of belief.

---

[1] Add. MSS., 4912.
[2] Acton to Blennerhassett, 1872, *Correspondence*, p. 117.
[3] ibid.

Acton did not carelessly or easily arrive at this judgment. In the years after 1870 he turned over the evidence again and again. He reread the official literature of the council and the mass of pamphlets it had inspired. He asked Gladstone to make available to him the stenographic reports of the debates that were in the possession of the French government. He corresponded with the minority bishops who had submitted and with the Old Catholic priests who had not. And he continued his research in the history of the medieval and post-Reformation Church. By 1874, when he was publicly challenged to state his position, his ideas were in order and his stand taken.

INFALLIBILITY RECONSIDERED

It was Gladstone who revived the slumbering issue of Infallibility and so precipitated the next crisis in Acton's life. In November 1874, four and a half years after the promulgation of the decrees, Gladstone attacked them in a thirty-five page pamphlet carrying the dignified title, 'The Vatican Decrees in their Bearing on Civil Allegiance: a Political Expostulation'.[1] It was odd that the renewal of the controversy should be brought about by an intimate friend of Acton, and odder still that the friend should be Gladstone, the high churchman for whom Roman Catholicism was an ally in the struggle against the greater evils of secularism and atheism, and who alternated, during the Vatican Council, between trying to dissuade Rome from proceeding with the decrees and dissuading the English from curtailing Catholic rights. Yet in 1874, when he could no longer hope either to divert Rome or to sustain the minority, when the passions of Englishmen had subsided and Rome was contemplating no new affront, he launched the bomb that erupted all the old grievances and suspicions. Perhaps he did not realize how explosive a weapon he had created or that in two months 145,000 copies of the pamphlet would be sold.

Acton had tutored Gladstone too well, for the main argument of the 'Expostulation' might have been taken verbatim from Acton's letters to him during the council—the argument

[1] Ed. Philip Schaff (New York, 1875).

that papal Infallibility was inimical to freedom in history, science and society. For his own part Gladstone was most fearful lest the temporal pretensions of the Pope undermine the civic allegiance of Catholics. Just what he hoped to accomplish by rekindling this controversy is difficult to see, unless he thought that it might drive the Liberal Catholics into the arms of the Old Catholics, in whom he took a benevolent interest. If so, he misjudged the situation. In the years that had elapsed since the passage of the decrees, most Liberal Catholics who were unable to come to terms with them theologically or historically could at least take comfort in the pacific and conservative spirit that seemed to have descended upon Rome. The publication of the pamphlet had two results, neither of which Gladstone could have desired: non-Catholics were once again tempted to revoke Catholic emancipation, and Liberal Catholics were burdened with the disagreeable task of publicly defending the Church and the Pope. The replies of Newman and Acton in particular were read with great relish by those who delighted in the embarrassment of these two prominent opponents of Infallibility.

Acton's was the first reply. Prepared some days in advance in the form of a letter to the editor of *The Times*, it only awaited the release of Gladstone's pamphlet, which he had read in manuscript and had vainly urged Gladstone not to publish. He was in the familiar position of having to conduct a campaign on two fronts, this time against Gladstone and against Rome. Indeed it was only by convicting Rome of sin that he could convict Gladstone of error. Rome, he argued, had tolerated abuses and immorality compared to which the decrees were trifles. For three centuries the canon law, through numerous revisions and editions, had affirmed that the killing of an excommunicated person was no act of murder and that allegiance need not be kept with heretical princes. Yet in spite of these well-publicized evils, in spite of the extensive power claimed by the Pope long before the Vatican Council, Catholic emancipation had been voted for. It was felt then, as it should be now, that Catholics could be trusted to abide by the generally accepted canons of morality. Gladstone seemed to think that the council had replaced haphazard evil by systematic, organized evil in the form of Ultramontanism. This was not so, Acton replied. 'There is a waste of power by friction even in well-constructed machines, and no machine can enforce that degree of unity and harmony which you apprehend.'[1] Thus Fénelon could publicly aver his orthodoxy and privately protest the truth of his condemned views; or Copernicanism could be officially condemned and universally tolerated in private. Similarly Catholics could be exposed to doctrines having distinctly disloyal implications without being guilty of actual disloyalty. Yet the demonstration of loyalty Gladstone asked of them, Catholics had to refuse. They could neither deny the Pope's right to vast discretionary powers, which was legally his, nor pledge themselves to resistance if he exercised that right, for this 'is not capable of receiving a written demonstration'.[2] Only experience would prove Gladstone's misgivings to be unwarranted.

The ordinary *Times* reader, it may be presumed, found Acton's letter bewildering. The non-Catholic must have been vexed to see him go so far in criticism of the papacy without crossing the line into defiance of the Pope, while the conventional Catholic must have been furious that a public letter ostensibly in defence of Catholicism should give so much ammunition to the enemy. Only the Liberal Catholic could appreciate the gymnastics involved in straddling the fence between submission and resistance, and even he might fear that Acton was teetering dangerously on the side of resistance. It is no wonder that *The Times*, in an editorial comment, concluded that Acton had, in plain words, rejected the decrees or had decided to treat them 'as a nullity'.[3] Acton composed a denial of this imputation but, for some reason, failed to send it. Instead he wrote three more letters to *The Times* documenting the facts he had earlier adduced, the first of which concluded, after five thousand words of quotations and bibliographical references, with a plea for truth and honesty, and an intimation of other more grievous and still unknown episodes in the history of the Church.

It is unfortunate that Acton chose to terminate the public phase of the controversy on this note. He might have said

[1] London *Times*, 9 November 1874.   [2] ibid.   [3] ibid.

much more in clarification of his position. In denying to the 'post-July' Church the stigma of Ultramontanism, he might have gone on to explain, as he did in private,[1] that the council had not so unalterably tied itself to Ultramontanism as to preclude entirely an acceptable Catholic interpretation of the decrees. The decrees were certainly a victory for the Ultramontanes and an expression of Ultramontane prejudices, but they were not binding, legally and formally, in their extreme Ultramontane sense. When a high church functionary could deny that the Syllabus of Errors was 'literally and certainly' sanctioned in the decrees, because of some technical flaw in formulation, then honest men had the right to avail themselves of the benefit of this doubt. If Manning was justified in saying, as he did when the argument redounded in his favour, that apostolic constitutions were technical, legal documents, then the Liberals were justified in claiming that they need be accepted only in their technical, legal sense, that they could be 'minimized', rather than, as was Manning's custom, 'maximized'. It was because Acton, like Newman (another notorious 'minimalist'), felt it possible to subscribe to a minimal interpretation of the decrees that he could make the remarkable statement, on one occasion, that nothing in his letters 'contradicted' any doctrine of the council. (He had at first intended to use the word 'inconsistent', but replaced it with 'contradicted' when it was suggested to him that inconsistent might imply assent, whereas contradicted had the more limited connotation of non-dissent.)[2]

What positive content Acton may have assigned to the decree of Infallibility, according to this minimal interpretation, is suggested in one of his notes:

'It [the decree] might have been corrected if the council had continued. A declaration that it did not mean to innovate; that the decree shall not be understood or interpreted otherwise than in harmony with all tradition; that no change was intended in the constant and universal doctrine of Catholics,

[1] Acton to Simpson, 18 December 1874, Gasquet, p. 336; Acton to Gladstone, 30 December 1874, *Correspondence*, p. 150.
[2] Acton to Simpson, 10 December 1874, Gasquet, p. 365.

might still be expected. But the council closed without it. There was always room for this, und es versteht sich eigentlich von selbst.'[1]

Apart from this special interpretation of the decree, Acton also clung to the right to reserve judgment upon the ecumenicity of the council. The list of ecumenical councils had never been definitely established, and it was not even certain that the Council of Trent was among them, so that it was permissible to entertain the same suspicions about the Vatican Council. For this reason Acton did not feel obliged to retract his published criticism of the council or even to exercise reticence in the future.

Acton and Newman were the two famous exponents of the minimalist position. But their differences are, in some ways, more instructive than their similarities. When Newman published his 'Letter to the Duke of Norfolk' in reply to Gladstone's 'Expostulation', his only concern was to provide a minimal interpretation of the decrees that would not fall into heresy. Acton's letters to *The Times* were a more complicated affair, for while he was arguing against Gladstone that the decrees need not be accepted in an Ultramontane sense, he was also denouncing in the most unequivocal fashion the principles and practices of Ultramontanism. His purpose, which was no part of Newman's, was to 'make the evils of Ultramontanism so manifest that men will shrink from them, and so explain away or stultify the Vatican Council as to make it innocuous'.[2] Under the most trying circumstances, Acton did not permit himself to relax his offensive against Rome.

The Catholic Archbishop of Westminster might allow Newman's letter, however distasteful, to pass without comment, but he could not afford to ignore Acton's, particularly since *The Times* had taken pains to spell out its heretical implications. Besides, Manning had long harboured suspicions of Acton's unorthodoxy. He had hoped that the promulgation of the decrees would bring to their knees the proud, self-righteous

[1] Add. MSS., 5600.
[2] Acton to Gladstone, 19–20 December 1874, *Correspondence*, p. 147.

opponents of Infallibility, who thought they were wise men and the Ultramontanes fools. 'At last', he had rejoiced, 'the wise men have had to hold their tongues, and, in a way not glorious to them, to submit and to be silent.'[1] But Acton was conspicuous neither by his submission nor by his silence, and when it began to look as if the moral victory as well as the patent intellectual superiority was with him and his party, Manning decided it was time to assert his authority.

Three days after Acton's first communication to *The Times*, Manning addressed two questions to him: Did his letter have any heretical intent, and did he accept the decrees? The reply was satisfactory on the first score but not on the second. Acton, Manning deduced, was one of those who adopt 'a less severe and more conciliatory construction'[2] of the decrees—in which case Manning wanted to know what construction that was, or more simply, whether he adhered to them as defined by the council. This was the critical moment for Acton. To answer Manning in his own terms would be a total capitulation, and for this he was unprepared. Should he say that he 'submitted' to the decrees without difficulty or examination, meaning, he explained, 'that I feel no need of harmonizing and reconciling what the Church herself has not yet had time to reconcile and to harmonize?'[3] He decided against it, settling on a formulation which avoided the objectionable word. His letter, dated the 18th, read:

'My dear Lord,—I could not answer your question without seeming to admit that which I was writing expressly to deny, namely, that it could be founded on anything but a misconception of the terms or the spirit of my letter to Mr. Gladstone.

'In reply to the question which you put with reference to a passage in my letter of Sunday, I can only say that I have no private gloss or favourite interpretation for the Vatican Decrees. The acts of the Council alone constitute the law which I recognize. I have not felt it my duty as a layman to pursue the comments of divines, still less to attempt to supersede them

[1] George W. E. Russell, *Portraits of the Seventies* (London, 1916), p. 331.
[2] Manning to Acton, 16 November 1874, *Correspondence*, p. 152.
[3] Acton to Simpson, 17 November, 1874, Gasquet, pp. 359–60.

by private judgments of my own. I am content to rest in absolute reliance on God's providence in His government of the Church.—I remain, my dear Lord, yours faithfully, Acton.'[1]

The reply had overtones that Manning's sensitive ear could hardly have missed. Acton was politely informing him that he did not feel obliged to answer any question not specifically arising from the letter to Gladstone, for it was only his public acts that Manning had the right to challenge. As Simpson less delicately put it, Manning had the right to know whether Acton's letter had any heretical intent, but not the right to question his acceptance of the decrees. Only Acton's bishop had that authority, and Acton had already satisfied him. Dr. Brown, Bishop of Shrewsbury, in whose diocese Aldenham was located (and formerly one of Acton's masters at Oscott), knew Acton as a conscientious and pious man, whose unwillingness to be separated from the Church was assurance enough of his orthodoxy. But Manning was less easily persuaded. In his opinion Acton was a heretic who desired to remain in the Church for subversive reasons of his own: 'He has been in and since the council a conspirator in the dark, and the ruin of Gladstone. His answers to me are obscure and evasive. I am waiting till after Sunday, and shall then send one more final question. We need not fear this outbreak for our people. Some masks will be taken off, to our greater unity.'[2]

For the third time Manning requested from Acton an unequivocal declaration of submission, and again Acton took refuge in Bishop Brown. It was probably upon Manning's prompting that Brown then called upon Acton for a confession of belief. After consulting with several friends, Acton composed a respectful but firm statement:

'To your doubt whether I am a real or a pretended Catholic I must reply that, believing all that the Catholic Church believes, and seeking to occupy my life with no studies that do not help religion, I am, in spite of sins and errors, a true Catholic, and I protest that I have given you no foundation for your doubt. If you speak of the Council because you suppose

[1] *Correspondence*, p. 153.
[2] Manning to Bishop Ullathorne, 27 November 1874, Leslie, p. 232.

that I have separated myself in any degree from the Bishops whose friendship I enjoyed at Rome, who opposed the Decrees during the discussion, but accept them now that it is over, you have entirely misapprehended my position. I have yielded obedience to the Apostolic Constitution which embodies those Decrees, and I have not transgressed, and certainly do not consciously transgress, obligations imposed under the supreme sanction of the Church. I do not believe that there is a word in my public or private letters that contradicts any Doctrine of the Council; but if there is, it is not my meaning, and I wish to blot it out.'[1]

This may not have been the whole of Acton's letter; a handwritten draft contained among his manuscripts includes a passage that probably concluded the letter: 'You bear testimony to the [orthodoxy—deleted] Catholicity of my doctrine, and you are willing to assume the truth of my statements, and I am grateful to you for it; but I will not relinquish the hope that, in resisting tactics which are dishonourable and [ruinous to the Church—deleted] injurious I retain your sympathy as my bishop and your confidence as a friend.'[2]

Brown, no Ultramontane, was apparently willing to let the matter drop there, particularly when Thomas Green, Acton's private chaplain at Aldenham (and another former Oscott master), came to Acton's support. But Manning was obdurate. Early in January he delated the case to Rome, and Acton, who was spending the winter at Torquay, prepared for a siege of research in order to defend his position. As late as 13 April 1875, he wrote to Lady Blennerhassett: 'It is simply at the choice of the authorities, Pope, Cardinal, bishop or priest, when I am excommunicated. . . . It can only be a question of time.'[3]

As his strategy of defence was revised, first to take shelter behind Brown and then behind the bishops of the minority, so his strategy of offence shifted: the target was no longer the decrees themselves but Ultramontanism and Ultramontanes. By interpreting the decrees in a minimal sense, he put them

---

[1] Probably 12–15 November 1874, Leslie, p. 233.
[2] Add. MSS., 4863.
[3] *Correspondence*, p. 155.

out of the range of discussion, which permitted him at the same time to persevere in his war against Ultramontanism and to remain within the Church by accepting the decrees. The new strategy might have succeeded had Manning been willing to recognize the legitimacy of this minimal interpretation or to appreciate the fact that a revelation of Ultramontane corruption was a matter of historical truth and not of dogmatic authority. As it was, Manning suspected, and rightly, that Acton's distinction between the decrees and Ultramontanism was only a formal device of polemic, that in fact he was using Ultramontanism as a club to beat down the decrees. Privately Acton admitted that he wanted to 'stultify the Vatican Council' and 'make it innocuous',[1] so that the decrees would eventually be nullified. When he wrote to Manning that he would rely upon 'God's providence in His government of the Church' (to which was added, in the first draft, '[and] the construction she herself shall adopt in her own true time',[2]) Manning must have recognized the indomitable theory of development that Acton and Döllinger knew how to wield so dexterously. It was because Acton had faith in the power of the Church to regurgitate the unwholesome material fed it by zealots that he could reconcile himself to the temporary discomfort of yielding to the decrees. The important thing, he felt, was to create the conditions which would promote a quick recovery, and this meant proceeding against Ultramontanism 'in the root and stem' of immorality, rather than in the 'flowering top'[3] of the decrees:

'What I want people to understand is that I am not really dealing with the Council, but with the deeper seat of the evil, and am keeping bounds with which any sincere and intelligent bishop of the minority must sympathize. If I am excommunicated—I should rather say *when* I am—I shall not only be still more isolated, but all I say and do, by being in appearance at least, hostile, will lose all power of influencing the convictions of common Catholics.'[4]

[1] See above, p. 122.
[2] Acton to Manning, 18 November 1874, *Correspondence*, p. 153.
[3] Acton to Gladstone, 16 December 1874, ibid., p. 49.
[4] Acton to Gladstone, 19–20 December 1874, ibid., p. 148.

Acton under-estimated the prudence of Rome, for he was not excommunicated. As an influential layman, peer and associate of Gladstone, he was too valuable to be discarded. Bishop Brown declared himself satisfied with Acton's statement, and Rome took that to be adequate. Grant Duff, Acton's good friend, thought that the interview between the bishop and Acton must have resembled the historic one described by Byron, when 'Betwixt his Darkness and his Brightness. There passed a mutual glance of great politeness.'[1] Politeness, at least on the side of Rome, henceforth also characterized the relations of Acton and Rome. Although Acton continued his frank examination of Church history and neither retracted nor recalled any of his writings on the Vatican Council, he was never again seriously troubled by the ecclesiastical authorities.

Acton had yielded obedience to Rome, but on his own terms, so that it was less a submission than an assertion of independence. It is stretching a point to claim, as his Catholic biographer, Lally, does, that Acton accepted the issue of the Vatican Council with 'filial piety', and that the question of papal Infallibility, as a point of faith, was 'closed for him for ever after 1870'.[2] But this is no less a travesty of Acton's dilemma than a common non-Catholic opinion, best expressed by the popular historian, Lytton Strachey. To Strachey, Acton was that ludicrous phenomenon, 'an historian to whom learning and judgment had not been granted in equal proportions, and who, after years of incredible and indeed well-nigh mythical research, had come to the conclusion that the Pope could err'. If he could swallow the camel of Roman Catholicism, why should he strain at the gnat of infallibility? So Strachey wondered, as he watched 'that laborious and scrupulous scholar, that life-long enthusiast for liberty, that almost hysterical reviler of priestcraft and persecution, trailing his learning so discrepantly along the dusty Roman way'.[3] Yet there were some who knew how to wear their Catholicism with a difference, Strachey admitted, and Acton was one of them.

[1] Mountstuart E. Grant Duff, 'Lord Acton's Letters', *Nineteenth Century and After*, LV (1904), 773.

[2] Lally, p. 128.

[3] Strachey, *Eminent Victorians* (New York, n.d.), pp. 101–2.

Neither the ordinary pious Catholic, who saw the controversies of 1869–74 as a blot upon Acton's memory to be thoroughly erased before the process of rehabilitation could get under way, nor the scoffing non-Catholic, for whom the controversies themselves were as meaningless as Acton's ambiguous submission, could appreciate the difficulty of his problem and the delicacy of his solution. Neither could understand how Acton, in the words of his friend, Lord Bryce, could have 'remained all his life a faithful member of the Roman communion, while adhering to the views which he advocated in 1870'.[1] The traditional Catholic would be quick to expose the weaknesses of Acton's arguments, while the non-Catholic might find it hard to credit the sentiment, the conviction and the personal sense of propriety which were his ultimate justification. Belief, for Acton, admitted of many shades and variations, so that it was possible to give formal adherence to a decree while reserving judgment on its meaning, wisdom, and even legitimacy. For a while, when pressed about the decrees, he considered saying nothing beyond, 'I do not reject',[2] which was all the council required under its extreme sanctions. Instead he used the more gracious formula, 'I have yielded obedience', a euphemism for 'I do not reject' and a far cry from the 'I assent' that Manning would have liked to hear. And because belief was a delicate thing, not to be summoned at will or rejected lightly, he perhaps felt that its private complexion need not be identical with its public, and he could take comfort in the example of Fénelon, who was finally obliged to assert publicly what he denied privately. The Anglican priest, Frederick Meyrick, who saw a good deal of Acton at Torquay in the critical winter of 1874–5, recalled his state of mind: 'Lord Acton told me that he did not believe, and could not believe, the Infallibility of the Pope, as defined, any more than Döllinger, who declared that he could as soon believe that two and two made five. He said that he should appoint a private chaplain with the same sentiments as himself, and proceed just as if the Vatican Council had not been

---

[1] James Bryce, *Studies in Contemporary Biography* (New York, 1903), pp. 385–6.
[2] Acton to Simpson, 10 December 1874, Gasquet, pp. 363–4.

held.'[1] If Meyrick's memory can be trusted, Acton was indeed prepared to follow in the path of Fénelon. Convinced that the Vatican decrees, if not already made innocuous by vague wording and conflicting interpretations, would become so in the course of time, he decided that it was the way of wisdom and piety to 'yield obedience' to the Church.

The final word may rest with Lord Acton's daughter, who observed, in obvious reference to her father, that the part played by the Pope and the hierarchy in the thoughts of lay Catholics could be much exaggerated, and that a man's relationship to the Church is governed by his inner sentiments, his love for the sacraments and respect for the traditions.[2]

[1] Meyrick, *Memories of Life at Oxford, and Experiences in Italy. . . .* (London, 1905), pp. 287–8.
[2] Coulton, *Papal Infallibility*, p. 223.

VI

THE HISTORY OF LIBERTY

'THE HISTORY OF LIBERTY'

IN 1875, when the last echoes of the Vatican Council were dying away, Acton was forty-one, not an advanced age for the historian he aspired to become, but well past the prime of precocious youth. For twenty years he had contemplated the writing of a universal history, and had ordered his life to that end. Under Döllinger he had served an exacting apprenticeship as professional historian, a career which he carefully distinguished from the more casual one of man of letters. He had mastered a variety of disciplines related to the history of politics, culture, ideas and religion. His style combined the sharp, colourful writing, the sense of immediacy and timeliness, of the informal essay, with the precision (degenerating occasionally into pedantry) and the susceptibility for the ancient and the universal of academic history. In addition to some 400 reviews and short articles, he had already published or delivered in the form of lectures the equivalent of almost 1,000 pages of serious essays ranging in subject from the early Christian Church to the American Civil War and the Italian Revolution.

Yet it was beginning to be apparent that by trying to embrace too much, he ran the risk of dissipating everything. Döllinger had already been heard to observe that if Acton did not write a great book before he was forty, he would never do so.[1] A dozen schemes for great books had suggested themselves and a dozen programmes of research had been begun

---

[1] Bryce, p. 392.

and often completed, only to be abandoned, in most cases, just at the point where another historian would have committed them to paper and posterity. As early as 1857, he was known to be engaged in an ambitious historical work on some aspect of ecclesiastical history in connection with which he sought to consult the Vatican documents on the trial of Galileo;[1] of this project Granville expressed the hope that it would not be as it was admiringly described by Lady Camden, 'so clever that nobody will be able to understand it'.[2] Two years later Acton described his work-in-progress as a study of the modern history of the Popes, adding that if only he could spare half a year among his books at Aldenham, he could complete his research[3]—a refrain that became familiar as the years went by. In 1863, provoked by the American Civil War, he thought of writing a history of the origin of the American constitution and a comparison with the democracies of the ancient world. At the same time he conceived the idea of an historical reader in English in which texts from German historians would be so arranged as to reveal the general progress of world history. After the failure of the *Home and Foreign Review* in 1864, he renounced periodical literature in favour, he said, of substantial books on less 'controversial' subjects—of which the first was to be a large history of the Index![4] For at least a year he worked seriously on this, but the only material results were several notebooks of data,[5] and valuable additions to his library in the form of copies of thousands of documents, some made available to him by Cardinal Antonelli from the papal archives, others discovered, together with Döllinger, in the libraries and archives of Vienna.[6]

The history of the Index was never written because other projects came to distract him. He played with the idea of publishing a collection of historical letters. He found that in the course of his research he had accumulated enough original

---

[1] Add. MSS., 5751.
[2] Granville to Canning, 24 October 1857, Fitzmaurice, I, 262.
[3] Acton to Simpson, 28 November 1859, Gasquet, p. 152.
[4] Woodward, p. 255.
[5] Add. MSS., 5765, 5766, 5767.
[6] Add. MSS., 4992; Friedrich, *Döllinger*, III, 370.

material about James II to fill three volumes, and had un-
covered new sources for the life of Cardinal Pole which would
help elucidate the course of the Reformation in England and
Italy. He also contemplated lecturing on the relation between
Christianity and paganism, emphasizing particularly the state
of religious knowledge in pre-Christian times. His resolution
not to become involved in periodical writing went the way of
other similar resolutions when the *Chronicle* was founded in
1867. It was then, while producing a host of articles of contemporary and historical interest and ransacking the papal
archives, that it occurred to him to establish an English
Catholic historical society, for which, he told Döllinger,
he could produce six or eight volumes *De Rebus Catholicis in
Anglia*.[1]

Acton's attention was now turning to the Council of Trent,
and this time it was Cardinal Theiner who fed him documents
from the papal archives and library. But the material he collected, enough to fill many volumes, he estimated, was used for
the enlightenment of the minority bishops rather than for the
documentation of a scholarly work of history. His reticence
to publish it occasioned some surprise, as he himself noted,
among those who could not understand why 'anyone should
take so much trouble for nothing, or for nothing better than
his own instruction'.[2] The following years, dominated by the
North British Review and the Vatican Council, taught Acton a
good deal about history and more about the psychology of
men and political movements, but left him little opportunity
to transmit his extraordinary fund of knowledge to the world.

With Infallibility no longer an urgent issue, and relieved of
the obligation to defend himself or clarify his position, he was
able to take stock of his accomplishments and strike out on a
fresh course for the future. A history of the Popes, of James II,
of the Index, no longer seemed adequate to his resources and

[1] Woodward, p. 256.
[2] Add. MSS., 4979. It was probably the documents gathered at this
time, plus those in Döllinger's collection, that were later edited by
Döllinger's secretary, Philipp Woker, and were published in 1876 in two
volumes under the title of *Sammlung von Urkunden zur Geschichte des Konzils
von Trent: ungedruckte Berichte und Tagebücher.*

interests,[1] and he reverted to the plans of his youth, the composition of a universal history. He now knew just what the theme of such a history must be: the progress of freedom. This, he explained, would permit him to 'concentrate in one focus'[2] the particular subjects which had engaged him; he added, characteristically, that he had only to consult a number of books in Munich before proceeding. It was another two years, however, before the history of freedom was cast in even provisional form.

The Bridgnorth Institution, to which he had addressed his discourse on the Civil War in America eleven years earlier, was now favoured with his sketch of the history of freedom. The two lectures on 'The History of Freedom in Antiquity' and 'The History of Freedom in Christianity', delivered on 26 February and 28 May 1877, together with an article in the *Quarterly Review* of January 1878 reviewing Sir Erskine May's *Democracy in Europe*—100 pages of text in all—represent the most systematic statement of Acton's theme. In one way or another, however, most of his essays, correspondence and notes bear upon the subject, so that although the 'History of Liberty' has come down to us as the 'greatest book that never was written',[3] it is possible to reproduce in broad outline the pattern of that history.

The opening words of Acton's first lecture set the theme: 'Liberty, next to religion, has been the motive of good deeds and the common pretext of crime, from the sowing of the seed at Athens, 2,460 years ago, until the ripened harvest was gathered by men of our race.'[4] In the course of time, constitutions were perverted, charters became obsolete, parliaments abdicated and peoples erred, but the idea of liberty survived. That idea is 'the unity, the only unity, of the history of the world, and the one principle of a philosophy of history'.[5] Whatever

---

[1] In regard to James II, he satisfied himself with editing the *Letters of James II to the Abbot of La Trappe* ('Miscellanies of the Philobiblon Society'; London, 1872–6).

[2] Woodward, p. 258.   [3] See above, p. 10.

[4] Reprinted in *Essays on Freedom and Power*, p. 30.

[5] Add. MSS., 4991.

institutions or forms of government have been devised through the ages, the idea of liberty has remained constant: the right of each man to consult his conscience without reference to authorities or majorities, custom or opinion. The security of conscience enjoyed by the individual has its parallel in the security of minorities within the State; in both cases liberty is the safeguard of religion.

In the history of antiquity, Acton found confirmation of two of his favourite theories, that liberty is ancient and despotism modern, and that the history of liberty is in large measure the history of religion. The government of the Israelites, the first demonstration of political liberty, was a voluntary federation of self-governing tribes and families. When monarchy was finally instituted, it was only after much resistance, and the prophets kept alive the idea of equality before the law and the subservience of all before God. 'Thus the example of the Hebrew nation laid down the parallel lines on which all freedom has been won—the doctrine of national tradition and the doctrine of the higher law; the principle that a constitution grows from a root, by process of development, and not of essential change; and the principle that all political authorities must be tested and reformed according to a code which was not made by man.'[1] The first of the many disasters to befall liberty occurred when Babylonia conquered Judah and freedom under divine authority made way for absolutism under human authorities.

From the degradation of tyranny, inequality and oppression, the world was rescued by the most gifted of ancient cities, Athens. Solon inaugurated a revolution in philosophy and politics when he introduced the idea of popular election, 'the idea that a man ought to have a voice in selecting those to whose rectitude and wisdom he is compelled to trust his fortune, his family and his life.'[2] Government by consent replaced government by force, and those who ruled were made responsible to those who obeyed. It was then discovered that political power, once concentrated in the interest of good order, could be distributed at no risk to order and at great gain to liberty. This process of democratization was hastened by Pericles.

[1] *Freedom and Power*, p. 33.   [2] ibid., p. 36.

With popular religion disintegrating, morality liberating itself from mythology, and a growing scepticism of moral authority, the people became the effective arbiters of good and evil. In consideration of this, Pericles installed them in the seat of power. All the props that artificially bolstered up property and wealth were destroyed, and it was a duty as well as a right for Athenians to participate in public affairs. Government became a matter of persuasion and rhetoric the instrument of popular rule, so that the 'ascendancy of the mind'[1] was established together with the ascendancy of the people.

In the zeal for the popular interest, however, there was no provision for the unpopular, and the minority soon found itself at the mercy of the majority. The people, now sovereign, felt themselves bound by no rules of right or wrong, no criteria except expediency, no force outside of themselves. They conducted wars in the marketplace and lost them, exploited their dependencies, plundered the rich, and crowned their guilt with the martyrdom of Socrates. The experiment of Athens taught that democracy, the rule of the most numerous and most powerful class, was an evil of the same nature as monarchical absolutism and required restraints of the same sort: institutions to protect it against itself and a permanent source of law to prevent arbitrary revolutions of opinion. Men learned for the first time what later history was to confirm again and again: 'It is bad to be oppressed by a minority, but it is worse to be oppressed by a majority. For there is a reserve of latent power in the masses which, if it is called into play, the minority can seldom resist. But from the absolute will of an entire people there is no appeal, no redemption, no refuge but treason.'[2]

The Roman Republic experienced the same problems as Greece. Aristocratic governments alternated with democratic ones, until Caesar, supported by an army flushed with victories and a populace seduced by his generosity, converted the republic into a monarchy. In spite of the fact that the empire was an 'ill-disguised and odious despotism',[3] it made an important contribution to liberty. As Frederick the Great, though a despot, could promote the freedom of religion and

---

[1] ibid., p. 39.　　　　[2] ibid., p. 40.　　　　[3] ibid., p. 43.

speech, and the Bonapartes, though tyrants, could win the love
of the people, so the Roman Empire aroused genuine loyalty
because it satisfied deep needs. The poor fared better than they
had under the Republic and the rich better than under the
Triumvirate, the provinces acquired citizenship, slavery was
mitigated, religious toleration was instituted, a primitive law
of nations was devised, and the law of property was perfected.
But what was given to liberty with one hand was taken away
with the other when the people, by a voluntary act of delega-
tion, transferred its sovereignty to the emperor and supported
his tyranny because they thought of it as their own.

In terms of institutions and legislation, Greece and Rome
had an imperfect conception of freedom. They knew how to
manipulate power, but not how to achieve liberty. 'The vice
of the classic State was that it was both Church and State in
one. Morality was undistinguished from religion and politics
from morals; and in religion, morality, and politics there was
only one legislator and one authority.'[1] The citizen was subject to the State as the slave was to his master, and nothing was
deemed sacred apart from the public welfare. But where their
institutions failed, their philosophy succeeded. At a time when
their governments were most absolute, their theories called for
a mixed constitution. They saw that any single principle of
government standing alone, whether monarchy, aristocracy
or democracy, was apt to be carried to excess, and that only
in a distribution and balance of powers was liberty secure. All
the philosophers of antiquity displayed the same theoretical
boldness and practical timidity. Socrates urged men to submit
all questions to the judgment of reason and conscience, and to
ignore the verdict of authority, majority or custom. Yet he
would not sanction resistance. 'He emancipated men for
thought, but not for action',[2] and he fell victim to the old
superstition of the State. Plato taught the supremacy of a
divine law 'written in the mind of God',[3] and Aristotle applied
it, in the form of the doctrine of a mixed constitution, to practical government. But neither Plato nor Aristotle dared to

[1] ibid., p. 45.
[2] 'May's "Democracy in Europe",' reprinted in *Freedom and Power*,
p. 137. [3] Add. MSS., 4991.

conceive of liberty as justice rather than as expediency. Plato 'perverted'[1] the divine law when he limited it to the citizens of Greece, refusing it to the slave and the stranger. Aristotle perverted it by putting good government higher than liberty. They did not see that liberty was not a means to a higher political end but was itself the highest end, that 'it is not for the sake of a good public administration that it is required, but for security in the pursuit of the highest objects of civil society and of private life'.[2]

The Stoics pushed the theory of liberty one step forward with the doctrine of a law of Nature that was superior to the law of nations and the will of the people. 'The great question', they taught, 'is to discover, not what governments prescribe, but what they ought to prescribe; for no prescription is valid against the conscience of mankind.'[3] And the conscience of mankind knows no distinctions between Greek and barbarian, rich and poor, slave and master. Men are equal in rights as in duties, and human legislation can neither detract from the one nor add to the other. Thus the Stoics 'redeemed democracy from the narrowness, the want of principle and of sympathy, which are its reproach among the Greeks'.[4] Augustine testified to their wisdom when he remarked, after quoting Seneca, 'What more could a Christian say than this Pagan has said?'[5]

The Christian had, indeed, little more to say. There was hardly a truth in politics or ethics that had not already been enunciated before the new dispensation was revealed. It was left for Christianity, however, to animate the old truths, to make real the metaphysical barrier which philosophy had erected in the way of absolutism. The only thing Socrates could do in the way of a protest against tyranny was to die for his convictions. The Stoics could only advise the wise man to hold aloof from politics and keep faith with the unwritten law in his heart. But when Christ said, 'Render unto Caesar the things that are Caesar's, and unto God the things that are God's', he gave to the State a legitimacy it had never before enjoyed, and set bounds to it that it had never yet acknowledged. And he not only delivered the precept but he also forged the instru-

[1] ibid.   [2] *Freedom and Power*, p. 51.
[3] ibid., p. 52.   [4] ibid., p. 140.   [5] ibid., p. 53.

ment to execute it. To limit the power of the State ceased to be the hope of patient, ineffectual philosophers and became the perpetual charge of a universal Church.

The strange thing was that for long Christianity itself was unaware of its real mission. It hoped to avoid conflict with the State by remaining aloof from political disputes, and in the first centuries the doctrine of passive obedience and the temper of political quietism prevailed. When Constantine the Great converted the Empire to Christianity, he thought to strengthen his throne without relinquishing any of his authority. He and his successors used all the resources of Roman civilization, the reasonableness and sublety of Roman law, and the heritage of pagan authority to make the Church serve as a 'gilded crutch of absolutism'.[1] What enlightenment there was in the philosophy of Socrates, in the wisdom of the Stoics or in the faith of Christianity could not withstand the incorrigible practices of antiquity. A tradition of self-government was lacking, and that tradition finally came into the West with the barbarian invasions.

The Teutonic migration introduced a kind of primitive republicanism in which monarchy was an incidental, almost accidental, feature. The idea that the permanent and ultimate factor in government is the collective supremacy of free men was the germ of modern parliamentarianism. But another novel aspect of the new communities was the personal loyalty exacted from the circle surrounding the king. The first principle tended to dissolve society by its radical limitations on government, the second tended to destroy freedom by its dangerous dependence upon persons. It was a system in which learning, literature, the arts, even the material culture, were decadent. To bring order out of chaos not liberty but force was required, and the great names of the next centuries—Clovis, Charlemagne and William the Conqueror—were those of men of action unencumbered by scruples.

The growth of liberty, the great achievement of the Middle Ages, came not from the forests of Germany, as one theory had it, nor from the Christian Church itself, but from the conflict between the two:

[1] ibid., p. 59.

'To that conflict of 400 years we owe the rise of civil liberty. If the Church had continued to buttress the thrones of the kings whom it annointed, or if the struggle had terminated speedily in an undivided victory, all Europe would have sunk under a Byzantine or Muscovite despotism. For the aim of both contending parties was absolute authority. But although liberty was not the end for which they strove, it was the means by which the temporal and the spiritual power called the nations to their aid. The towns of Italy and Germany won their franchises, France got her States-General, and England her Parliament out of the alternate phases of the contest; and as long as it lasted it prevented the rise of divine right.'[1]

The three-cornered struggle of Pope, emperor and feudal lords left no room for ideas of absolute sovereignty. Pope and lords joined in denying the indefeasible title of kings; occasionally, as in the contest between the houses of Bruce and Plantagenet for possession of Scotland and Ireland, the king and the Pope found themselves in temporary coalition against the nobility; more often, Guelphs and Ghibellines competed for the favour of the nobility. From these cross-currents of interests there emerged a fund of constitutional principles: representative government, no taxation without representation, the moral right of insurrection, the extinction of slavery, trial by jury, local self-government, ecclesiastical independence, even the ideas of the Habeas Corpus Act and the income tax. If there was any notion of sovereignty, it adhered primarily to the corporation, and it was in the immunity enjoyed by the corporation, by powerful classes and privileged associations, that liberty took refuge.

The treasure stored up by the Middle Ages was dissipated by the Renaissance, when religion declined in influence and the State reasserted the sovereignty it had possessed in antiquity. Machiavelli's principle, that the end justifies the means, became the arch-stone of politics. Statecraft, it was discovered, was too perilous an undertaking to be hampered by the precepts of the copy-book. Even men of goodwill were persuaded by the logic of Machiavelli:

[1] ibid., pp. 62–3.

'They saw that in critical times good men have seldom strength for their goodness, and yield to those who have grasped the meaning of the maxim that you cannot make an omelette if you are afraid to break the eggs. They saw that public morality differs from private, because no government can turn the other cheek, or can admit that mercy is better than justice. And they could not define the difference, or draw the limits of exception; or tell what other standard for a nation's acts there is than the judgment which Heaven pronounces in this world by success.'[1]

Kings embraced his doctrine with so much zeal that it was no longer possible to distinguish between good and bad. Not by isolated crimes, but by a studied philosophy of evil and a thorough perversion of the moral sense was absolute monarchy inaugurated.

The Church made no attempt to resist the current of absolutism. Constitutionalism was in disrepute there as it was in the State, and Popes feared it no less than kings. Reverting to the Byzantine pattern, the ecclesiastical hierarchy entered into an association with royalty which soon became a subjection to it. In France the absolute monarchy was built up by twelve political cardinals, while the kings of Spain revived and appropriated the tribunal of the Inquisition. The Reformation, after a brief flirtation with Liberalism, settled down to a marriage of convenience with royal absolutism. Luther's boast, that he was the first divine to do justice to the civil power, was entirely warranted. But whether princes welcomed the Reformation or fought it, they used it as an occasion for the increase of their power. Nations outbid each other in their zeal to invest their rulers with all the prerogatives necessary for the preservation of their faith, and the great work of past ages, the distinction between Church and State, was forgotten. Religious passion became the instrument of many atrocious deeds, and policy of State the motive. 'Calvin preached and Bellarmine lectured, but Machiavelli reigned.'[2] No one, with the exception of Richard Hooker, thought of politics as the impartial arbiter of justice, holding court over all religions alike.

[1] ibid., p. 68.   [2] ibid., p. 71.

For a short while Grotius seemed to have brought liberty to life again by reviving the philosophy of natural law. With law independent of any national or even revealed code, and all men united under a single common law, politics would have been free to consult only principle and conscience. Unfortunately, however, natural law was swept back into the hinterlands of speculation by the irresistible tide of seventeenth-century royalty. All over the Continent, assemblies, provinces and privileged classes were making their obeisance to the throne, which they worshipped as 'the constructor of their unity, the promoter of prosperity and power, the defender of orthodoxy, and the employer of talent'.[1] Theology, with its doctrines of divine right and passive obedience, provided the rationale for absolute monarchy, and the new religion of the State was fostered by ecclesiasts and philosophers, who agreed that only an absolute monarchy could maintain order, that the State was the natural guardian of religion, and that there was no justice apart from the king's justice.

When the English parliamentarians finally rebelled against this order of things, they compromised their cause by the 'fanatical treachery'[2] with which they brought about the death of King Charles and by the illiberalism and inconsistency of the revolutionary government. Yet it was the revolutionary sects which, after Grotius, gave the impetus to the movement for liberty. The principle of religious liberty, which was their unique contribution, was second only to that of natural law in the history of freedom. Religious liberty had made its appearance earlier, but only as a temporary concession in the warfare of religions. What the seventeenth-century sects did was to establish toleration as an absolute right: 'It is one step to show that it is useful, expedient. A second step makes it a religious duty. A third makes it a political right. . . . Argument from right alone completes it.'[3] Religious and civil liberty were mutually dependent, for only by abridging the authority of States could religious liberty be secured, and only with the security of religious liberty was civil liberty meaningful.

Unlike the Radical experiments of 1640–60, the Revolution of 1688 was undistinguished by any great principle or fanatical

[1] ibid., p. 74.   [2] ibid., p. 78.   [3] Add. MSS., 5006.

devotion to liberty. The English political lineage has the misfortune to include men who were in the service of foreign
kings, who did not scruple to invent slanderous lies about the
Catholics in order to persecute them, who were not averse to
slavery, and whose conception of liberty (Acton had Locke in
mind) involved nothing more spiritual than the protection of
property. The main result of 1688 was that the divine right of
freeholders succeeded to the divine right of kings.

It took the American Revolution to emancipate liberty from
property and expediency by striking out boldly for right and
justice. At this point of history, the typically modern despotism of the Renaissance and Reformation gave way to a typically
modern Liberalism. America made all previous attempts to
capture the secret of liberty look like the futile grapplings of
shadows. In the strictest sense the history of liberty dated from
1776, for 'never till then had men sought liberty knowing what
they sought'.[1] The Revolution pursued liberty as an end in
itself, and the Constitutional Convention created a democracy
that was unique in also being Liberal. 'It established a pure
democracy; but it was democracy in its highest perfection,
armed and vigilant, less against aristocracy and monarchy than
against its own weakness and excess.'[2] The third of the modern
revolutions was less fortunate. France adopted the moral fer-
vour of America without its political wisdom, and the grandiose
promise of liberty contained in the French Revolution ended
in bleak tyranny. Eventually America too fell victim to the same
lassitude of spirit. As on the Continent, democracy became, next
to absolute monarchy, the most formidable enemy of liberty:

'The true democratic principle, that none shall have power over
the people, is taken to mean that none shall be able to restrain
or to elude its power. The true democratic principle, that the
people shall not be made to do what it does not like, is taken
to mean that it shall never be required to tolerate what it does
not like. The true democratic principle, that every man's free
will shall be as unfettered as possible, is taken to mean that the
free will of the collective people shall be fettered in nothing.'[3]

It is as unavailing to try to summarize Acton's 'History of
[1] Add. MSS., 4870.   [2] *Freedom and Power*, p. 150.   [3] ibid., p. 159.

Liberty' as to paraphrase a lyric poem. History, to Acton, was the intricate arrangement of a multitude of episodes, facts, persons and ideas. To give the barest outline of his thought culled from essays and notes which he himself insisted did not begin to scratch the surface of his subject, and which were even far from exhausting his own speculations, is to risk making a travesty of his most serious enterprise. Legal codes, social theories, theological doctrines, popular opinions, literary sentiments, political principles, economic institutions, great books and curious pamphlets, exceptional men and commonplace men were all grist for his mill. Almost everything worked its way through his restless, recondite mind to emerge as part of the texture and pattern of the history of liberty. He once criticized Sir Erskine May, author of the two-volume *Democracy in Europe*, for neglecting to track down the basic democratic dogmas that all men are equal, that thought and speech must be free, that each generation legislates for itself alone, that endowments, entail and primogeniture are illegitimate, that the people are sovereign and can do no wrong. These were the kinds of problems Acton would have put to himself had he been writing such a book. And he would also have found place for the many details of 'antiquarian curiosity', as he ironically put it: 'how M. Waddington has emended the *Momentum Ancyranum*, what connection there was between Mariana and Milton, or between Penn and Rousseau, or who invented the proverb *Vox Populi Vox Dei*'.[1]

Yet even in the most skeletal outline, some features of Acton's character are revealed. He was not the optimistic historian like Buckle, who conceived of history as the invariable victory of truth over error, the progressive conquest by the intellect of physical and human nature. In his fundamental values—his respect for religion, approval of aristocracy, and distaste for democracy—he had more in common with Toqueville. Yet he did not share Toqueville's fears that religion and aristocracy, the necessary conditions of liberty, were obsolete in the modern world, and that democracy, equality and centralization were in danger of submerging men in a slough of despotism. He was less facile than Buckle, less apprehensive

[1] ibid., p. 165.

than Toqueville. The history of liberty for him was a succession of gains and losses, but he was confident that the idea of liberty could no more be lost for ever than the idea of morality. Liberty depended upon no single idea or institution; all ideas and institutions depended upon it: '[It was] not prosperity or material progress, not happiness or [material] civilization, not science or religion, not democracy or nationality. All these things have been its tributaries and servants, but they have, in turn, been rivals and obstacles'.[1] Moreover liberty was no primitive quality that could be swallowed up in the welter of a complex civilization; on the contrary, it was the delicate product of a mature culture. Liberty is ancient, to be sure, but only in an undeveloped, untried form. Just as societies untroubled by religious diversity are not given to religious persecution, so societies undisturbed by the complex problems of civilization may find it easy to avoid despotism. It is civilization that makes despotism tempting—and makes liberty meaningful. 'Those nations are happy', Acton observed, 'which do not resent the complexity of life'.[2]

In the 1870's, when Acton sketched some of the highlights of the 'History of Liberty', he had not thought out the full implications of all his ideas. It was a time of transition for him, when his early pragmatic view of politics was slowly yielding to his later moralistic view. In 1859 he had proclaimed Burke as 'the law and the prophets'[3]—the older Burke, master of the art of practical politics and antagonist of the French Revolution, rather than the younger Burke, friend of the American Revolution. Abstract, metaphysical principles he had then denounced as the bane of politics, and natural rights and natural law as empty formulas at best, and at worst, traps in which lurked the despotic instincts of fanatical men. He had described slavery as a good as well as an evil in the providential order of the world, had execrated the abolitionists for their 'abstract, ideal absolutism',[4] and had extolled the Church for its willingness to accommodate itself to varying times, circumstances and ideas.

In the course of the 'seventies, much of this Burkian heritage

[1] Add. MSS., 4944.　　　　[2] Add. MSS., 4870.
[3] Acton to Simpson, 4 February 1859, Gasquet, p. 60.
[4] See above, p. 79.

was abandoned. Practical politics, Acton discovered, had its vices and ideal politics its virtues. He now decided that the American Revolution was the greatest Liberal event in the history of the world, that the idea of natural rights and natural law was the basic motif in the history of liberty, and that the abolition of slavery was a symptom and a symbol of moral emancipation. But the break with his earlier views was not yet conscious or irreparable. He had not yet formulated the moral principle in its most radical sense, nor discovered the urgency of political and social reform, nor explored the relation between the idea of liberty and the institutions of Liberalism. He concluded the second of his lectures by suggesting that the law of free States was the doctrine known as development, evolution or continuity, the doctrine that constitutions are not made but grow. Several years later he was to be converted to the view that constitutions must sometimes be made rather than allowed passively to grow, and that it was occasionally desirable that revolutions break the continuity of history.

LIBERTY, MORALITY AND RELIGION

In 1878 Acton was full of plans for the expansion of his lectures into a book on the history of liberty. He regaled his friends with dramatic, extemporaneous recitals of some of its episodes, but he delayed writing. Mary Gladstone wrote after one of these narrations: 'It is extraordinary the way he tingles with it to his fingers [sic] ends and yet can sit patient and quiet over wife and children and wait and wait another year before writing it. What an extraordinary man.'[1] By 1882 the waiting was largely a formality. It had become clear to some of his friends that although the 'History of Liberty' would continue to be the focus of Acton's life, it would never acquire an independent reality. He took to referring to it as his 'Madonna of the Future', a title suggested by the Henry James story of an artist who had dedicated his life to the creation of a single magnificent painting and on whose easel, after his death, was discovered a blank canvas.

[1] 8 October 1879, Mary Gladstone (Mrs. Drew), *Her Diaries and Letters*, ed. Lucy Masterman (London, 1930), p. 173.

Döllinger used to complain of the temptation to prolong research at the expense of writing,[1] but Acton was even more incorrigible than his master. He could not bring himself to take less than all of history for his province, and even the concept of liberty was intended not so much as a limitation of his subject than as a convenient perspective from which to survey it. And Acton went far beyond Döllinger in his fastidious treatment of data, the compulsion to exhaust all the material remotely related to his problem and to dissect it with every critical instrument available to the historian. He had been invited by the German historian, Wilhelm von Giesebrecht, to write three volumes on England for the historical series initiated by Heeren and Ukert, but demurred, explaining that if he was to compete with Guizot, Ranke and Macaulay, he would have to be original, scientific and comprehensive, which would make it too great an undertaking. Although he later volunteered to do the volume on 1509–62, like so many other projects this too went unfulfilled. Writing of his 'Madonna of the Future' to Mary Gladstone, he explained that every week brought new publications to throw fresh light or fresh difficulties on his subject.

Yet the sheer physical magnitude of the project was not Acton's main obstacle. He could have found ways of coping with it or getting around it; the most obvious course would have been simply to plunge into some one chapter of the history. What he could not get around, however, and this faced him wherever he turned, was the problem of judgment. Liberty was itself a moral concept, and the history of liberty was necessarily a record of good and evil. Unfortunately there was no agreement among historians regarding moral values, or an accepted convention governing their use in the writing of history. The history of ideas was still something of a novelty; the history of a moral idea, written by a respectable historian and not a party hack, was even less common. And when that idea trespassed on all of the most cherished and controversial values of religion, party, nation and class, it is no wonder that Acton felt his charge weigh heavily upon him.

Only slowly had Acton become conscious of the gravity

[1] Döllinger to Acton, 29 December 1872, Add. MSS., 4911.

of moral questions. His experiences during and after the Vatican Council had taught him that the important issues separating men hinged not upon disagreements of fact but upon differences of value, and it was then that he discovered that his values did not have the consensus of all men, or even of all well-thinking men. For some time he was able to take comfort in the knowledge that Döllinger at least was of his mind. When that knowledge failed him, he was left with a profound despair of his work and a wretched sense of isolation.

For twenty years Acton had been the faithful disciple of Döllinger. There was nothing obsequious in his devotion, but only a generous recognition of his teacher's ability. In 1866 Acton confessed: 'I am nothing but what you have made of me, and I subsist on what falls from your abundant table. The lustre of your name, the memory of your words, the study of your ideas gives me a reputation here [in England] that I do not deserve.'[1] The slight hint of discord in 1869, when Acton quarrelled with Janus for being too lenient to the Ultramontanes, was soon forgotten, and Döllinger wrote to assure him that he was 'the only one with whom I can completely be open and express my innermost thoughts'.[2] During the Vatican Council they worked harmoniously together, and the fact that Döllinger was excommunicated and Acton was not reflected a difference of situation rather than of opinion. Even after Döllinger, largely for want of an alternative, became involved with the Old Catholics, Acton continued to regard him as the spokesman of Liberal Catholicism, and in September 1874, he urged him to undertake the most important work left to Liberals, the task of exposing the roots of Ultramontanism.[3] By 1876, however, a more significant and permanent divergence of views had become evident. Gladstone was perhaps the first outsider to realize that, as he confided to his diary, Acton 'seems in opinions to go beyond Döllinger, though in certain things he stops short of him'.[4] Where Acton had stopped short of Döllinger was in not inviting excommunication,

[1] Woodward, p. 249, translated from the German.
[2] 27 June 1869, Add. MSS., 4911, translated from the German.
[3] Acton to Döllinger, 19 September 1874, Add. MSS., 4914.
[4] 2 November 1876, Morley, *Gladstone*, II, 558.

but he had gone far beyond him in the intensity with which he had rejected Ultramontanism.

Until 1879 the differences between Acton and Döllinger seemed trivial, the passing disagreements, more verbal than real, of men who had been influenced by the same books, had pondered the same problems, and had lived through the same intellectual and religious experiences. In the beginning of 1879, Döllinger was preparing to write a paper on one of Acton's favourite subjects, the Massacre of St. Bartholomew, and Acton was full of plans for his 'History of Liberty'. In February the blow fell that for Acton almost assuredly meant the abandonment of the history and the beginning of a period of creative impotence. For six years he was to write nothing except one short review.

In the *Nineteenth Century* for February 1879, there appeared an article commemorating the recent death of Dupanloup, written by Lady Blennerhassett and prefaced with a short letter by Döllinger. The article was not the conventional memorial eulogy, but neither was it critical, and in explaining Dupanloup it often seemed to be exonerating him. Acton was repelled by the tolerance accorded to a man who had defended the Syllabus of Errors, had assumed a position of compromise at the Vatican Council and had then unhesitatingly submitted to the decrees, a man who, in his opinion, fully merited the odious title of Ultramontane. He was not so much distressed, however, by the article itself as by the defection of Döllinger. When Lady Blennerhassett had asked Acton for his recollections of Dupanloup, he had been frankly critical and disapproving, but Döllinger, approached with the same request, had politely refrained from adverse judgment. As soon as Acton received the February issue of the *Nineteenth Century*, he wrote to Lady Blennerhassett reproachfully. He had expected her to discount his remarks about Dupanloup as naïve. But that Döllinger should regard a defender of the Pope, of the Syllabus and of the temporal power as a genuine Christian, capable of receiving the benefits of the sacraments, was a great shock. 'That gives me cause for reflection and opens up to me unforeseen horizons.'[1]

Acton was forty-five when the disillusionment with Döllin-

[1] 17 February 1879, *Correspondence*, p. 53, translated from the French.

ger set in, but he took it with the emotional intensity of an adolescent. The disagreement over Dupanloup he now saw as only a minor incident in a long, dreary history of misunderstandings, and he racked his memory to discover when the divergence had begun and what its early symptoms had been. 'Men', he pessimistically observed, 'are always divided on more points than they know of. Time brings on occasions that bring out their differences. Every colleague of to-day is a future opponent, if he only lives a few years.'[1]

Reconsidering the past, Acton decided that the original sin from which Döllinger could never redeem himself was romanticism. The moral relativism that was part of the romantic tradition persuaded Döllinger that the historian must immerse himself in the mood of each age, nation and ideology, and must try men by their own codes and authorities.[2] In typical romantic fashion he wanted to explain rather than judge, and when judgment was inevitable to temper justice with mercy,[3] which had the unfortunate effect of 'blunting the edge of his thought'.[4] He refused to see all the evil there was in man, and ascribed what evil he did find to a false speculative system or a defect of knowledge rather than to moral turpitude: 'It suited his way to distribute blame so that nobody suffered. He hated moral imputations. Folly, stupidity, ignorance, moral cowardice, the deceived conscience, did duty as long as possible. [It] suited him to trace the gradual growth of things, so that no one was really responsible.'[5]

The habit of rigorous judgment, which for Acton was the mark of moral integrity, was interpreted by Döllinger as moral righteousness, the complacency of the historian not tried by the real problems of power and politics. Döllinger, Acton knew, 'saw want of discernment as well as want of charity in excessive zeal in condemning'.[6] To this Acton retorted that his was no excessive zeal to condemn, no esoteric or unreasonable criterion of judgment. He proposed, as the obvious, decisive test to eliminate subjectivity in judgment, that found in all codes of law, the test of murder. In politics as in criminal

[1] Add. MSS., 4939.
[2] Add. MSS., 4914, 4907, 4905.
[3] Add. MSS., 4992, 4905.
[4] Add. MSS., 4905.
[5] Add. MSS., 4908.
[6] Add. MSS., 4909.

law murder was the 'low-water mark'.[1] It was the 'weakest link'[2] in a man's character, and if that link broke, there was no use tinkering elsewhere with the chain. Döllinger rejected this test of the weakest link, preferring to judge men by the whole of their lives. 'He refused', Acton noted, 'to test the author of 100 volumes by the matter of a single page.'[3] Döllinger assumed that a man's intentions might mitigate his actions and his good deeds compensate for his bad; but for Acton there was no mitigation, no compensation.

Even to the fact of the Inquisition, Acton discovered, Döllinger did not respond unambiguously. Not until his sixty-eighth year, after almost forty years of lecturing and the publication of fifteen volumes, had he begun to reflect seriously upon the theory and history of persecution.[4] And when he had finally set his mind to it, it was too late to change the habits of a lifetime. While he did not defend the Inquisition or the inquisitors, he remained on good terms with men who did, with Hefele, Theiner and Dupanloup, each of whom had been less than intransigent in his treatment of persecution.[5] The distance in the chain that connected Dupanloup, Hefele or Theiner (none of them Ultramontane by the conventional standard) with the Inquisition was immaterial to Acton; to be contaminated however remotely, was fatal. To say a good word for a persecutor was tantamount to condoning murder, and the accessory after the fact was guilty as surely as the original perpetrator of the deed.

For the eleven years separating the death of Acton's first teacher (Dupanloup) and his last, the controversy between Acton and Döllinger raged, now by correspondence, now in conversations at Tegernesee or Munich, often in the form of monologues which later found their way into Acton's notes. One issue after another was raised, agitated at length, and finally dropped, only to come up again at some later time. The

[1] Add. MSS., 4914.
[2] Add. MSS., 4909, 4914.
[3] Add. MSS., 4911.
[4] Add. MSS., 4908. Acton fixed the date by a conversation in August 1864, but either that date or Döllinger's age must be in error, for in 1864 Döllinger was sixty-five, not sixty-eight.
[5] Add. MSS., 4904.

propriety of making of the historian a judge, and a 'hanging judge'[1] at that; the case of ecclesiasts and statesmen who came under his jurisdiction; the question of the superiority of Jansenists and Gallicans over Jesuits and Ultramontanes—these were the staples of debate. No compromise was possible because ultimately, as Acton and Döllinger both knew, the difference was one of moral sensibility, not to be reconciled by superficial concurrence on definitions or facts.

It is unfortunate that Acton's correspondence with Döllinger has not been published in full.[2] Because of its suppression, the full extent and effect of the quarrel has rarely been appreciated. The disagreement over a memorial essay in honour of Dupanloup ramified until it attained the proportions of a major conflict of *Weltanschauungen*, involving all of history, religion and morality. What an unsympathetic observer might describe as the two dominant characteristics of Acton's later life—an obsessive fixation upon a private brand of moral idealism, and a hysterical paralysis of the creative faculty were the immediate results of the rupture with Döllinger. Two documents, the first a letter to Lady Blennerhassett and the second a set of notes which were probably a draft of that letter, give evidence of the spiritual torment which seemed to Acton to be making of his past a delusion and of his future a desolation.

To Lady Blennerhassett, Acton related the 'simple, obvious,

[1] *Freedom and Power*, p. 18.

[2] A translation of that correspondence was made by Professor E. L. Woodward in 1914, and had been announced for publication by Longmans, Green & Co., London, as Volume II of the *Correspondence*. Lady Acton subsequently decided against having it published, however, so that Volume I of the *Correspondence* now stands alone. It is hoped that the forthcoming edition of Acton's collected works will include the whole of these letters. In the meantime, quotations from some of them may be found in Woodward's article in *Politica*. Other more provocative excerpts from these letters and notes of conversations with Döllinger are to be found among Acton's manuscripts in the Cambridge University Library. Several letters bearing on this subject addressed to Gladstone and his daughter and to Lady Blennerhassett are included in the *Correspondence* and *Letters to Mary Gladstone*; unfortunately most of the explicit references to Döllinger seem to have been omitted from these, probably because they were intended for a separate volume.

and not interesting' story of his life: 'It is the story of a man who started in life believing himself a sincere Catholic and a sincere Liberal; who therefore renounced everything in Catholicism which was not compatible with Liberty and everything in Politics that was not compatible with Catholicity.'[1] In religion and in politics he was prepared to sacrifice the real to the ideal, interest to duty, and authority to morality. But the Church would have none of this. On the theory that much wrong may be done for the sake of saving souls, the Church had abrogated the common precepts of morality, and men had become demons in the service of religion. The papacy in particular had encouraged this perversion: 'The papacy contrived murder and massacred on the largest and also on the most cruel and inhuman scale. They were not only wholesale assassins, but they made the principle of assassination a law of the Christian Church and a condition of salvation.'[2] The papacy was the 'fiend skulking behind the Crucifix.'[3] What, then, was the serious, moral Catholic to do?

'Was it better to renounce the papacy out of horror for its acts, or to condone the acts out of reverence for the papacy? The Papal party preferred the latter alternative. It appeared to me that such men are infamous in the last degree. I did not accuse them of error, as I might impute it to Grotius or Channing, but of crime. I thought that a person who imitated them for political or other motives worthy of death. But those whose motive was religious seemed to me worse than the others, because that which is in others the last resource of conversion is with them the source of guilt. The spring of repentance is broken, the conscience is not only weakened but warped. Their prayers and sacrifices appeared to me the most awful sacrilege.[4]

This letter has never been printed in full and the original is not available, but from the duplication of one paragraph in the published version of the letter and in the manuscript notes, it seems likely that the letter was composed from the notes, or, at the very least, that they were both written at about the same

[1] *Correspondence*, p. 54. [2] ibid., p. 55.
[3] ibid., p. 56. [4] ibid., p. 55.

time, probably early in 1884.[1] The notes, however, have a personal character that a reticent Acton, or possibly a reticent editor, thought fit to expunge from the letter. Elliptical, carelessly phrased, and hastily scrawled in pencil on small index cards, they are more moving and revealing than any other single document left by Acton. The argument is the familiar one: Döllinger opposed Ultramontanism as one might legitimately oppose protectionism, as an error rather than a crime; he was entangled in sympathy with Gallicanism, not realizing that it was no more an instrument of moral reform than Ultramontanism; and he thought that Ultramontanes might be in a state of grace, 'that they carry with them, weakened and impaired, but still efficacious, the sacramental gifts'.

It is when the notes venture beyond argument into personal confession that they testify to the depth of the spiritual crisis through which Acton passed in the five years following the publication of the seemingly innocuous looking essay on Dupanloup:

'When in reply to Gladstone I said, there is no indictment short of wilful murder, you must either hang or absolve, I became aware that the Professor was not in harmony. It did not make a deep impression on me, I know not why. Two or three years later, you published your paper on Dupanloup. You asked me for reminiscences, and afterwards told me that you had made no use of them. I concluded that it was because I was hard upon him, and such $\begin{cases} \text{ideas} \\ \text{views} \end{cases}$ could not be worked into your own. And I imagined that your judgment on him was more favourable, treating him perhaps as a man who was mistaken, but not as a common rogue and imposter.

'Every summer since, I have spent all my time and energy in trying to discover whether we [Döllinger and Acton] really differ so widely. I met with great difficulty. The response was not always the same, or even consistent, nor always clear. I

[1] Figgis and Laurence, editors of the *Correspondence*, assumed that the letter was written in February 1879, as soon as the Dupanloup article appeared, but nothing in the published part of the letter justifies their assigning it to that early date. The notes, on the other hand, can be dated, by internal evidence, as 1884.

made very little way, and had to meet *des fins de non revceoir*—as when you are older; or, if you mean to bring a new doctrine of Christianity into the Church; or, consider the advantage of your position; or, what should we have done in like circumstances; or, men must have men to look up to.

'Often it appeared that the Professor did not give me of his best; but rather put me off with imperfect statements of fact. Very often he was disposed to treat my points not as the result of many years' incessant study, and varied observation, but as a hasty paradox or prejudice, not worthy of very serious treatment. The general effect was that the thing became distasteful to him the more definite I became. And at last, in 1883, he made it very clear that it was time for our conversations to cease, for this world.

'As he afterwards spoke to my wife and her sister otherwise, as not being so far apart, I made a slight attempt this year in writing; and received an answer which to me is ambiguous and contradictory. As now advised, I must think either that he does not like me to know his real mind, or that he is really of the opinion which I reject. For if we really agreed, we should not have taken five years to find it out.

'Therefore, so far as I can see, I have thoroughly misunderstood the Professor, have been in opposition when I thought myself his disciple, and have had to spend five years in merely trying to find out his real sentiments.

'First: I must say to myself that I have probably mistaken many other people, whom I had fewer opportunities of knowing and questioning.

'2. Others also may have misunderstood him.

'3. I have deceived people, by sailing under false colours.

'4. I have renounced public life, and a position favourable to influence in my own country, to pursue an object I cannot attain.

'5. I am absolutely alone in my essential ethical position, and therefore useless. Not because one wants support or encouragement but because anyone who asks who agrees with me, will learn that no one agrees, and that no one disputes my view with anything like the energy with which the Professor disputes it.

'6. No other person can ever be so favourably situated as the Professor. He seeks nothing, knows more, and had, assuredly, a prejudice in my favour. People whose prejudices are the other way, who know less, who are less perfectly independent will certainly not listen to me better than he.

'The probability of doing good by writings so isolated and repulsive, of obtaining influence for views, etc., is so small that I have no right to sacrifice to it my own tranquillity and my duty of educating my children. My time can be better employed than in waging a hopeless war. And the more my life has been thrown away, the more necessary to turn now, and employ better what remains.[1]

This was Acton's statement of abdication. His 'History of Liberty' would go unwritten because he despaired of receiving a sympathetic hearing, and more decisively, because the experience of losing the key to Döllinger's mind and finding himself 'in outer and increasing darkness'[2] was disabling him for creative work. To say that Acton's emotional reaction was excessive is to say only what Acton would have readily admitted, that he alone took seriously the problem of liberty and morality, that it was for him, as it was for the victims of tyranny and persecution, a matter of life and death. To Acton the cultivation of moral inflexibility was the necessary consequence of a genuine humanitarianism; to Döllinger it was the escape of a fanatically inhuman mind. One can sympathize with Döllinger, who submitted to Acton's constant badgering for four years until he was driven to propose that their conversations 'cease for this world'.[3] But on his own terms at least,

---

[1] Add. MSS., 5403. The cards, included in a file labelled, 'D. Table Talk', had been numbered, probably by a Cambridge University librarian. The only remaining ones are those numbered 19 through 35, 67, and one unnumbered card obviously belonging to the same series. What happened to the others is not known. Of these I have transcribed 29, 26, 25, 24, 21, 20 and 19, in that order (the reverse order preserves the continuity of thought), altering the punctuation in only minor respects and spelling out the numerous abbreviations.

[2] Acton to Lady Blennerhassett, 31 January 1886, *Correspondence*, p. 269.

[3] This was the way Acton reported it. Döllinger apparently meant that their discussions of that subject were to cease, for he and Acton continued to meet at Tegernsee in the summer or early autumn of every year from

Acton was no less worthy of sympathy. He had worried over the problem long and earnestly, and it was humiliating to find Döllinger making light of his arguments, as it was demoralizing to discover that the precepts of morality could be so casually relaxed.

The irony of the situation, as Döllinger and Acton's friends were acutely aware, was that it was the Catholic Acton who chose to lecture the excommunicate Döllinger on the evils of Ultramontanism. Acton had apparently forgotten the controversies of 1872-4, when he had rebuked Gladstone for suggesting that Ultramontanes were evil in all they did and that Ultramontanism was a consistently effective scheme of thought. At that time it was Döllinger who had insisted, with Gladstone, upon the full measure of Ultramontane guilt, and it was Acton who had found logical gaps through which Ultramontanes might escape perdition. Or perhaps Acton remembered that episode and regretted the concessions he had then made. In one sense, the Acton-Döllinger conflict can be interpreted as cancelling out part of the Acton-Gladstone controversy. Whatever symptoms there were, in the earlier controversy, of a more mellow, tolerant Acton were erased in the later one, as he reverted to the simple moral intransigence that had possessed him at the Vatican Council.

There were other and more serious moral perverts in Acton's universe than Döllinger. One outstanding member of what Acton called 'a very grotesque company of professing Christians'[1] was Newman, who reached the height of his career with the offer of a cardinal's hat in the same month that the Dupanloup article plunged Acton into the depths of despair.

Newman was generally conceded to be one of the distinguished men of the age and certainly the most distinguished and influential Catholic. Yet Acton, his contemporary, compatriot and co-religionist, disparaged him as a feeble intellec-

1884 to 1889. There are references to these meetings in Add. MSS., 4914, 6871, and 5003; *Letters to Mary Gladstone*, p. 305; Friedrich, *Döllinger*, III, 674; Morley, *Gladstone*, III, 351–2; George Leveson Gower, *Years of Endeavour* [London, 1942], p. 1; Kobell, p. 88.

[1] Add. MSS., 4914.

tual counterpart of the Munich theologians and a feeble moral counterpart of the Ultramontanes. That Newman was no fanatical devotee of religious Liberalism had become clear in the early days of the *Rambler*, when he alternately lashed out at the 'dull tyranny of Manning and Ward',[1] and chided the *Rambler* for a Protestant-like irreverence towards authority. In later years his prejudice against political Liberalism as the modern form of devil worship made him even less congenial to Acton. During the Vatican Council much was made of Newman's attack upon the 'aggressive and insolent'[2] faction that had introduced the new decrees, but he was furious when his words became known and later explained that he accepted and believed the dogma of Infallibility although he was 'unable to reconcile it with well-ascertained historical facts'.[3] In 1874, when the Vatican controversy was revived, Newman congratulated Acton for coming to the defence of historical truth,[4] but Acton took care to dissociate his own position from Newman's.

'The most cautious and artful of apologists'[5] was the way Acton thought of Newman. Only one with Döllinger's habitual benevolence, he felt, could assume that Newman sincerely believed what he said.[6] The fact was, according to Acton, that Newman had no idea of truth or right apart from expediency. His sophistry and opportunism identified him as an Ultramontane in temperament, while his adulation of authority and acquiescence in the principle of the Inquisition marked him as an Ultramontane in policy:

'He defended the Syllabus, and the Syllabus justified all those atrocities. Pius the Fifth held that it was sound Catholic doctrine that any man may stab a heretic condemned by Rome, and

---

[1] Newman to Acton, 18 March 1864, Add. MSS., 4989.
[2] Newman to Bishop Ullathorne, 28 January 1870, Ward, *Newman*, II, 288.
[3] Newman's remarks were paraphrased by Sir Roland Blennerhassett in a letter to Acton (10 April 1871, Add. MSS., 4989).
[4] Charlotte Blennerhassett, *Edinburgh Review*, CXCVII (1903), 527.
[5] Add. MSS., 4908.
[6] Add. MSS., 4915.

that every man is a heretic who attacks the papal prerogatives. Borromeo wrote a letter for the purpose of causing a few Protestants to be murdered. Newman is an avowed admirer of Saint Pius and Saint Charles [Borromeo], and of the pontiffs who canonized them. This, and the like of this, is the reason for my deep aversion for him.[1]

To Döllinger Acton explained that the difference between the persecutor, Charles Borromeo, and the tolerator of persecution, Newman, was 'a difference of times, not of persons'.[2] If Newman quarrelled with the Ultramontanes, it was for personal rather than ideological reasons; if he chafed at authority, it was because that authority happened to interfere with his plans. That he was not an enthusiastic Ultramontane said little in his favour, for, as Acton observed, 'there is no real difference between reluctance and enthusiasm when once the ethical objection is surmounted'.[3] Privately he sometimes professed to be a religious Liberal, but the public, official Newman, the Ultramontane, was the real one.[4] Even his death in 1890, at the venerable age of eighty-nine, did not dispose Acton to greater charity: after ranking Newman with Napoleon, Bismarck and Hegel, Acton told Gladstone that he could not say half of what he really thought of 'that splendid Sophist'.[5]

If Döllinger did not conform to Acton's ideal, it is no wonder that Newman fell outside the pale. Döllinger had the commonplace notion that although there were such things as absolute truth and absolute morality, these were generally beyond the reach of fallible men, bound by their environment, by ignorance and by temptation. Newman had the more subtle theory that truth itself was an ambiguous concept and that intellectual and moral excellence were not identical. Belief and conviction, he held, were too circuitous, too dependent upon emotion, will and character, to be comprehended by logical syllogisms or empirical demonstrations. 'The edge of truth',

[1] 21 March 1882, *Letters to Mary Gladstone*, pp. 242–3.
[2] 28 January 1881, Add. MSS., 4992.
[3] Acton to Gladstone, 9 February [1884], *Correspondence*, p. 262.
[4] Add. MSS., 5646.
[5] 14 August 1890, *Correspondence*, p. 59.

he wrote, 'is so fine that no plain man can see it.'[1] Most of
Acton's contemporaries, like Acton himself, had little patience
with this theory and less faith in Newman's personal honesty.
Thomas Huxley, not so demanding as Acton, wrote after re-
reading Newman: 'After an hour or two of him I began to lose
sight of the distinction between truth and falsehood,' and to
another correspondent: 'That man is the slipperiest sophist I
have ever met with.'[2] Acton, for whom truth was a sturdy axe
to be wielded vigorously about the heads of immoral men, had
no use for the delicate instrument Newman was trying to
fashion.

The one time Acton appeared in print between 1878 and
1885, it was to do battle once again for morality. On this
occasion his contestant was Mandell Creighton, an Anglican
priest (later bishop) and author of the *History of the Papacy
During the Period of the Reformation*, of which Acton reviewed
the first two volumes in the *Academy* of December 1882.
Creighton had suggested that the books be given to Acton for
review, because, as he later explained, 'I wanted to be told my
shortcomings by the one Englishman whom I considered capable of doing so.'[3] The main shortcoming of which Acton
complained was the familiar one, the laxity of moral standards
in the writing of history. Creighton took the criticism with
good grace, and his reply opened up a long and thoughtful correspondence between the two.[4]

Three years later Acton was one of the small group who
helped found the *English Historical Review*, of which Creighton
was made editor. When the next two volumes of Creighton's
History appeared in 1887, he asked Acton to review them, this
time for the *Review*. With more space at his disposal and a more

[1] Newman to F. Rogers, 8 April 1835, *Letters and Correspondence of John
Henry Newman*, ed. Anne Mozley (2 vols.; London, 1891), II, 97.
[2] Huxley to Knowles and to J. Hooker, 14 April and 30 May 1889,
Leonard Huxley, *Life and Letters of Thomas Huxley* (3 vols.; London, 1903),
III, 111–12.
[3] Creighton to Acton, 9 December 1882, Add. MSS., 6871.
[4] Fortunately almost the whole of this correspondence, unlike that with
Döllinger, has been preserved and is available in the Cambridge University Library, Add. MSS., 6871.

serious journal as his vehicle, Acton gave free rein to his critical instincts, and the first draft of his review lacked even the conventional courtesies that generally serve to draw the sting of academic controversy. Creighton was prepared to publish the review, which he privately regarded as an ill-natured, passionate and almost incoherent piece of writing, and in spite of the fact that he was put in the absurd position of an editor inviting and printing an attack upon himself. Acton later volunteered to modify the review, so that when it finally appeared in print its tone was somewhat chastened although its point was by no means dulled.

The worst thing Acton could say about the work was that parts of it might have been taken from Newman. These were the passages in which Creighton was unduly sympathetic to the pre-Reformation Church and impatient with the reformers, and in which he seemed willing to ignore the atrocities of the Inquisition and the scandals of the Popes. (Creighton had casually remarked that Pius II 'stood high in all men's estimation, though he was the father of a large family of children'.)[1] In other respects Acton must have been reminded of Döllinger, for it was Creighton's wish to make his way through the passion of history with an untroubled curiosity and a suspended judgment. Acton felt that this prejudice against the advocate, the judge and the prophet threatened not only to debase the moral standard in history but to eliminate the standard altogether.

Creighton, a more patient audience than Döllinger, received the confidences that Döllinger had repulsed. 'You must understand', Acton told him of his *History*, 'that it is the work of an enemy.'[2] To this Creighton replied that he respected Acton's views even if he could not share them, and that he admired him for keeping faith with an unpopular philosophy of history. Warming to Creighton's sympathy, Acton complained of the isolation to which his philosophy had condemned him: 'I find that people disagree with me either because they hold that Liberalism is not true, or that Catholicism is not true, or that both cannot be true together. If I could discover any one who

[1] *Historical Essays*, p. 435.
[2] 22 March 1887, Add. MSS., 6871.

is not included in these categories, I fancy we should get on very well together.'[1]

Creighton, like Döllinger, must have been amused to find, himself in the role of whipping boy for the papacy and successor to the long line of antagonists—including Ward, Manning, Dupanloup and Newman—with whom Acton had drawn swords. Acton's perennial 'Conflict with Rome' had settled down, in recent years, to a steady, plodding campaign, less dramatic than the battles of the 'sixties and early 'seventies but no less real. As early as 1874 Acton had given notice of a change in battle-front from the 'flowering top' of the contemporary papacy to the 'root and stem' of all immorality. And immorality now appeared to him to be less insidious in the overt Ultramontanes like Ward and Manning than in ostensible Liberals like Döllinger and Creighton, who could resist corruption when it appealed to their intellect and interests, but not when it invoked their sentiments and sympathies. In spite of his excommunication, Döllinger persisted in the effort to understand and forgive the Ultramontanes. And now Creighton, not even a Roman Catholic, was offering up the same puerile excuses to absolve the papacy from its own self-confessed principle that 'killing was no murder'.[2]

The Inquisition, Acton argued against Creighton as he had also argued against Döllinger, was the article by which the medieval papacy must stand or fall. Just as a man is hanged because of a single episode in his life and the fact of his having been a good husband or a fine poet is deemed irrelevant, so the Popes of the thirteenth and fourteenth centuries must be convicted on the one ground of the Inquisition, which they deliberately instituted, protected with every spiritual and temporal sanction, and used to inflict death and damnation on all who resisted them. From this murderous act there was no appeal. Creighton had said that men in authority could not be 'snubbed or sneezed at from our pinnacle of conscious rectitude'.[3] In a memorable passage, Acton disposed of this fallacy that rank can mitigate murder and power create right:

[1] 29 March 1887, ibid.   [2] *Academy*, XXII (1882), 408.
[3] Acton to Creighton, 5 April 1887, Add. MSS., 6871, reprinted in *Freedom and Power*, p. 363.

'I cannot accept your canon that we are to judge Pope and King unlike other men, with a favourable presumption that they did no wrong. If there is any presumption it is the other way against holders of power, increasing as the power increases. Historic responsibility has to make up for the want of legal responsibility. Power tends to corrupt and absolute power corrupts absolutely. Great men are almost always bad men, even when they exercise influence and not authority: still more when you superadd the tendency or the certainty of corruption by authority. There is no worse heresy than that the office sanctifies the holder of it. That is the point at which the negation of Catholicism and the negation of Liberalism meet and keep high festival, and the end learns to justify the means. You would hang a man of no position, like Ravaillac; but if what one hears is true, then Elizabeth asked the gaoler to murder Mary, and William III ordered his Scots minister to extirpate a clan. Here are the greater names coupled with the greater crimes. You would spare these criminals, for some mysterious reason. I would hang them, higher than Haman, for reasons of quite obvious justice; still more, still higher, for the sake of historical science.

'The standard having been lowered in consideration of date, is to be still further lowered out of deference to station. Whilst the heroes of history become examples of morality, the historians who praise them, Froude, Macaulay, Carlyle, become teachers of morality and honest men. Quite frankly, I think there is no greater error. The inflexible integrity of the moral code is, to me, the secret of the authority, the dignity, the utility of history. If we may debase the currency for the sake of genius, or success, or rank, or reputation, we may debase it for the sake of a man's influence, of his religion, of his party, of the good cause which prospers by his credit and suffers by his disgrace. Then history ceases to be a science, an arbiter of controversy, a guide of the wanderer, the upholder of that moral standard which the powers of earth, and religion itself, tend constantly to depress. It serves where it ought to reign; and it serves the worst cause better than the purest.'[1]

Acton was hard put to it to decide whether the greater guilt

---

[1] ibid., pp. 364–5.

attached to the medieval papacy or to its defenders. Sometimes he would damn them equally: 'For many years my view of Catholic controversy has been governed by the following chain of reasoning: 1. A crime does not become a good deed by being committed for the good of a Church. 2. The theorist who approves the act is no better than the culprit who commits it. 3. The divine or historian who defends the theorist incurs the same blame'.[1] Elsewhere he seemed to operate on the principle that culpability went with self-consciousness and that the advocate, therefore, was more guilty than his client: 'To commit murder is the mark of a moment, exceptional. To defend it is constant, and shows a more perverted conscience.'[2] But in either event the source of the evil and its judgment were not in doubt: 'To a Liberal, the papacy was murderous and there's an end on't.'[3]

MORALITY WITHOUT RELIGION

If religion had proved so ineffectual a guardian of morals, if the final word to be said of the papacy, the highest authority in the most dogmatic of religions, was that it was 'murderous', then it was high time to cast about for a non-religious system of ethics. In his lectures on the history of freedom, Acton had credited paganism with anticipating the main principles of what modern civilization generally regards as Christian ethics. This was no novel thesis. Professor Lasaulx had first suggested it to Acton a quarter of a century earlier in Munich, and at one time in the 'sixties Acton had played with the idea of writing on the relation between Christianity and paganism. Döllinger had not then encouraged the idea, and it was only after their quarrel that Acton reverted to the theme.

His main adversary now was Gladstone. Again Acton found himself in the anomalous position of a Catholic urging upon an Anglican the merits of a non-Catholic, even non-Christian system of ethics. In ethical matters, he held, Christianity 'was not progress all along the line'.[4] The example of the Jewish Essenes and of the pagan Stoics stood as a reproach to many

[1] Add. MSS., 5631. [2] Add. MSS., 4939.
[3] Add. MSS., 4996. [4] Add. MSS., 4938.

Christians, and the seventeenth-century Socinians and Quakers, who rejected the sacraments, boasted the soundest system of ethics in Christendom. Rome, on the other hand, had the weakest. Acton once made out a case for an Anglican convinced of the truth of the Catholic dogmas and doctrinally prepared for conversion, but who nevertheless chose to remain in the Church of England. The Anglican might have been persuaded of this course, Acton thought, by some credible line of reasoning such as this: Roman Catholics hold that the Thirty-Nine Articles of the Church of England may be interpreted as consistent with Catholic doctrine, while Anglicans believe that they are not literally binding on the clergy, much less on the laity. To remain in the Anglican communion, therefore, would not involve a layman in dogmatic error. It would involve him in dangers and difficulties, to be sure, but these would be no greater than the dangers and difficulties attending his conversion. Because the authorities of the Catholic Church not only sanction but enforce opinions that are perhaps perilous to the soul, the moral risk entailed in embracing Catholicism was greater than the dogmatic risk in remaining an Anglican. It was easier, Acton concluded, to escape heresy in Anglicanism than to escape the 'ungodly ethics'[1] of the papacy, the Inquisition and Catholic casuistry.

Catholicism was more corrupting than Anglicanism, Anglicanism more than deism, and deism more than secularism— the line of morality, Acton found, was leading straight away from religion:

'A Liberal does not believe that Catholicism, Lutheranism, Calvinism, Aug[ustinism], Arm[inianism] offer a sufficient security against moral error. They all have promoted persecution Therefore he gives higher value to Socinians, Independents, Baptists, and to systems of philosophy which do not persecute. He holds that a sound morality and escape from sin is more easy to find in philosophy than in religion. He checks his theology with philosophy. Therefore he is essentially secular. He grounds himself, not indeed against the lower types of clergy, but against the priesthood of the great Churches.'[2]

[1] 4 March 1882, *Letters to Mary Gladstone*, p. 234.
[2] Add. MSS., 4973.

Religion, which had forfeited its claim to moral superiority, had also lost control over the minds of men. It was a time, as Acton put it, when 'unbelief in the shape of doubt is yielding to unbelief in the shape of certain conviction'.[1] Most thoughtful men were made uneasy by the prospect of a people without faith, and awaited anxiously the moral disintegration that would set in when old hopes, fears, and beliefs grew dim. It is ironic that Acton, a Catholic, should have been somewhat less apprehensive than an unbeliever like Morley. But both Acton and Morley joined in paying homage to one of the great moralists of the age, George Eliot. Upon her work, a generation of fearful men could focus as upon a beacon of inspiration and a portent of salvation.

When Eliot died in December 1880, Acton wrote to Mary Gladstone: 'You cannot think how much I owed her. Of eighteen or twenty writers by whom I was conscious that my mind has been formed, she was one.'[2] Eliot, he felt, had hit straight at the main problem of the age, the reconciliation of the ethics of belief with the state of unbelief. Hers was a gallant attempt to salvage virtue and happiness from the ruins of obsolete dogmas and authorities. Abandoning the old site without regrets, she made the bold experiment of grounding ethics in the uncongenial soil of atheism. She was surrounded by vulgar free-thinkers, crude materialists and 'boisterous iconoclasts';[3] she committed the grave social offence of living with a man to whom she could not be legally married. Yet she contrived, out of the unpromising conditions of her intellectual and social life, to become a great moral teacher, and to make atheism, morally and intellectually, the rival of Christianity. In some ways, her brand of atheism was even superior to the traditional religions, for unlike almost all the Christian communions, 'it had no weak places, no evil champions, no bad purposes to screen or to excuse'.[4]

[1] 16 October, 1887, *Letters to Mary Gladstone* (2d. ed., London, 1913), p. 181.
[2] 27 December 1880, ibid. (1st ed.), p. 155.
[3] 'George Eliot's "Life",' *Nineteenth Century*, XVII (1885), reprinted in *Historical Essays*, p. 294.
[4] Acton to Lady Blennerhassett, 9 July 1885, *Correspondence*, p. 292.

To a generation distracted by 'the intense need of believing and the difficulty of belief',[1] Eliot provided a new sanction for morality. Others before her—Butler, Rousseau, Kant and Fichte—had substituted conscience for authority as 'the great resource of unbelief'.[2] But Eliot was the first to supply conscience with an objective, practical test in the form of the doctrine of earthly retribution. The idea that men's actions breed their reward in this world, that justice and reason prevail in life and not in death, was the keystone of her atheistic ethics. This was her strongest point, but it was also her weakest, Acton felt. By making punishment more fearful and immediate, she converted atheism from esoteric philosophy to a way of life for masses of people. The philosophy itself, however, was neither sound nor safe. It was not sound because it was contradicted by the facts of history and experience—but then the majority of men were no more gifted with historical insight or experience than she. And it was not safe because it tended to emphasize the obvious, external sins by which men are related to men, at the expense of the more private and subtle sins which disturb their relations with God. Her genius, to be sure, might reveal the consequences of even these secret sins of conscience, although Acton had his doubts: 'The inclination of a godless philosophy will be towards palpable effects and those about which there is no mistake. Especially in a doctrine with so little room for grace and forgiveness, where no God ever speaks except by the voice of other men.'[3] Since most men however, were not susceptible to the finer appeals of sensibility contained in religion, society could no more do without the idea of retribution than dispense with the services of the policeman. Eliot might not satisfy an Acton, but Acton hoped she would satisfy the masses.

More than anything else, perhaps, it was Eliot's insights into the minds of men that fascinated Acton. His own forte was the history of ideas, and Eliot had succeeded in translating that history into personal, emotional terms. The 'inner point of view' he was always seeking, the *raison d'être*[4] that made men

[1] *Historical Essays*, p. 303. [2] Add. MSS., 5395.
[3] 25 January 1882, *Letters to Mary Gladstone* (1st ed.), pp. 227–8.
[4] 21 January, 1881, ibid., p. 158.

act and think as they do, the combined workings of religion, philosophy and politics—all these Eliot had grasped with a certainty and profundity that escaped the mere historian. She was a 'consummate expert in the pathology of conscience'.[1] 'George Eliot', he wrote to Mary Gladstone, 'seemed to me capable not only of reading the diverse hearts of men, but of creeping into their skin, watching the world through their eyes, feeling their latent background of conviction, discerning theory and habit, influences of thought and knowledge, of life and of descent, and having obtained this experience, recovering her independence, stripping off the borrowed shell, and exposing scientifically and indifferently the soul of a Vestal, a Crusader, an Anabaptist, an Inquisitor, a Dervish, a Nihilist, or a Cavalier without attraction, preference, or caricature.'[2]

What Acton admired in Eliot, it would seem, was what he execrated in Döllinger and Creighton. First to sympathize and even identify oneself with one's characters and then to report on them objectively and impartially was exactly the method he deplored in the writing of history. And, paradoxically, he chose to be indulgent to the novelist who most closely approximated the historian, whose aim was the reproduction of a real, not fanciful, world, and who sometimes, as in the novel *Romola*, even used authentic historical characters and situations (and Acton particularly praised Eliot for seeing more clearly than any historian the key to Savonarola's character). The paradox, however, was more apparent than real, for behind Eliot's sympathy and objectivity was a structure of moral judgments of which Acton could approve. And so he contrived to have his cake and eat it too, to retain the moral rigour of the historian without depriving himself of the sympathy of the novelist.

This question of judgment, however, was a trivial matter compared with the revolutionary character of the enterprise as a whole, the founding of a non-religious morality. Religion had once been, for Acton, the apex towards which history, liberty and morality converged. It no longer occupied that exalted position. Religious liberty was still a necessary condi-

[1] *Historical Essays*, p. 277.
[2] 21 January 1881, *Letters to Mary Gladstone* (1st ed.), p. 159.

tion of liberty, but it was not the sufficient condition or even the paradigm of all liberties. Nor was morality dependent upon religion; indeed the man who had no moral test of duty apart from religion Acton now termed a fanatic. And while religion still had its subtleties and profundities which no secular philosophy of history could reproduce and which were indispensable to Acton personally, the rest of the world, he thought, seemed to manage fairly well without them. He could only hope that what spiritual impoverishment was suffered would be more than offset by the gain in freedom and morality, for it was unhappily true that, as he had remarked in his youth, 'a certain intolerance [is] inseparable from religion'.[1]

It was in this state of mind that Acton received, in 1888, eight years after the death of Eliot, the report of a new literary sensation exploiting the old theme of religion and morality. Mrs. Humphry Ward's *Robert Elsmere* was one of the best-sellers of the age; its three volumes went through seven editions in five months and soon exceeded the million copy mark. Where Eliot's *Middlemarch* had tried to found ethics upon atheism, the more popular *Robert Elsmere* tried to found it upon theism, a Christianity without dogmas. Gladstone, taking up the cudgels for revealed religion in an article in the *Nineteenth Century* entitled 'Robert Elsmere: the Battle of Belief', succeeded rather in increasing the sales of the offending volume than in demolishing its argument. He denied that the miracles of the Scriptures and Gospels had been disproved by science and philosophy, or that Christian faith and morality could survive without its miracles, rituals, dogmas and authorities. To get ammunition for his attack, he turned as usual to Acton, expecting confirmation of his theories and facts. Instead Acton reproached him for exaggerating the moral superiority of Christianity over paganism, for not taking seriously the Biblical criticism of Strauss and Renan, and for ignoring the fact that it took deists and unbelievers to sweep away 'that appalling edifice of intolerance, tyranny, cruelty' by which Christians had hoped to perpetuate their belief.[2]

Acton had little interest in this particular 'Battle of Belief' and refused to be drawn into it. He felt that *Robert Elsmere*

[1] Add. MSS., 5527.   [1] 2 May 1888, *Correspondence*, p. 217.

made no significant contribution to the problem of religion and morality, and that Gladstone's polemic was as little to the point as the book itself. Gladstone and Mrs. Ward seemed to share the opinion that Christianity stood or fell with the truth or falsity of miracles. They thought only to quarrel about the metaphysics of Christianity and not about the more important question of its practical ethics. Acton could get enthusiastic about Eliot because hers was a severe conception of morality grounded in a bold and serious metaphysics. He could not be provoked by the vapid sentimentalities of Mrs. Ward.

Every shade of opinion from belief to unbelief, religion to secularism, had its adherents in late Victorian England, and the consensus everyone clamoured for was no nearer. Even individuals found it difficult to abide by opinions they had once heatedly defended. Comte had traced a new path in the circuit of unbelief and belief by creating a positivist religion, appropriately dubbed 'Catholicism without Christianity'. When Mill felt his utilitarianism becoming flat and insipid, he tried to spice it with a dash of Comtism, but wiser counsels prevailed and at the end he called only for a 'religion of Humanity'. Morley, Mill's disciple and the sanest advocate of secularism and naturalism, announced in 1888, the year made memorable by *Robert Elsmere*, that the worship of humanity could never be expected to satisfy men's deepest needs and that only a genuine spiritual belief would suffice. That same year Matthew Arnold died and with him went the faith in a religion that would be 'morality touched with emotion', a Christianity without dogma that would somehow make its peace with official Anglicanism. Shortly afterwards, Thomas Huxley, having coined the word 'agnosticism', went on to shatter the illusions of his disciples when he espoused, in distinction to Comte, a kind of 'Calvinism without Christianity' that would pay homage to the religious insights of original sin, predestination, and the eternal conflict between morality and nature.

In this universal attempt to reconcile opposites, Acton's flirtation with scepticism, in the shape of George Eliot, was only another evidence of the confusion of the times and the dissatisfaction of all honest thinkers with the conventional answers. What distinguished Acton from the others was the fact that, compared with them, he was travelling backwards. Their progress was from unbelief to belief; Acton, having started in the citadel of belief, Roman Catholicism, journeyed in the opposite direction. And just as they dropped some of their optimistic illusions about science and progress along the way, so he unburdened himself of the scandals of Christianity.

The scepticism of Eliot was a haven for a conscience tortured by memories of persecution, intolerance and immorality. But the place of refuge was itself built upon a sham foundation. Like the boldest of the nineteenth-century atheists, Eliot was living on the ethical capital of Christianity, as a later generation learned to think of it. Her atheism was viable because it was steeped in an austere Calvinism. In the strictest sense, she was not even an atheist: later in life she went so far as to disavow the philosophies of Renan and Strauss, a fact that Acton seems not to have known. The experiment of removing all the props of Christianity had not, then, succeeded, for some of the pinnings remained to give a precarious support to the structure of morality. But some important ones had gone, including that which Catholics generally thought of as indispensable, the idea of authority. This was a loss Acton did not regret. All the sins of the Church, he believed, had originated with the representatives of authority and had been defended by the principle of authority. Whatever personal compromises he might make with the idea and its agents, he would not recommend them for others, least of all for society as a whole.

VII

POLITICS AND POLITICIANS

THE POLITICS OF LIBERALISM

O NE of Acton's contemporaries, Sir Henry Maine,
coined the term 'Irreconcilables' to describe those who
held political opinions with the same intensity of belief,
immunity from doubt, and expectation of salvation that once
characterized the disciples of a religious faith. In many ways,
Acton was the prototype of the 'Irreconcilable'. Certainly this
was his own image of himself. To Mary Gladstone he once
wrote: 'Have you not discovered, have I never betrayed, what
a narrow doctrinaire I am, under a thin disguise of levity? . . .
Politics come nearer religion with me, a party is more like a
church, error more like heresy, prejudice more like sin, than I
find it to be with better men'.[1] There is a mock humility in the
last remark. It is not true that Acton found better men to think
otherwise. On the contrary, he broke with the heroes of his
youth because they did not think as he did—with Döllinger
who refused to take politics as seriously as religion, and with
Burke who treated politics naturalistically, empirically, as if
men did not 'lose their souls by political, as they do by
domestic, error.'[2]

Upon politicians and their parties Acton trained the same
critical eye that he habitually turned upon the actors and events

[1] 18 December 1884, *Letters to Mary Gladstone* (1st ed.), p. 314.
[2] 16 October 1887, ibid. (2d ed.), p. 180. For a more complete discussion
of the change in Acton's attitude to Burke, see my article, 'The American
Revolution in the Political Theory of Lord Acton', *Journal of Modern
History*, XXI (1949).

of history. He once told Bryce that, except for liberty, there was no subject he wanted to treat extensively as much as that of party.[1] At a time when some of his more frivolous contemporaries were satirizing the party system as one in which 'half the cleverest men in the country [were] taking the utmost pains to prevent the other half from governing',[2] Acton preached the sober doctrine that party was an instrument of salvation or damnation. He protested against the popular view of the party struggle as an amiable contest between two friendly teams, conducted in an atmosphere of 'understanding, compromise, mutual toleration'.[3] If the 'laws of the game'[4] were sacred, he pointed out, nothing else was sacred, and the tacit agreement that neither party would completely prevail was the warrant of death for political principles.

The conflict of parties was no aimless game, but neither was it, for Acton, a battle of social classes and interests. The great vice of the Conservative Party was its identification with a special economic interest; the virtue—and the meaning—of Liberalism lay in its disinterested pursuit of principles, its superiority to sectarian motives. Therefore Acton judged that 'the best [i.e. the most complete] Conservative is an American Republican, the best Liberal is a divine'.[5] A Liberal Party might sometimes derive momentum from an interest, but it always received its original motion from an idea, and only as long as it continued to be moved by that idea was the party justified. The moral climax in the life of almost every great statesman came when his party, having lost its ideological inspiration, had to be abandoned.

By far the greatest man thrown up by contemporary politics, in Acton's opinion, was Gladstone. The early distrust of Gladstone had given way to admiration and intimate friendship, in spite of the fact that Acton occasionally still felt the need, as he once confessed, to 'admonish his [Gladstone's]

[1] James Bryce, 'The Letters of Lord Acton', *North American Review*, CLXXVIII (1904), 703.
[2] Henry Sumner Maine, *Popular Government* (London, 1918), p. 99.
[3] Add. MSS., 5689.
[4] *Lectures on the French Revolution*, ed. J. N. Figgis and R. V. Laurence (London, 1910), p. 27.
[5] Add. MSS., 4952.

LORD ACTON

conscience'.[1] And although he admitted that Gladstone had
the irritating habit of reversing his position without relaxing
for a moment his invariable attitude of moral righteousness,[2]
he nevertheless venerated him for being one of the few men
who knew that politics was philosophy in action, and who
appreciated the 'religious sanctity of the Liberal cause'.[3]

There were other endearing traits in Gladstone: his religious
seriousness and intellectual drive, for example. But more than
these—for Gladstone's religion was Anglican and his intellectual interests, however prodigious for a busy statesman,
were those of a dilettante compared with Acton's—Acton was
gratified by the political tendency represented by the Prime
Minister in his later years. He saw Gladstone as maintaining
the balance, in programme and in his own person, between the
old Liberals, descendants of the Whigs, and the new Radicals,
precursors of the Socialists. He saw in him the only public
figure capable of reconciling democracy with liberty.

For all of his fears about democracy, Acton was no prophet
of doom. Unlike many of his contemporaries—among the
historians, Sybel and Lecky were typical—he did not believe
that universal manhood suffrage heralded the end of parliamentary government and the inauguration of a democratic
tyranny. On the contrary, disliking the idea of a State catering
to the interests of a single class and cherishing the vision of a
disinterested government meting out justice impartially, he
welcomed the Reform Acts of 1867 and 1884. He did not fear
the venality, ignorance, drunkenness and violence of the lower
classes that so exercised the imagination of his contemporaries.[4] Nor did he believe that the upper classes had a monopoly
of political wisdom and virtue, or even sufficient wisdom and
virtue to rule justly over the lower. 'It is easier to find people
fit to govern themselves than people fit to govern others,' he

[1] Woodward, p. 256.
[2] Stephen Gwynn and Gertrude M. Tuckwell, *Life of the Right Hon. Sir
Charles W. Dilke* (2 vols.; New York, 1917), II, 62.
[3] Arthur D. Elliot, *Life of George Joachim Goschen, 1st Viscount Goschen*
(2 vols.; London, 1911), I, 205.
[4] See a speech by Robert Lowe delivered in the House of Commons on
13 March 1866 (Hansard [3rd series], CLXXXII, 147-8).

observed.[1] 'Every man [is] the best, the most responsible, judge of his own advantage.'[2]

The Reform Acts were not only an obvious measure of justice; they were also an indispensable ingredient of liberty. Acton was always quick to insist that democracy, carried to its logical extreme, is a threat to liberty, for where liberty tends to the division of power, democracy tends to its unity, and where liberty undertakes to protect minorities, democracy comes to enforce the will of the majority. But it was one thing to say that the minority must be protected in its rights and liberties against the majority, another to think that the majority has no rights or liberties against the minority. And to a certain extent, liberty and right mean power, power for the minority to ward off the encroachments of democracy, and power for the majority to satisfy its own needs. Moreover, liberty has both a positive and a negative dimension: it is a 'mode of action'[3] as well as a means of restraint. The positive dimension, participation in power, is what is meant by democracy. In this sense it is 'liberty given to the mass'.[4] Thus, 'where there is no powerful democracy freedom does not reign'.[5]

One of Acton's letters to Mary Gladstone deserves to be included among the great documents of democratic philosophy —of philosophy, not of rhetoric, for its passion derives not from the exuberance of a bountiful optimism but from a sober commitment to a political faith that carries forebodings of disaster as well as the promise of salvation.

Democracy, Acton wrote, has perils that a true Liberal keeps always in mind. With masses of new electors ignorant of affairs of State and inclined to prejudice, the stability of public policy, the security of public credit and of private property, were in genuine danger. But the Liberal also knows that one cannot make an omelette without breaking eggs, 'that politics are not made of artifice only, but of truths, and that truths have to be told'. The most important of these truths stems from the discipline of political economy. Of the two proposi-

---

[1] Add. MSS., 4941.
[2] Add. MSS., 4939.
[3] Add. MSS., 4908.
[4] Add. MSS., 4945.
[5] ibid.

tions established by Adam Smith—that contracts ought to be free between capital and labour, and that labour is the source of wealth—the Liberals had adopted the first and the Socialists the second. Socialists reasoned that if labour is the source of national wealth, it should also be the source of national power. Liberals learned another lesson, that if labour and capital were to meet freely in the open market, it could not be right for one of the contracting parties to have exclusive control over the making of laws, the keeping of peace, the administration of justice, the levying of taxes and the expenditure of income. That all these securities should be on one side, and on the side that had least need of them, was monstrous. 'Before this argument, the ancient dogma, that power attends on property, broke down. Justice required that property should—not abdicate, but—share its political supremacy. Without this partition, free contract was as illusory as a fair duel in which one man supplies seconds, arms and ammunition.'

To the Conservative retort that the lower classes have not the ability or knowledge to participate in public affairs, Acton countered with the observation that the most prosperous nations in the world, France and America, were democracies. Wealth, education, even intelligence, appeared to prevent certain faults of conduct but not errors of policy. 'The danger', Acton insisted, 'is not that a particular class is unfit to govern. Every class is unfit to govern.' When the rich and propertied ruled alone, they ruled selfishly and inhumanly. Not until their monopoly was broken did social legislation come into being. Liberals, who valued that legislation, would seek to foster in the lower classes the sense of their responsibility by reminding them of the enemy behind them and the goals before them. It was also part of the Liberal strategy to see to it that 'political antagonism should not degenerate into social envy', and this distinguished Liberalism from Radicalism and Chartism. But it was possible to go too far in repudiating Radicalism. This Gladstone had done, early in his career, when he denied the principle of progressive taxation, pampered the landed aristocracy, and granted to the Irish landlords 'an absolution ampler than they deserve'. Only recently had the Prime Minister come to realize that it might be right to legislate 'not quite impartially for the whole nation, but for a class so numerous as to be virtually equal to the whole'.[1]

The letter to Mary Gladstone put the issue clearly. Democracy, in the sense of the participation of the people in government, was both a moral right and an assertion of liberty. When the franchise was extended to the working class in 1884, Acton rejoiced in this 'advent to power of principles, the commencement of disinterested policy'.[2]

Yet principles too had their limits. Confronted with the prospect of women's suffrage, Acton went the way of many other Victorian gentlemen who hastily abandoned their most precious beliefs—that the weak should be protected against the strong, principles transcend expediency, and the interests of humanity prevail over the interests of party. In 1891 he assured Gladstone 'that there is no higher law deciding the question and that it falls within the computations of expediency', in which case, since the votes of women would be largely Tory, he did not feel bound to sacrifice 'the great interest of party'. 'If it can be shown', he cautiously added, 'that the majority of women will probably be Liberal, or that they will divide equally, I should say that the balance is, very slightly, in favour of giving them votes.'[3] He denied that his motives were, as he put it, sordid, and explained that a few years earlier he would have agreed that the balance of power should be redressed in favour of the 'perpetual victim of man', but that he had since discovered that the position of women might be ameliorated without political emancipation. On this subject, Acton's memory, like his principles, must have failed him, for as early as 1884 he had argued, in identical fashion, that women, subject to Tory and clerical influence, could not be trusted with the vote.[4] Women's suffrage, in spite of the earnest efforts of Mill and others, was still a political curiosity in Victorian England, so that Acton's repudiation of his own principles is more a quaint weakness than a serious apostasy.

The question of social reform, even more than political re-

[1] 24 April, 1881, *Letters to Mary Gladstone* (1st ed.), pp. 193–4.
[2] Add. MSS., 4869.
[3] 26 April, 1891, *Correspondence*, p. 235.
[4] 30 March, 1884, *Letters to Mary Gladstone* (1st ed.), pp. 293–4.

form (if women's suffrage be excepted), shows Acton at his most radical. Political reform, it was generally conceded, was consonant with the English political tradition; social reform, however, introduced a new and incalculable factor into public life of which both Liberals and Conservatives were wary. Yet Acton was, if anything, more enthusiastic about social and economic changes than about political ones. Towards those economists for whom the laws of Smith, Ricardo and Malthus were the Bible of modern man, he felt something of the same repulsion once expressed by Ruskin, that it was horrifying how ready men were to declare 'that the laws of the Devil were the only practicable ones, and that the laws of God were merely a form of poetical language'.[1]

Acton had not always been so easily shocked. In the *Rambler* and *Home and Foreign Review*, he had been fond of quoting the precepts, 'The poor we have always with us', and 'If any man will not work, neither let him eat'.[2] He had then been not so much worried about the conditions of the poor as about the possibly deleterious effect of poor relief upon the rest of society. He had feared that excessive philanthropy, and certainly a compulsory poor law, would encourage pauperism: 'Indiscriminate almsgiving is as contrary to Christ's teaching as to political science.'[3] During a London building trades strike, the current events columns of the *Rambler* (most of which were composed by Acton) had vindicated the employers on every ground, had condemned the benefit societies as coercive and illegal, and had insisted that the issue between labour and capital be decided by the normal operation of supply and demand.[4]

In his later years, Acton decried such views as the shameful expression of Tory immorality. He warned that to accept the principle of *laissez-faire* economics as the supreme arbiter of

[1] John Ruskin, *Modern Painters* (Sterling ed.; Boston, n. d.), p. 432.
[2] 'Cavour', *Historical Essays*, p. 177.
[3] Acton to Simpson, 17 December 1861, Gasquet, p. 246. A passage in this letter, of which this sentence is part, is almost identical with a 'Current Events' article, not previously attributed to Acton, in the *Rambler*, VI (1862), 417.
[4] *Rambler*, II (1859), 116–18.

politics was to open the way for such monstrosities as the defence of slavery wherever it happened to be economically
sound.[1] *Laissez-faire*, he noted, had been valuable in an earlier
age in promoting the concept of a disinterested, Liberal State
that had no design upon society, but once this concept became
prevalent, thoughtful men set about to correct its exaggera-
tions.[2] *Laissez-faire* economics had created a social order
that did not benefit the masses of the people: wealth had in-
creased without relieving their wants, and the progress of
knowledge had left them in ignorance. The laws of society,
made by the upper classes, proclaimed that the poor should
not have been born at all, and if born should better have died
in childhood; failing both, they were destined for a life of
misery, crime and pain. Civil liberty itself was jeopardized, for
among the obstacles to liberty were 'not only oppression,
political and social, but poverty, ignorance'.[3] 'Seeing how
little was done by the wisdom of former times for education
and public health, for insurance, association, and savings, for
the protection of labour against the law of self-interest, and
how much has been accomplished in this generation, there is
reason in the fixed belief that a great change was needed, and
that democracy has not striven in vain.'[4]

When Gladstone's retirement was once rumoured, Acton
contemplated the future with misgivings. No one else, he said,
could be expected to appreciate both the virtues and the vices
of democracy, to give due respect to existing institutions and
traditions and yet realize that the men who pay wages were not
the political masters of those who earned them, and that laws
should be made to accommodate those with the heaviest stake
in the country. And the heaviest stake was not riches but
poverty; it was the burden of those 'for whom misgovernment
means not mortified pride or stinted luxury, but want and
pain, and degradation and risk to their own lives and to their
children's souls'.[5] The economists were blind to these moral
d spiritual considerations. They regarded man as a utility

[1] Add. MSS., 4953.   [2] Add. MSS., 5486.
[3] Add. MSS., 4941.
[4] 'May's Democracy in Europe', *History of Freedom*, pp. 94–5.
[5] 14 December, 1880, *Letters to Mary Gladstone* (1st ed.), p. 147.

and commodity, a means of production to be bought and sold. Only the Liberal of Gladstone's variety could be trusted to treat man as an end in himself. The Liberal, unlike the economist, took progress to mean not the discarding of inefficient units of production, but the preserving and protracting, at infinite cost, of the life of the cripple, the idiot and the madman, the pauper and the culprit, the old and the infirm, the curable and the incurable.[1] His was a philosophy of the 'survival of the unfit',[2] in which the social doctrine of 'liberality towards the weak'[3] corresponded to the political doctrine of respect for the minority.

What Acton lacked and what both the Manchester Liberals and the traditional Conservatives had in great abundance was the ability to worship property, either in the form of money or of land. He reproached Döllinger for believing, with Locke and Burke, that representation must always depend upon property; this, Acton said, was to ignore the very essence of Liberalism, 'that man owns something besides property'.[4] Property was a negative rather than a positive claim to virtue. It could relieve want and so promote spiritual ease, but it did not itself ensure spiritual superiority:

'Property is not the sacred right. When a rich man becomes poor it is a misfortune, it is not a moral evil. When a poor man becomes destitute, it is a moral evil, teeming with consequences injurious to society and morality. Therefore, in last resort, the poor have a claim on the wealth of the rich, so far that they may be relieved from the immoral, demoralizing effects of poverty.'[5]

Society had a definite moral claim upon property; property only had a claim upon society when it was in the interest of liberty to sponsor that claim. In general, to be sure, liberty was well disposed to property. During the long periods when

---

[1] Add. MSS., 4993 and 5399, and *Lectures on Modern History*, ed. J. N. Figgis and R. V. Laurence (London, 1906), p. 33.
[2] Add. MSS., 5399.
[3] *Lectures on Modern History*, p. 33.
[4] Add. MSS., 4912.   [5] Add. MSS., 4869.

conscience was in abeyance, property had been the only effective check upon a power-hungry State. When the House of Commons threatened to become the omnipotent organ of an omnipotent State, the House of Lords, in effect the agent of landed property, had been a valuable counterbalance, and for this reason Acton deplored the movement for its abolition. But he was also insistent upon the need for drastic reform. The virtue of the upper house, its determination to protect its own interest against the pressure of a hostile democracy, was also its vice. Because it represented only the one interest of land, and because as a corporation having neither 'body to kick nor soul to save'[1] it was not accessible to ideals that might have influenced its individual members, it was moved by the grossest of motives. It felt a duty only to its eldest sons and none to the people as a whole, and it resisted all measures intended for the good of the poor. Whether from prejudice, fear and miscalculation, or from a too alert instinct of self-preservation, it had in recent times almost always managed to be in the wrong. For the most part, because it could be overruled by the lower house, it was capable of inflicting only temporary injury upon society, and this was its plea for existence. But the injury might prove to be irreparable. In 1881, thirty years before the event, Acton argued that the reform of the House of Lords would be an act of great political wisdom: 'If we have manifest suffering, degradation, and death on one side, and the risk of a remodelled senate on the other, the certain evil outweighs the contingent danger. For the evil that we apprehend cannot be greater than the evil we know.'[2]

The chasm that separated the young Acton from the mature Acton can be measured by his changing opinion of primogeniture. In 1867 he had rebuked Goldwin Smith for deprecating the importance of primogeniture: liberty, he had then argued, depended upon inequality, inequality implied an aristocracy, aristocracy required property, and property could only be protected by primogeniture.[3] By 1881, liberty, instead of leading inexorably to primogeniture, led just as inexorably away

[1] 7 May 1881, *Letters to Mary Gladstone* (1st ed.), p. 206. [2] ibid., p. 207.
[3] 'Mr. Goldwin Smith on the Political History of England', *Chronicle*, I (1867), 543.

from it. Not the democrat Goldwin Smith but the Conservative Sir Henry Maine was now Acton's adversary. Maine had described primogeniture as of great political service, and Acton retorted that while this may once have been true, modern primogeniture only served to confuse authority with property and so prepared the way for the theory of legitimacy, the great resource of Toryism. Maine innocently commented upon Acton's use of 'Tory' as a term of reproach, to which Acton replied: 'I was much struck by this answer—much struck to find a philosopher, entirely outside party politics, who does not think Toryism a reproach, and still more, to find a friend of mine ignorant of my sentiments about it.'[1]

It is startling to find that Toryism was more consistently a term of reproach in the vocabulary of Acton, at least in his later years, than Socialism. Socialism generally took its place among the enemies of liberty together with such varied evils as Toryism, positivism, racism, nationalism, imperialism, legitimacy, determinism, *laissez-faire*, and the survival of the fittest. But occasionally Acton relented, even going as far as to suggest that a loose usage of the word might find him in that category. The sense in which the French economist, Emile de Laveleye, was a Socialist, was congenial to him, for Laveleye differed from the orthodox economists in being more anxious about the condition of society and the suffering of the poor than about party, power or wealth. Laveleye was an academic Socialist, a '*Kathedersozialist*', Acton explained, adding that the most illustrious English representative of the school was Gladstone.[2]

That Acton should have regarded Gladstone as something of a Socialist says more about Acton's state of mind than about Gladstone's. What Acton was particularly pleased with was Gladstone's sponsorship of the Irish Land Act in 1881. The principles of a fair rent, fixed tenure, and right of free sale hardly seem, to-day, to warrant the label of Socialist, but at the time they were branded as revolutionary. Acton, however, set

[1] 17 January 1882, *Letters to Mary Gladstone* (1st ed.), pp. 225–6.
[2] 19 February 1881, ibid., p. 176; 9 February 1884, ibid., pp. 287–8. See also 11 November 1885, ibid., p. 328.

his sights far beyond the 'three F's' of the Land Act. Without yielding the conviction that a thoroughgoing, practical Socialism would subvert liberty because it could be realized only by a thoroughgoing despotism, he gave it credit for being morally and intellectually superior to *laissez-faire* economics. The Socialists solved the problem of wealth and distribution, which orthodox economists had disastrously fumbled, and they made the important discovery 'that what the speechless masses of the poor need is not political privileges which they cannot enjoy, but comfort, without which political influence is a mockery or a snare'.[1] By these achievements, Socialism revealed the contemptibility of conventional politics.

It is not true, as has sometimes been suggested, that Acton was oblivious of the existence of one of his greatest contemporaries, Karl Marx. Certainly he was not so impressed by him as a later generation might consider proper, but in this he was only reflecting the general indifference of his age and country. The *Rambler* was not alone in ignoring Marx's *Zur Kritik der politischen Ökonomie* in 1859, or the *Chronicle* in failing to review the first volume of *Das Kapital* in 1867—although both journals, pretending to a special interest in Continental literature, had less excuse than the more provincial English periodicals. Although Marx lived and worked in England from 1849 until his death in 1883, his name was familiar to few Englishmen. Even the editors of the Radical *Fortnightly*, after being introduced to Marx by a friend, rejected an article contributed by him in 1871, four years after the publication of *Das Kapital*.

In 1873, occasional references to Marx's works and excerpts from them began to appear in Acton's notes. His library contained underscored copies of both *Das Kapital* and *Zur Kritik*. *Das Kapital*, 'the Koran of the new Socialists', he recommended to Gladstone as a 'remarkable book', but he was otherwise noncommittal.[2] Like many of his contemporaries, he tended to assign to Engels much of the credit that to-day is given to Marx. Under the caption, 'That the Materialistic Socialists will improve H. [History] for the poor,' he noted:

[1] Add. MSS., 5487.
[2] 17 November 1873, *Correspondence*, p. 169.

'Their best writer, Engels, made known the errors and the horrors of our Factory System'.[1] It was Engels whom he regarded as the only one of the German Socialists capable of creating a new philosophy of history, and whom he praised as knowing the history of economic science better than any living man except Wilhelm Roscher, father of the historical school of political economy.[2]

These occasional testimonials to Marx and Engels, casually thrown up in the course of Acton's voluminous reading and notetaking, point up his essential indifference more effectively than if he had completely ignored them. It is more significant that neither Marx nor Engels appears among the many 'to be read' memoranda and 'great books' lists among his notes than that Acton, who prided himself on reading everything, should have read a few of their works. Acton touched Marx only tangentially, at the point where both met with the 'academic' and utopian Socialists—the point of moral protest. It took imagination and moral insight for Acton to see through the class character of so many of the institutions in his own society; it would have been folly for him to embrace a philosophy that aspired to do nothing but substitute one class for another. To one who was repelled by the materialist bias of Adam Smith, Marx could not have been a congenial thinker. What Acton sought was not a Socialist saviour who would lead the way to a dictatorship of the proletariat, but a slightly modified version of the Liberal Prime Minister, who would show a little more daring than Gladstone in matters of social reform, a little more generosity and sympathy in his feelings for the lower classes, a more lofty, spiritual approach to political economy.

On contemporary issues, Acton's thinking was all of a piece. He was a Liberal whose vision of man was not blurred by the conventional categories of class, race and nation. It was only the individual man, created in the image of God and partaking of His sanctity, who possessed moral and political rights. Classes, races and nations had no rights. At best they were

[1] Add. MSS., 4981.
[2] Add. MSS., 4929 and 5487.

fortuitous groupings of individuals whose ideas and interests happened, for the time, to coincide. At worst they were monsters of human invention that had run amok.

It was sometimes convenient, Acton admitted, to think of men as belonging to different races. But the cultivation of racism as a philosophy and a programme was a more serious threat to liberty than any that had yet been conceived. Gobineau's doctrine of race, he noted, was 'one of many schemes to deny free will, responsibility, and guilt, and to supplant moral by physical forces'.[1] In the category of race, the free, moral personality lost its identity and, in consequence, its liberty.

Nationality was a fiction of the same order as race. One could assume the existence of something that might be called a 'national character'—'nobody doubts it who knows schools or armies'[2]—but it should not be taken as a determining factor in history or politics. Nationality may have been decisive in an early, primitive and material stage of society, but its importance has been progressively diminished by the action of culture. 'The process of civilization depends on transcending Nationality. . . . Influences which are accidental yield to those which are rational.'[3] Liberty, the rational end and fulfilment of man, owed little or nothing to nationality. 'The nations aim at power, and the world at freedom,'[4] Acton noted.

Modern nationality was associated with its twin evil, the modern State created by Machiavelli—'a vast abstraction above all other things', to which all men were subject and for which they were all expendable.[5] Prussia was the modern nation-State at its worst, pursuing the criminal object of power and using the criminal methods of oppression and war. Perhaps because of a normal Catholic prejudice against Prussia, Acton saw sooner than most men the insidiousness of Bismarck's strategy. He saw the connection between Prussian expansion abroad and unification at home, between the Kulturkampf and the suppression of the Social-Democratic Party, between pro-

[1] Add. MSS., 4940.   [2] Add. MSS., 4939.
[3] Add. MSS., 4908.   [4] Add. MSS., 4981.
[5] Add. MSS., 4982.

tectionism and imperialism. However impatient he was with French ineptitude during the Franco-Prussian War, he was careful not to go the way of so many Englishmen, the historian Lecky among them, who hoped for a German victory as retribution against an insolent and vainglorious France. His successor at Cambridge, J. B. Bury, wrote of him: 'Men during the World War used to recall the prescience of Acton when he declared that the bayonets of Berlin constituted the most serious menace to our Empire.'[1]

With most men a prescience of German aggression would have given rise to a demand for a more vigorous military and imperial policy. But Acton was not a practitioner of *Realpolitik*, for whom evil can only be fought with evil. If counter-aggression was the only way of resisting aggression, he preferred to retire from the struggle. He had not always been so pacific. One of his early journals had contained blatantly Nietzschean sentiments on the life-giving virtues of war,[2] and in the *Rambler* he had urged England to expand its imperialist programme in India so as to incorporate society, religion, culture and manners as well as politics and administration.[3] His militancy, however, vanished with his youth, and the 'eighties and 'nineties found him an exponent of the 'Little Englandism' he had once so bitterly condemned. In the fashionable theory of the 'white man's burden' he saw nothing but a confession of immorality and an invitation to tyranny. Nor did he hesitate to inculpate England together with Germany in the civilization-destroying mania of imperialism. 'In judging our national merits', he wrote, 'we must allow much for our national hypocrisy. . . . We were the best colonists in the world, but we exterminated the natives wherever we went. We despised conquest, but annexed with the greed of Russia.'[4] He rejoiced at Gladstone's concessions to the Boers and at his evacuation of Egypt, and was distressed by the rumour of a war with

[1] J. B. Bury, *History of the Papacy in the Nineteenth Century* (London, 1930), p. xxiv.
[2] Add. MSS., 5528.
[3] Review of Vol. I of Edwin Arnold's *The Marquis of Dalhousie's Administration of British India*, in *Rambler*, VI (1862), 535.
[4] Add. MSS., 4954.

Afghanistan; to his 'cheap and pacific mind', he wrote, the war would be a disaster which no military victory could mitigate, for the conflict itself would be degrading and brutalizing.[1] That a man of Acton's persuasion should have succeeded the ardent imperialist, Sir John Seeley, was one of the ironies attending his appointment to the Regius Professorship. It was also the subject of some criticism, so that the London *Times*, in an otherwise laudatory obituary notice of Acton, felt obliged to remark that perhaps one of his imperfections was a 'want of national fibre'.[2]

If Acton's compassion was aroused by injustice in India and Africa, it was even more aroused by the case of Ireland, where political oppression was aggravated by religious and economic abuse. It was not as an admirer of Ireland or even as a Catholic that he was so enthusiastic about Gladstone's Home Rule Bills, for he had no great faith in the political wisdom of the Irish. If they did win their independence, he expected, they would proceed against the English and Protestants within their borders with much the same rancour and bigotry that Protestant England had displayed against them, and he warned that any measure for independence should include a guarantee of the rights of Ulster. 'Especially in a country where religion does not work, ultimately, in favour of morality',[3] where 'the assassin is only a little more resolutely logical or a little bolder than the priest',[4] he could not be sanguine about the eventual success of Home Rule. But these reflections, he said, did not detract from Ireland's claim for independence: 'It is with a mind prepared for failure and even disaster that I persist in urging the measure'.[5] The whole of the political baggage with which he set out on the Irish expedition, as he put it, was the conviction that the ends of liberty were the true ends of politics.

[1] 22 April 1885, *Letters to Mary Gladstone* (1st ed.), p. 323.
[2] London *Times*, 20 June 1902.
[3] Undated, *Letters to Mary Gladstone* (1st ed.), p. 74.
[4] 21 March 1883, ibid., p. 276.
[5] Undated, ibid., p. 74.

THE POLITICIAN MANQUÉ

Acton was that familiar and often comic figure in recent times, the politician *manqué*. Like so many other historians and philosophers, he liked to think that an understanding of the course of history and an articulate system of philosophical values would equip a man for a career as lawmaker or administrator. Some of his most illustrious contemporaries shared the same illusion: Alexis de Tocqueville hoped that a manipulator of words and ideas might also be an effective manipulator of men, and Adolphe Thiers is reported to have said that he would willingly have sacrificed the writing of ten good histories for one successful session in Parliament. As political aspirant, if not as political philosopher, Acton was in good company.

Acton was well situated to exercise the political influence he sought. His stepfather, Lord Granville, had worked his way up the political ladder to the Foreign Secretaryship; it was by his doing that Acton was thrust into a parliamentary career (for which, however, he proved to have little taste and less talent). Gladstone himself, the Grand Old Man of English politics, was said to influence all around him but Acton: 'It is Acton', Matthew Arnold observed, 'who influences Gladstone'.[1] Because of his intimate association with both Gladstone and Granville and his numerous connections with the aristocracy and statesmen of the Continent (he was related to Marco Minghetti, twice Premier of Italy),[2] Acton was often credited with being the power behind the scenes of many political decisions. Dupanloup was among those who, at one time or another, supplicated him to use his influence with the government, in this case to secure the mediation of England in the Franco-Prussian War.[3]

After his elevation to the peerage in 1869, Acton began to be thought of as a candidate for high diplomatic positions. In April 1871, Odo Russell, against whom he had pitted his

[1] Charlotte Blennerhassett, *Edinburgh Review*, CXCVII (1903), 528.
[2] There is supposedly in existence a lengthy correspondence between Acton and Minghetti which has never been published.
[3] Woodward, p. 250.

strength in Rome the previous year, wrote to Granville about several diplomatic vacancies, and described it as his 'diplomatic dream' to see Lord Acton as Ambassador at Berlin, a task 'for which he is more admirably qualified than any man living'.[1] The appointment, however, went to Russell himself. Two years later, Acton's name was again mentioned for the Berlin post. Franco-German relations had come to a critical juncture, and Acton's advice to Granville is said to have been instrumental in sparing Europe another serious Continental war. Once again the coveted ambassadorship seemed to be his. It is unlikely that Acton declined the offer, as Lady Blennerhassett seemed to think.[2] More probably the offer was never made, perhaps, it has been suggested, because his Catholicism would have been embarrassing to both governments at a time when the Kulturkampf was at its height.[3] In spite of this failure, however, his diplomatic reputation continued to grow. As a friend of the Crown Prince of Prussia, later Frederick William III, and of his wife, formerly the Princess Royal of Great Britain, he was in a strategic position to influence German policy. At one time Queen Victoria turned to him with the request that he urge the German Emperor to check Bismarck's aggressiveness.

When Gladstone assumed office for the third time, in 1880, the perennial question of the ambassadorship was again raised. Before the campaign, Gladstone had intimated that Acton would share in a Liberal victory. Two months after that victory, having waited in vain for word from Gladstone, Acton wrote him and delicately put in his bid for the Berlin Embassy. But the embassy continued to be occupied by Russell, now Lord Ampthill. With Russell's death in 1884, the possibility of an appointment for Acton was again broached. Of two ambassadorial vacancies, in Berlin and in Constantinople, Acton was considered a likely candidate for the Berlin post. The

[1] Paul Knaplund, *Letters from the Berlin Embassy, 1871–4, 1880–5* ('Annual Report of the American Historical Association', II [Washington, 1942]), 47.
[2] Charlotte Blennerhassett, *Biographisches Jahrbuch*, VII (1902), 20.
[3] W. L. Blennerhassett, 'Acton: 1834–1902', *Dublin Review*, CXCIV 1934), 181–2.

German Crown Princess told her mother, Queen Victoria, that there were only two men whom she considered suitable for the position, Acton and Lord Arthur Russell.[1] But neither received it. Gladstone, or perhaps the Foreign Office, may have suspected that Acton's austere sense of morality was not appropriate to the proper diplomatic temperament. Or, more simply, the successful claimant, Sir Edward Malet, the son of an old friend of Bismarck, may have been more of an asset in Berlin. In either case, the prize continued to escape Acton.

His hopes died hard. In 1892, when Gladstone became Prime Minister for the fourth and last time at the venerable age of eighty-three, and when Acton, a generation his junior, was already fifty-eight, Acton was indiscreet enough to confide to friends his expectation of a Cabinet position.[2] But Gladstone remained impervious and instead recommended him for a position in the Royal Household. His friends were indignant that he should be 'fobbed off', as one put it, 'with the offer of an absurd appointment in the household which would have obliged him to play at being a soldier, and to wear a brass helmet with a horsehair plume'.[3] But even this proposal was withdrawn, apparently after Acton had already accepted it, and Acton was granted yet another position in the household, that of Lord-in-Waiting. Perhaps because he did not want to embarrass Gladstone, perhaps because he did not want to indulge in a petty display of feeling, Acton surprised his friends by accepting this offer. For almost three years, whenever his services were required at Windsor Castle or Buckingham Palace, he fulfilled the formal duties of his position, while indulging his taste for the royal libraries or passing the day with the celebrated callers of the Queen. In the House of Lords at this time, he represented the Irish office, then under the direction of John Morley, a responsibility which he discharged ably, if unenthusiastically.

Acton was never given the opportunity to prove himself as the statesman-philosopher of his visions. He might have been

---

[1] *Letters of the Empress Frederick*, ed. Frederick Ponsonby (London, 1908), p. 193.

[2] *Personal Papers of Lord Rendel* (London, 1931), p. 127.

[3] Russell, p. 132.

comforted by the thought, however, that he would probably have failed in the test (as even Gladstone occasionally failed), defeated by his own rigorous moral standards. 'The best political thinkers, often very poor politicians', he had noted, and he might have mentally appended his own name to the distinguished list that followed: Turgot, Joseph von Radowitz, Burke and Webster.[1]

[1] Add. MSS., 4938.

VIII

CAMBRIDGE

REGIUS PROFESSOR

ACTON was an anomaly in many worlds. He was a Catholic in bad standing with the hierarchy, a politician without portfolio, and, for the most part, an historian without academic status. Only in the last respect did his situation notably improve towards the close of his life. When it was beginning to appear that public recognition would permanently escape him, he was rewarded with the most coveted academic position open to the English historian.

Honours were late in coming to him, particularly in his own country. In 1872, the University of Munich, after putting the traditional question, 'Is there no Dalberg present?' conferred upon him the honorary degree of Doctor of Philosophy, and three years later he was elected to the Royal Academy of Munich, of which Döllinger was then president. It was not until 1888 and 1889 that Cambridge and Oxford thought to award him honorary degrees and only the following year, upon the suggestion of Gladstone, was he named Honorary Fellow of All Souls, Oxford, a distinction he shared only with his sponsor.

Acton's real laurels, however, came in the testimonials of his friends and in the familiar description of him as the most erudite man of his times. Casual acquaintances agreed with his best friends that he was 'the nearest approach to omniscience' they had ever seen.[1] They went to him, one friend observed,

[1] *Autobiography of Andrew Dickson White* (2 vols.; London, 1905), II, 412.

to settle disputes as to a dictionary,[1] and another spoke of him as 'an acknowledged final court of appeal'.[2] James Bryce once arranged a dinner party for Robertson Smith, the most eminent Hebrew and Arabic scholar in Britain, Mandell Creighton, then occupied with his history of the Popes, and Acton. 'The conversation', Bryce recalled, 'turned first upon the times of Pope Leo the Tenth, and then upon recent controversies regarding the dates of the books of the Old Testament, and it soon appeared that Lord Acton knew as much about the former as Dr. Creighton, and as much about the latter as Robertson Smith.'[3]

Even those who suffered harsh treatment at his hands conceded his genius and tried to promote his career. Creighton enlisted his help in the editing of the *English Historical Review*, and encouraged 'the most learned Englishman now alive'[4] to contribute to the journal. In the first issue of the *Review* in June, 1886, Acton was represented by a typical work of his later years, 'The German Schools of History', a learned, allusive discussion of nineteenth-century German historians and philosophers of history—'the sort of thing that takes your breath away', as Creighton described it.[5] For the next ten years, Acton abandoned himself to the congenial task of writing for professional colleagues. As a result, his style became increasingly weighty, elliptical and difficult, and it is unlikely that more than a handful of Englishmen fully understood his three articles and eight reviews. While the journal gave him an immediate incentive to write, it had the unfortunate effect of drawing him even further away from the ambitious projects to which he still clung. Thus a projected biography of Döllinger, which was apparently intended to occupy many volumes,[6]

[1] Oscar Browning, *Memories of Later Years* (London, 1923), p. 16.
[2] Thomas Thornely, *Cambridge Memories* (London, 1936), p. 117.
[3] Bryce, p. 387.
[4] Louise Creighton, *Life and Letters of Mandell Creighton* (2 vols.; London, 1904), I, 275.
[5] ibid., p. 339.
[6] The following files of notes were exclusively or largely devoted to Döllinger: Add. MSS., 4903–15, 4973, 4992, 4993, 5009, 5401–4, 5515, 5609, 5639–45, 5647, 5658, 5663, 5664, 5669–71, 5675, 5697, 5704.

became, in the pages of the *Review*, an article of 22,000 words, densely packed with little known information and subtle interpretive suggestions that must have escaped the vast majority of even his learned readers, and that made it absolutely unintelligible, as Creighton admitted, to the uninitiate.

While the *Review* confirmed Acton in his predilection for the difficult and elliptical, it did him a service in introducing him to an academic audience and giving him an academic reputation he had not previously enjoyed in his own country. In 1891, he was invited to stand for the Dixie Professorship of Ecclesiastical History at Cambridge, the chair vacated by Creighton when he became Bishop of Peterborough. It is not known whether Acton stood for the chair and was rejected, or whether he declined the invitation on the ground that it was improper for him, as a Roman Catholic, to occupy a position meant to represent orthodox Anglicanism. The latter has been suggested as the reason why Gladstone, the following year, passed over Acton in favour of Sir John Seeley to fill the vacant Regius Professorship of Modern History at Cambridge.

It was, ironically, only after the retirement of Gladstone, whose scruples, so much like his own, had unwittingly retarded his advancement, that Acton received the reward which was to be the crowning point of his career. Upon Seeley's death in 1895, Lord Rosebery, Gladstone's successor, recommended Acton for the Regius Professorship of Modern History at Cambridge. Acton was thought of as 'the dark horse'[1] for the position, and at one point he declined it in favour of a Cambridge professor, but the office was finally his.

For the first time since his youth in Munich, Acton found himself in the academic society which was the usual habitat of the scholar. The Regius Professorship dispelled the last lingering traces of the amateur, and gave him the official recognition and prestige that might have been expected to dull his sense of isolation and futility. Externally, at least, the pattern of his life had altered since the time, ten years earlier, when he had despaired of attaining a position in which he could exert moral

[1] H. A. L. Fisher, 'Lord Acton's Lectures', *Independent Review*, XI (1906), 225.

influence. The reward was a testimonial to his scholarship and perhaps even to his unorthodox views, both of which might now receive a sympathetic hearing. Yet even as he accepted the appointment and rejoiced in it, he realized that it would be no panacea, that his isolation would not yield to the genial society of academicians, and that his views were still too idiosyncratic to be taken seriously by more than a few. When Cardinal Vaughan, successor to Manning, congratulated him on the appointment, Acton replied that while it was full of promising opportunities, 'the danger is that it is almost more a platform before the country than a *cathedra* with serious students under it'.[1]

Acton found in Cambridge what he had found everywhere else: many came to hear him, respecting his learning and intrigued by his social position, but few understood him and still fewer, having understood, agreed with him. Although his lectures were extremely well attended, a suspiciously large part of the audience was composed of curious visitors— women, notably. To a certain extent, this was his own doing. Visitors could carry away an agreeable sensation of erudition and profundity, but students preparing for examinations were bewildered by the mass of esoteric facts and intricate theories with which Acton assumed familiarity. His colleague, Oscar Browning, who was grateful to him for inaugurating a 'great epoch in the Cambridge teaching of History',[2] deliberately paralleled Acton's lectures with more elementary ones on the same subjects.

With most of the undergraduates Acton had little to do. He once tried to conduct some conversation classes but soon had to abandon them, perhaps, as the misogynist Browning suspected, because 'the women who attended them asked such silly questions'.[3] For a few Trinity men, however—Acton was a fellow of Trinity—he was a revelation of what history might be and had never been. The Historical Tripos at Cambridge had traditionally been the haven of those who wanted a sub-

[1] J. G. Snead Cox, *Life of Cardinal Vaughan* (2 vols.; London, 1910), II, 299.
[2] Browning, p. 17.
[3] ibid., p. 18.

ject that would require no thought and little knowledge. Acton changed that, at least for some. G. M. Trevelyan, the present Master of Trinity and one of England's most esteemed historians, was an undergraduate at Trinity during Acton's professorship. When he succeeded to the chair once occupied by his teacher, he spoke of Acton's arrival at Cambridge three decades earlier as a renaissance of study, 'when learning like a stranger came from far'. Acton was that 'sage of immense and mysterious distinction' who had been famous in old Continental controversies, 'a traveller from the antique lands of European statescraft, religion and learning'. 'Under Acton's leadership', Trevelyan recalled, 'we did not care how proud we were, for he had excited the imagination of the whole University and indeed of the country at large.'[1]

THE HISTORIAN AS PHILOSOPHER

In his inaugural lecture, Acton commented on the irony of his having had to wait forty-five years before Cambridge would officially admit him. What he had the grace not to say was that as a result of his initial rejection by Cambridge, his intellectual character was shaped in the very different atmosphere of Munich. The difference might be measured by the contrast between Acton and his predecessor, Sir John Seeley, a conventional political historian to whom German cultural and intellectual history were as alien as the German methods of scholarship and research. To the task of bringing together the divergent traditions of Germany and England, of history and philosophy, Acton dedicated his inaugural lecture.

'A Lecture on the Study of History', as it was formally entitled, opened with a statement of the need for a philosophy of history that would help elucidate the 'unity of modern history'.[2] For Seeley's view of history as little more than an accessory to politics, Acton had no sympathy. He admitted that history was immensely useful to politics, but insisted that

---

[1] G. M. Trevelyan, *Present Position of History* (Cambridge [England], 1927), pp. 11–12.

[2] Reprinted in *Essays on Freedom and Power*, p. 3.

its peculiar genius was its ability to isolate the abiding issues
from the morass of the temporary and transient, which is why
ecclesiastical history has always claimed priority over civil
history. At its best, history is more than a mere record of the
course of events and far more than a record of political events;
it is a philosophy of origins and causes, the profound, spiritual
origins that determine events. The great heresy of modern
history is the attempt to reduce the profound to the superficial,
the holy to the profane, the spiritual to the material:

'If we are to account mind not matter, ideas not force, the
spiritual property that gives dignity and grace and intellectual
value to history, and its action on the ascending life of men,
then we shall not be prone to explain the universal by the
national, and civilization by custom. A speech of Antigone, a
single sentence of Socrates, a few lines that were inscribed on
an Indian rock before the Second Punic War, the footsteps
of a silent yet prophetic people who dwelt by the Dead Sea, and
perished in the fall of Jerusalem, come nearer to our lives than
the ancestral wisdom of barbarians who fed their swine on the
Hercynian acorns.'[1]

Just as history, properly understood, is more than a mere
succession of events and facts, so, Acton argued, modern history is more than a period of time marked off arbitrarily for the
convenience of the student. It had a definite, unmistakable
beginning. It was not the heir of medieval history, succeeding
by right of legitimate descent. It was born of revolution: the
revolution of Columbus who 'subverted the notions of the
world, and reversed the conditions of production, wealth and
power', of Machiavelli who 'released government from the
restraint of law', of Erasmus who 'diverted the current of
ancient learning from profane into Christian channels', of
Luther who 'broke the chain of authority and tradition at its
strongest link', of Copernicus who 'erected an invincible
power that set for ever the mark of progress upon the time
that was to come'.[2]

For good and for bad, the world was liberated from its

[1] ibid., p. 5.　　　[2] ibid., pp. 5–6.

past, and historical literature, the knowledge of that past, was one of the instruments of its liberation. The Middle Ages were content to live in a twilight of fiction in regard to their heritage; the modern world had need of all the wisdom stored up by its predecessors. Men no longer took for granted the conditions of their lives. They questioned their faith, their actions and their reasons. This 'advent of the reign of general ideas' was the Revolution.[1] And because ideas, unlike customs or conventions, had wings with which to traverse frontiers and seas, the historian had to follow in their wake and master the generalities of universal history and philosophy.

Modern history is of interest not only because it broke with the past, ensuring the predominance first of opinion over established belief and then of knowledge over opinion, but because it is a narrative about ourselves, with its themes still uncompleted and its problems unsolved. Religion is the most conspicuous of these themes, and one of the most urgent tasks for modern historians is the redeeming of religion from many unjust reproaches and from the graver fact of reproaches that are just. In the pursuit of this task, the historian invariably finds himself in the realm of politics. He discovers that the seventeenth-century sects, with their great reverence for the soul of the individual, were least reverent toward established institutions, and sought to replace public authority, external discipline and organized violence by the conscience and intellect of free men. Toleration, the plea of men who desired protection for their own beliefs, was converted by the sects into a political and moral belief in its own right. When religion was discovered to be the mother of freedom, freedom was adopted as the ideal of politics, and religion and politics together ordained that each man should be permitted to fulfil his duty to God undeterred by other men. This was the doctrine 'laden with storm and havoc, which is the secret essence of the Rights of Man, and indestructible soul of Revolution'.[2]

With religion the proud mother of freedom, Providence became the godparent of progress. The constancy of progress toward greater freedom, Acton felt assured, was the characteristic and unique aspect of modern history. Those who depre-

[1] ibid., p. 6.   [2] ibid., p. 12

cate progress, who deny the superiority of the present over the past, also deprecate freedom. Thus, Carlyle, Newman and Froude agreed that the ways of God would never become known to man and that 'the mere consolidation of liberty is like the motion of creatures whose advance is in the direction of their tails'.[1] Therefore they saw in the principle of checks and balances of power not a commendable precaution of liberty but a dangerous obstruction to effective government, and the theory that the sovereign is dependent upon the subject they regarded as an affront to the divine principle of authority. Against thinkers of this stamp, Acton affirmed his faith in history as the true demonstration of religion, in the wisdom of divine rule as seen in the progress of the world, and in progress as measured by the achievement of liberty.

The method of modern progress and liberty has been revolution: the revolution of commerce against land, labour against wealth, the State against society, conscience against authority, the living individual against the dead past. Here the historian meets with a serious dilemma:

'If the supreme conquests of society are won more often by violence than by lenient arts, if the trend and drift of things is towards convulsions and catastrophies, if the world owed religious liberty to the Dutch Revolution, constitutional government to the English, federal republicanism to the American, political equality to the French and its successors, what is to become of us, docile and attentive students of the absorbing past? The triumph of the revolutionist annuls the historian.'[2]

Yet by a strange twist of irony, the revolution that would annul the historian succeeded, perhaps inadvertently, in reaffirming history. The romantic or Conservative school of history, with its headquarters in Germany, had chosen to regard revolution as an alien episode, a disease to be cured before history could resume its normal course of organic evolution. The Liberal school in France, on the other hand, looked upon the revolution as the proper development and ripened fruit of history. The conflict of these two schools gave to the study of

[1] ibid., p. 13.　　　[2] ibid., p. 15.

modern history an importance analogous to the revival of ancient learning. And when added to this are the vast stores of documents recently made available by the archives of Europe, the advances in the techniques of criticism, and the peculiar combination of impartiality and judgment which the modern historian can bring to bear on his subject, the revolutionary character of modern historiography appears as dramatically as the revolutionary character of modern history itself.

The most recent, and least exploited, discovery of history is the idea that the 'hanging judge'[1] may be the most truly impartial judge. The generation following Ranke was so impressed by the difficulty of finding the truth and the even greater difficulty of persuading others of it that they respected everything and affirmed nothing. They hoped to raise history above contention by being coldly critical, colourless and disinterested, by treating as objective forces those ideas which in religion and politics are deemed to be truths. This discipline of objectivity, Acton felt, was one which it was well for men to undergo, but also wise eventually to abandon. Ultimately it should be recognized that the genuinely impartial historian was not the one who acquiesced in the immoralities of the age he described, but he who judged each age according to the clear and undisputed canons of eternal justice. 'The weight of opinion is against me', Acton said, 'when I exhort you never to debase the moral currency or to lower the standard of rectitude, but to try others by the final maxim that governs your own lives, and to suffer no man and no cause to escape the undying penalty which history has the power to inflict on wrong.'[2]

The mistake of Ranke was in supposing that Providence justifies every event, legitimizes every success, and sanctions the theory that what it is, is right. The true sense in which history is providential, however, is not that it transforms all evil into good, but that it permits us to distinguish between evil and good. Men must learn to resist history as well as to respect it, to realize that it is 'the part of real greatness to know

[1] ibid., p. 18.
[2] ibid., p. 25. 'Debasing the Moral Currency' was the title of an essay in George Eliot's *Impressions of Theophrastus Such*, published in 1879.

how to stand and fall alone, stemming, for a lifetime, the contemporary flood'.[1] The unhappy fact is that there is more sin
than virtue in the past, more criminals than saints.

'If, in our uncertainty, we must often err, it may be sometimes better to risk excess in rigour than in indulgence, for
then at least we do no injury by loss of principle. As Bayle has
said, it is more probable that the secret motives of an indifferent action are bad than good; and this discouraging conclusion
does not depend upon theology, for James Mozley supports
the sceptic from the other flank, with all the artillery of Trac-
tarian Oxford. "A Christian", he says, "is bound by his very
creed to suspect evil, and cannot release himself. . . . He sees
it where others do not; his instinct is divinely strengthened; his
eye is supernaturally keen; he has a spiritual insight, and senses
exercised to discern. . . . He owns the doctrine of original sin;
that doctrine puts him necessarily on his guard against appear-
ances, sustains his apprehension under perplexity, and pre-
pares him for recognizing anywhere what he knows to be
everywhere." There is a popular saying of Madame de Staël,
that we forgive whatever we really understand. The paradox
has been judiciously pruned by her descendant, the Duke de
Broglie, in the words: "Beware of too much explaining, lest we
end by too much excusing." History, says Froude, does teach
that right and wrong are real distinctions. Opinions alter,
manners change, creeds rise and fall, but the moral law is
written on the tablets of eternity.'[2]

However well or ill founded were Acton's fears that the
Regius Professorship was more a public platform than a chair
of learning, certainly the inaugural lecture was traditionally as
much a public pronouncement as an academic discourse. The
university acclaimed it for what it was, one of the best lectures
of its kind ever to be delivered, and even to-day it is spoken
of as one of the greatest inaugural lectures in the history of the
Regius Professorship. What dissenting voices there were came
from laymen. The *Spectator* commented: 'It is possible for a
historian to know too much, and, if we wished to be bitter, we
might say that Lord Acton was himself a living example of the

[1] ibid., p. 27.   [2] ibid., p. 28.

new trouble.'[1] The *Saturday Review*, determined, as usual, not to be intimidated by what it did not understand or to be abashed by the insinuation of philistinism, was even more outspoken. Acton, the *Saturday Review* loftily judged, did not have a firm grasp on the immense mass of materials with which he pretended to deal, and what theories he did have were drowned in an 'overpowering deluge of verbiage' and in the 'laboured and pretentious style' which he affected. Even the most nimble mental gymnast, it predicted, would fail to reach the meaning 'which this inarticulate teacher has cunningly concealed'. The least that could be expected of the Regius Professor was intelligibility. It was intolerable that the unfailing lucidity of Seeley and the brilliant historic imagination and prose of Kingsley should be succeeded by the 'Batavian splutterings of Lord Acton's awkward pen'. The *Saturday Review* sincerely hoped that Acton would resign the post which he seemed in no way qualified to fill.[2]

On the subject of Acton's ideas, which should have been the real subject matter of controversy, the *Saturday Review* was silent. Ideas were not its forte, as may be surmised by its comparison of Acton with Seeley and Kingsley, to Acton's disfavour! Lucidity, urbanity and good humour were its criteria of intellectual excellence; enthusiasm or an excess of moral earnestness were its bugbears. But even favourable commentators shied away from a consideration of Acton's philosophy of history, preferring to praise his erudition and profundity rather than dispute his philosophy. The only idea to arouse serious controversy was his theory of the historian as a hanging judge. Henry C. Lea, the American historian whose work on the Inquisition Acton had once reviewed, summed up the prevailing objection when he wrote: 'The historian who becomes an advocate or a prosecutor instead of a judge forfeits his title to confidence, and, if he aspires to be a judge, he should not try a case by a code unknown to the defendant'.[3]

Yet there was much else in the lecture to provoke an atten-

[1] *Spectator*, LXXIV (1895), 807.
[2] *Saturday Review*, LXXIX (1895), 822.
[3] Henry C. Lea, 'Ethical Values in History', in *Minor Historical Writings*, ed. A. C. Howland (Philadelphia, 1942), p. 60.

tive listener. One point that might have invited comment was the ambiguous use of the word history to mean both the events of the past and the record of the past. Sometimes this was a simple verbal confusion that could have been removed by distinguishing between history and historiography, as this summary has attempted to do. But more often the ambiguity went too deep for merely verbal manipulation. For Acton there was no mechanical way to distinguish the fact of the past from its reproduction in the writing of the present. Past and present were united by a metaphysical bond, and it was this bond that condemned the criminal in history to eternal perdition in the works of historians.

Those historians, who tried to break the bond between past and present, thought to do so by ruling everything out of nature but documents. They effaced their own personalities, ignored the whole realm of social facts not to be found in documents, and, most important, neglected the vital ideas that impel men along paths they often neither foresee nor voluntarily choose. Acton explained his theory of history as essentially the history of ideas: 'The great object, in trying to understand history, political, religious, literary or scientific, is to get behind men and to grasp ideas. Ideas have a radiation and development, an ancestry and posterity of their own, in which men play the part of godfathers and godmothers more than that of legitimate parents'.[1] This was his quarrel with Seeley. Seeley saw only Whigs where he should have seen Whiggism. And he wondered at the mistakes of the Whigs, instead of following up the development of their doctrines. What was needed was neither the picturesque scenery of some historians nor the narrowly political history of others, but rather a forthright examination of the impersonal forces that govern the world—predestination, equality, divine right, secularism, congregationalism, nationality, and the many other ruling ideas propelling men.

The kinds of ideas Acton had in mind were not to be found only in conventional works of philosophy and theology, although these were important sources for them. They might be dug up in old manuscripts—and Acton's respect for manu-

[1] 15 March 1880, *Letters to Mary Gladstone* (1st ed.), p. 99.

scripts was second to no one's. Or they might be discovered on the backstairs of history, in the informal recesses of the home where the private lives of men were spun out. But whether in the shadows of the backstairs or in the spacious galleries generally inhabited by philosophers and historians, Acton's purpose was the same, to ferret out 'the little fact that makes the difference'.[1] And the particular fact he sought was that which would enable the historian to assess responsibility for the many evils in the world:

'The passage from histories to documents, from that which is public to that which is secret, is also the transition from complacent and conventional narrative to the disclosure of guilt and shame.'[2]

'History is an iconoclast, not a $\begin{cases} \text{teacher} \\ \text{school} \end{cases}$ of reverence.[3]

'You have to treat the greatest power, antiquity and fame as unceremoniously as a dismissed writer or a saucy apprentice.'[4]

It was the weakness of Ranke, Acton felt, to be too circumspect. By abstaining from the details of men's private lives, just as by abstaining from the controversies of doctrine, Ranke made of history an assemblage of great men attired in their most formal and least revealing costumes, with the historian as a benign and discreet attendant.

Just how the historian was to make the passage from the impersonal forces, the abstract ideas, that govern men to the secrets of the backstairs that illuminate their souls Acton did not say. Would the historian competent to analyse Whiggism as a philosophical doctrine also be competent to judge the Whigs as fallen men? Acton himself tended to solve the problem by taking doctrines, like men, personally, ascribing to them lives of their own and judging them much as one might judge a mortal. But the solution was not entirely successful. Men were free moral agents who could be called to account; the persecutor, it might be said, could have willed another course of action. But ideas, as Acton was quick to see, are less tractable. They are carried along, and carry men along, by an

[1] F. W. Maitland, *Collected Papers* (3 vols.; Cambridge, 1911), III, 517.
[2] Add. MSS., 4905. [3] Add. MSS., 4981. [4] Add. MSS., 4993.

irresistible tide which often takes them far from their place of birth. By Acton's own account, the theory of divine right started out as a principle of divine justice and ended up as an instrument of Stuart absolutism—yet the evil was an inevitable consequence of the good. A man, Acton was fond of saying, must be judged by his 'low-water mark', the one act of evil that outweighs all good. But if ideas are held to a low-water mark, then no idea is immune from the most damnable charge. Even Acton would not have said that religion was the Inquisition in the same sense in which Torquemada was the Inquisition.

Another point on which Acton might have been challenged, had his audience been less concerned with his delivery and more critical of his ideas, was the apparent contradiction between the idea of the historian as an iconoclast and the idea of history as the work of Providence. He sometimes seemed to think of history as more the work of the Devil than of God: 'Great men are almost always bad men';[1] 'power tends to corrupt and absolute power corrupts absolutely';[2] 'it is more probable that the secret motives of an indifferent action are bad than good';[3] history is the 'disclosure of guilt and shame'.[4] But if history is so liable to corruption that the historian must be eternally vigilant and men must learn to 'stand and fall alone' rather than be carried away by the contemporary flood, then how can God be supposed to be implicated in history?

The answer lies in distinguishing between Acton's theory of providence and that familiar in the philosophy of 'historicism'. The *Volksgeist* of Savigny, which implicitly sanctioned whatever forms had been developed by a nation in the course of its history, did for jurisprudence what Hegel's *Weltgeist* did for philosophy. For Savigny, as for Hegel, providence manifested itself in the event and nothing was more deserving than success. Acton's theory, on the other hand, derived from the eschatological tradition present in all great religious philosophies. Thus he conceived of God as being outside of history as well as in it. History did not have meaning or purpose in itself; it acquired meaning only by comparison with a fixed

[1] See above, p. 161. [2] ibid.
[3] ibid., p. 200. [4] ibid., p. 203.

moral standard outside of it, and purpose by fulfilling a moral end imposed upon it. God was also in history, to be sure. 'God in Nature', Acton noted, '[is] more manifest than God in History. Yet History leads to him and Nature away from him,'[1] God was in history by the fact of having fixed the distinctions between truth and error, virtue and sin, and so making it possible for error and sin to be eventually eliminated from history. 'The world exhibits the hand of Providence—the action of Christ—. . . .not by being good, but by becoming better, not by its perfection but by its improvement.'[2] Ultimately, God was neither outside of history nor in it but at its end, awaiting the era of true liberty. Just as providence could not be taken to sanction indiscriminately whatever exists, so progress was not whatever happens to come about; for Acton it was progress to a particular end, the end of liberty.

The ideas of progress and providence were as necessary to Acton as they were, in radically different ways, to Hegel. To Acton they gave a metaphysical security to liberty that was wanting in a purely secular philosophy, for they permitted an optimism regarding the future to be joined to a scepticism regarding the past. The attractiveness of German history was its assurance of salvation. Acton too sought that assurance. But instead of finding it in the manifest evils of recorded history, he projected it into the indefinite future. Thus providence became the critic of the past and the present without ceasing to be the hope of the future.

THE PHILOSOPHER AS REVOLUTIONIST

Against historicism, Acton offered the alternative theory of Liberalism: 'Liberalism wishes for what ought to be, irrespective of what is.'[3] Where the historicist catered to the past, Acton ministered to the future. As early as the Bridgnorth lecture of 1877, he had made it clear that he would no longer lavish upon the past the kind of veneration Burke had thought proper. But not until the 'eighties and 'nineties did his philosophy develop to the point where the future was seen as the

[1] Add. MSS., 5011.   [2] Add. MSS., 5648.   [3] Add. MSS., 5422.

avowed enemy of the past, and where the past was allowed no authority except as it happened to conform to morality. To take seriously this Liberal theory of history, to give precedence to 'what ought to be' over 'what is', was, he admitted, virtually to install a 'revolution in permanence'.[1]

The 'revolution in permanence', as Acton hinted in the inaugural lecture and admitted frankly in his notes, was the culmination of his philosophy of history and theory of politics. That history was, in its most significant sense, the history of ideas—rather than of institutions, events or persons—was itself an affirmation of revolution, for ideas are, at least potentially, subversive of institutions and critical of events and persons. And Acton carried this devotion to ideas into politics with his insistence upon a 'political science' that would assert the sovereignty of ideas over the conventional motives of 'habit, condition, interests, passion'.[2] History in the hands of a critical historian, and politics in the hands of a political scientist, were a record of the 'conscience of mankind'.[3] This idea of conscience, that men carry about with them the knowledge of good and evil, is the very root of revolution, for it destroys the sanctity of the past. 'The permanent and universal question is whether the living shall govern the dead,'[4] Acton noted, and he took his stand with the living. The Liberal, the 'breaker of ancestral images',[5] did not even hesitate to press force into the service of morality if that was necessary. 'Liberalism [is] essentially revolutionary,' Acton observed. 'Facts must yield to ideas. Peaceably and patiently if possible. Violently if not.'[6]

The *Saturday Review* had more reason for anxiety than it knew. 'The Batavian splutterings' of the new Regius Professor, had its reviewer listened carefully, might have been discovered to be the articulation of a philosophy of revolution. Early in his inaugural lecture Acton had made it clear that modern history owed its deliverance from evil and error to 'the advent of general ideas which we call the Revolution',[7] and his later lectures at Cambridge—a course on the French

---

[1] Add. MSS., 5432. [2] Add. MSS., 4941.
[3] 'German Schools of History', *Historical Essays*, p. 383.
[4] Add. MSS., 5468. [5] Add. MSS., 5655.
[6] Add. MSS., 5654. [7] *Freedom and Power*, p. 6.

Revolution first delivered in 1895-6 and another on modern history in 1899-1900—elaborated on the theme. The history of liberty, it appeared, was almost identical with the history of revolution.

Modern history began, in Acton's account, with the resurgence of the absolute State in the fifteenth century, a State fashioned in the image of Machiavelli, knowing no law outside of itself and no right apart from might, and supported by a Church that neither the Reformation nor the Counter-Reformation had succeeded in reforming. The moral revolution had to await the era of national revolutions: 'By a series of violent shocks the nations in succession have struggled to shake off the Past, to reverse the action of time and the verdict of success, and to rescue the world from the reign of the dead.'[1]

The first major revolutionary situation appeared in England. There the Stuarts were attempting to perpetuate a government based upon the most respectable theories of the time: the Lutheran dogma that kings rule by divine right, and the Machiavellian idea of a State ruled by its own experts for its own ends, catering neither to the interests of society nor to the claims of public opinion. The Stuarts had in their favour the successful example of the Tudor monarchy and the sanction of the most popular divines, philosophers and jurists. Yet by a higher test than law and custom, by the test of 'the idea of progress towards more perfect and assured freedom',[2] the revolutionists were in the right. Eventually their revolution failed, partly for the reason Harrington gave, that in neglecting to redistribute property they preserved the aristocratic character of the State, and for the more obvious reason that the death of Cromwell deprived them of their only real leader. But although the Puritans left more political ruins than creations behind them, they bequeathed to the world the ideas that were to generate the great revolutions of modern times.

The rise of the Whigs saw the transformation into a political principle of what had been for the Puritans a theological dogma—the dogma that salvation was a private affair and the Church a voluntary association of men. With the Revolution

[1] *Modern History*, p. 32.   [2] ibid., p. 202.

of 1688, the right of the people to govern the Church was secularized to mean the right to govern the State. It was agreed that the king would rule only with the approval of Parliament, and the moral right of resistance became a tacit limit upon all future governments. This revolution was accomplished without bloodshed or fanaticism. But the same spirit that eschewed bloodshed was also responsible for the inconsistencies, compromises and evasions of the revolutionary settlement. Whiggism was as much a Conservative as a revolutionary doctrine, as much a monarchical as a democratic movement.

The distinction between Toryism and Whiggism was central both to Acton's interpretation of English history and to his own philosophy of history. Toryism he consigned to the depths of political immorality. He had no respect for the theory, prominent among Whigs themselves, that both parties were right, that each was complementary to the other and both were necessary counter-balances in the constitutional structure.[1] He was appalled by Döllinger's suggestion that the Whig and the Tory might meet in heaven.[2] Because political differences, even more than religious differences, were based upon an ultimate moral conflict, the Tories were irrevocably damned. On this point, Acton was unrelenting: 'Toryism=negation of Liberty';[3] 'The Tory Party is no more than an association for the preservation of office and the distribution of patronage.'[4] The 'legitimate' tyrant favoured by Tories, who owed his title to no higher authority than the prescription of time, was no less odious than the illegitimate tyrant, for the principle of authority itself was at fault; and authority, Acton held, 'has been the main actor in history and is mainly responsible for its horrors'.[5] The Tory had a great many sins to atone for: 'A close chain of prejudices and errors connects the Conservative of to-day with the Legitimist and the absolutist, with the Royalist of the seventeenth century, [with] the persecutor of the sixteenth, with the advocate of Feudalism, with the party of Sulla, the slayers of Gracchus.'[6]

Toryism (with its somewhat less depraved neighbour, Con-

[1] Compare Acton's earlier view on this subject, p. 9.
[2] Add. MSS., 4905.   [3] Add. MSS., 4949.   [4] Add. MSS., 4869.
[5] Add. MSS., 4973.   [6] Add. MSS., 4949.

servatism) occupied the lowest rungs of the political ladder, Liberalism the top, and Whiggism the intermediate stages. The distinction between Whig and Liberal had been familiar to Acton since his earliest ventures in political thinking. But in the *Rambler* and *Home and Foreign Review*, the advantage had been with the 'constructive, positive' Whig[1] and against the 'abstract, ideal absolutism' of the Liberal.[2] Gradually he had reversed himself, until by 1877 he was chiding Burke and Macaulay for representing as the ancestors of modern liberty the leaders of the Whig Party—men whose only ideal was the preservation of their own power, for whom religious toleration was at best a temporary expedient, and for whom liberty meant nothing more than the security of property. Where the honest man, 'dreading the action of accidental surroundings', tried to escape from the influence of his age and country in order to be guided by eternal laws, the Whigs deliberately 'acquiesced in the existing order'.[3] 'A Whig was a reconciled Roundhead',[4] who wanted only to improve, not to reconstruct, to destroy little and innovate little. In his lectures Acton sometimes tended to be more gentle with the Whigs. So far as they went, he once suggested, they were in the right, ethically and politically: 'They saw that it is an error to ride a principle to death, to push things to an extreme, to have an eye for one thing only, to prefer abstractions to realities, to disregard practical conditions'.[5] But the general tenor of even this lecture, and much more of his notes, convicts this judgment of excessive generosity. The Whigs could not be ethically in the right if they preferred the realities of practical politics to the ideals of morality, and it was more than an accident that the great patriarchs of the party should have been 'the most infamous of men'.[6] In any event, Acton was certain that by 1770 whatever little virtue the Whigs had had was exhausted. The next great impetus to progress came not from the realistic, worldly-wise English, but from the immature, idealistic Americans.

[1] Review of Thomas Arnold's *A Manual of English Literature*, in *Home and Foreign Review*, II (1863), 253.
[2] See above, p. 79.
[3] Add. MSS., 4955 and 4949.   [4] Add. MSS., 4946.
[5] *Modern History*, p. 217.   [6] ibid., p. 218.

In the American Revolution, Liberalism finally emancipated itself from Whiggism:

'They [the Americans] claimed to draw from the pure wells of Whiggism. But they carried Whiggism from the stages of compromise to the crowning stage of principle.'[1]
'The Whig governed by compromise. The Liberal begins the reign of ideas.'[2]
'How to distinguish the Whig from the Liberal—One is practical, gradual, ready for compromise. The other works out a principle philosophically. One is a policy aiming at a philosophy. The other is a philosophy seeking a policy.'[3]

For the first time, in 1776, liberty was an end in itself, not a pawn in the hands of a suppressed religion or an abused interest. Absolutism, which previously had been inconvenient, injurious or illegal, was now simply and intolerably wrong. Where the Whigs had brought out ancient, illegible rolls of parchment to fortify their claims, the Americans called to witness nothing less than the universal law of nature. And where the Whigs had been inspired by a recital of economic abuses, the Americans regarded the economic abuse, the threepence tax, as only a symptom of the greater evil of absolutism, the imposition of taxation without representation. Legally America was probably in the wrong. Financially and materially the colonies had much to lose by the Revolution and little to gain. The problem posed by the Americans was, ultimately, this: Should a man risk his country and his family, his blood and his fortune, for a purely speculative and novel idea, sanctioned by no law, constitution or religion? 'The affirmative response', Acton replied, 'is the Revolution, or as we say, Liberalism.'[4]

Acton had no patience with those historians—James Bryce was one—who saw only 'the conservative, the traditional, the historic side of things' in the Revolution.[5] One of the few topics which he was rash enough to think had been adequately treated by historians, perhaps for all time, was the American

[1] Add. MSS., 4898.   [2] Add. MSS., 4949.   [3] Add. MSS., 4950.
[4] Acton to Lady Blennerhassett, no date, *Correspondence*, p. 278.
[5] Add. MSS., 6871.

Revolution, and he was certain that it was anything but traditional, conservative or historic. The revolutionist, like any good Liberal, was moved by an extreme and abstract conception of freedom, in which the most subtle usurpation of a right was as unendurable as the most shocking horror: 'He condemns, not Nero, or Ivan, or Lopez; but Charles V, Louis XIV, George III. He fights, he stakes his life, his fortune, the existence of his family, not to resist the intolerable reality of oppression, but the remote possibility of wrong, of diminished freedom.'[1] Because the Americans made the supreme sacrifice for an extreme idea, theirs was 'the abstract revolution in its purest and most perfect shape'. 'On this principle of subversion they erected their commonwealth, and by its virtue lifted the world out of its orbit and assigned a new course to history. Here or nowhere we have the broken chain, the rejected past, precedent and statute superseded by unwritten law, sons wiser than their fathers, ideas rooted in the future, reason cutting as clean as Atropos.'[2]

'We have to make up our minds to a breach of continuity,'[3] Acton argued against those who would have preferred, like Döllinger and Bryce, to wait upon the slow processes of evolution for the desired social changes. The American experience had demonstrated that nothing short of revolution could carry history so far and so quickly along the road to liberty. 'No course of obscure planting, of hidden growth, of gradual development, of venerable sanctions, of continuous progress have [sic] been more creative and constructive, more efficient in controlling events, directing progress, and moulding the future, than sudden decisions by which men have shaken off their past, have put off the old man, and turned their faces to the front.'[4]

A philosophy of history so radical and so explicit should surely have committed Acton to a defence of the last of the great modern revolutions, that of France. By extrapolating from his views of the English and American Revolutions, one would expect to find him even more enthusiastic about the

[1] Add. MSS., 4915.　　　　[2] *History of Freedom*, p. 586.
[3] Add. MSS., 4973.　　　　[4] Add. MSS., 4991.

French than about the American Revolution. If the government of George III was condemned, then the French monarchy, as Acton himself admitted, was condemned a hundred times over. And it was America that had prepared the way for France by providing a successful model of revolution and a ready-made ideology, an ideology glorifying resistance to tyranny and denying the legitimacy of all authority not derived from the people. The Liberalism of the American Revolution was an 'extra-territorial, universal' creed[1] that the French were quick to adopt.

The intellectual heritage of the French Revolution was respectable and its moral indignation was commendable. Its provocation, moreover—financial disorder, administrative corruption, and, most of all, the 'class government'[2] that was a relic of feudalism—was enormous. A generation tutored by Adam Smith, Turgot and Benjamin Franklin could hardly be expected to look kindly upon the irrational custom of making living men suffer because of social arrangements instituted by the dead. The ideals of political liberty and social equality were inextricably united, for liberty itself inspired the demand for equality: 'The real object of assault was not the living landlord, but the unburied past.'[3]

The Tennis Court Oath, the first act of political rebellion, typified the early history of the Revolution. The Oath gave promise of radical and infinite change, but it had come about more by the mismanagement of the court than by the conscious design of the revolutionists. When Louis rejected Necker's proposal for a constitution generous enough to propitiate the people and serious enough for genuine reform, he decreed 'that France, so near the goal in that month of June, should wade to it through streams of blood during the twenty-five most terrible years in the history of Christian nations'.[4] By his own wilfulness, the king, as Mirabeau said at the time, took the road to the scaffold.

Three days after the Tennis Court Oath the king offered terms of conciliation. At no time in English history would concessions so extensive have failed to pacify the people. And

1 *French Revolution*, p. 20.   2 ibid., p. 41
3 ibid., p. 58.   4 ibid., p. 72.

the French Physiocrats felt, like the English Whigs, that limited liberties conceded piecemeal were worth more than formal declarations of self-government; the first were certain, practical, of immediate advantage, while the second were in the dubious domain of theory. But the members of the Assembly thought otherwise. They knew better than to purchase a few political reforms at the cost of a comprehensive social programme. Because they acted on the larger principle that the law must be responsible to those who obey rather than to those who command, they had to reject the king's belated overture:

'It was the very marrow of the doctrine that obstruction of liberty is a crime, that absolute authority is not a thing to be consulted, but a thing to be removed, and that resistance to it is no affair of interest or convenience, but of sacred obligation. Every drop of blood shed in the American conflict was shed in a cause immeasurably inferior to theirs, against a system more legitimate by far than that of June 23. Unless Washington was an assassin, it was their duty to oppose, if it might be, by policy, if it must be, by force, the mongrel measure of concession and obstinacy which the Court had carried against the proposals of Necker.'[1]

The king alternately provoked the nation and showed himself incompetent to control it until, one month after the Tennis Court Oath, the first atrocities broke out. Revolutionists and their sympathizers argued that if these were excesses, they served the interests of liberty, reason and toleration. Jefferson in effect condoned them when he said that the arm of the people was a necessary, although not always accurate, instrument in the struggle for liberty, and that no prize of such a magnitude had ever been won with less innocent bloodshed. With the outbreak of violence, however, Acton's benevolent attitude to the Revolution disappeared. Murder was murder, he moralized, whatever its intentions and however sacred the cause, and crimes committed for the sake of liberty were no less infamous than those committed for love of power. In this righteous pronouncement, the

[1] ibid., p. 78.

ambivalence that lurked in the depths of Acton's thought came to the surface. Violence was inherent in the very idea of revolution, as he well knew. 'Burke was wrong to condemn the Revolution because of its crimes,' he had noted. 'No great cause could resist that test.'[1] By what right, then, could he acclaim the ideal of revolution and at the same time condemn the violence in it?

Perhaps to escape from this dilemma, Acton intimated that it was not the violence alone that he abhorred, but its motive, which was power rather than liberty, and its deliberate, systematic cultivation. 'The appalling thing in the French Revolution', he said, 'is not the tumult but the design.'[2] Behind the fire and smoke of the Revolution, he saw the hand of 'managers' and the evidence of 'calculating organization', of a long meditated plot.[3] And the managers were driven by 'brutal instinct and hideous passion', by a 'revolting and grotesque ferocity'.[4] Robespierre he singled out as 'the most hateful character in the forefront of history since Machiavelli reduced to a code the wickedness of public men'.[5]

Yet all of the horror of the Massacres and the Reign of Terror, and all of the wickedness of a Danton, Marat or Robespierre, should have been, on Acton's own principles, supererogatory. If the true Liberal, as he elsewhere argued, finds more to condemn in a George III than in a Nero, he should find the real villain of the French Revolution not in a Robespierre, who carried out the logic of terror to its ultimate conclusion, but in the moderate and Liberal Barnave, who, before he turned against the Revolution, justified the violence of July 1789 with the argument that the blood shed by the revolutionists was not, after all, so pure. 'It is by him and men like him, and not by the scourings of the galleys', Acton said, 'that we can get to understand the spirit of the time.'[6] Nor was it even the 'man of honour'[7] Barnave who initiated the course of events that culminated in the Terror. Before Barnave had come Sieyès, of whom Acton had said, in terms that were certainly intended to be complimentary, that he was 'essentially

[1] Add. MSS., 4967.   [2] *French Revolution*, p. 97.
[3] ibid.   [4] ibid., p. 226.
[5] ibid., p. 300.   [6] ibid., p. 91.   [7] ibid.

a revolutionist, because he held that political oppression can never be right, and that resistance to oppression can never be wrong'.[1] The best work of the Revolution was his doing; yet even he contributed to its degeneration. 'A long line of possible politics' ran from Sieyès to Robespierre, but 'the transitions are finely shaded, and the logic is continuous'.[2] To condemn Robespierre was also to condemn, according to Acton's own rigorous method, Sieyès. But how could one condemn Sieyès and still keep faith with Liberalism?

Sometimes Acton shifted his argument, hinting that it was not so much the fact of violence, the corruption of the ideal, that repelled him, as the nature of the ideal itself, the confusion of liberty with democracy. Even had violence not come to hasten the degeneration of liberty, he implied, democracy was there to poison it at the source. Democracy was fatal to liberty because it prescribed an economic revolution of such dimensions that anarchy threatened to be its permanent condition, and if not anarchy, then a Rousseauan variety of democratic despotism. Had the French looked more closely at their American predecessors, Acton reasoned, and particularly had they regarded the America of 1787 as carefully as the America of 1776, they might have been instructed on the methods of a Liberalism that was not democratic. They would have seen the aggressive, violent revolutionists of 1776 replaced by the 'eminently cautious and sensible'[3] leaders of the Convention who devised a multitude of checks and balances to curb democracy.

Yet democracy, like violence, had much to recommend it. Here too Acton's harsh and categorical judgments were tempered by the depth and range of his insights, suggesting mitigating explanations, subtle complications, unknown factors, all of which had the effect, despite his own severe intentions, of blurring his judgments. Thus, while calling down imprecations upon the heads of the democrats, he was ready to admit that democracy was not the idiosyncratic invention of vicious men. As a denial of privilege, whether legal, social or political, it was a perfect expression of the Declaration of the Rights of Man, for which Acton had nothing but praise:

[1] ibid., p. 161.   [2] ibid., p. 117.   [3] ibid., p. 34.

'The Declaration was the signal of those who meant to rescue France from the ancestors who had given it tyranny and slavery as an inheritance. Its opponents were men who would be satisfied with good government, . . . and would never risk prosperity and peace in the pursuit of freedom.'[1] Even about the constitution, which was less wise in its task of creating authority than the Declaration of Rights in its limiting of authority, Acton had something to say in favour and more in extenuation. The constitution was an attempt to realize the principle of Sieyès, that 'the law is the will of him that obeys, not of him that commands'[2]—a maxim which on other occasions Acton had acclaimed as the essence of Liberalism. The fact that the constitution provided neither for federalism nor for a division of powers was as much a reproach to the Conservatives as to the Democrats. It was the Conservative Mounier, Acton pointed out, who had been one of the first to reject federalism, and who then, by his exaggerated solicitude for the interests of the king, had rendered the idea of a division of powers suspect.

The Conservatives, indeed, were guilty of more than indiscretion. Acton found that it was the policy of many, including the king, to goad the revolutionists into excesses, hoping that in the resulting moral and military bankruptcy they might recoup their own losses. If Robespierre was the villain of the piece, Louis XVI was not its hero, for the king met his fate complacently, 'unconscious of guilt, blind to the opportunities he had wasted and the misery he had caused'.[3] He died a penitent Christian, which was in his favour, but he also died an unrepentant king. The queen was, if anything, more obdurate and incorrigible, and together they were the authors of their own disaster. The issue between a Liberal, constitutional monarchy and a democratic republic 'was decided by the crimes of men, and by errors more inevitably fatal than crime'[4]—the crimes being those of the Democrats, the errors those of the Conservatives. Elsewhere Acton delivered the less ambiguous judgment: 'The intellectual error of the Democrats vanishes before the moral error of the Conservatives.'[5]

[1] ibid., p. 103.   [2] ibid., p. 119.   [3] ibid., p. 255.
[4] ibid., p. 239.   [5] ibid., p. 122.

All the errors and crimes of the Revolution were not to be laid at the door of the Democrats, nor were all the errors and crimes of the Democrats to be ascribed to the perniciousness of their doctrines. Acton reproved Tocqueville for failing to distinguish between what was spontaneous and normal in the Revolution and what was done under the pressure of necessity, that is, for not separating 'the early movement towards liberty from the later movement towards power'.[1] The ancient system of local rights and liberties was swept away not only to satisfy the theory of equality but also to remedy the state of anarchy bequeathed by the Old Régime. Similarly the war of aggression and conquest, which was partly a logical deduction from the ideal of a superior, universal law (an ideal which was itself commendable—twenty years of war, Acton felt, was not too much to pay for a doctrine of international law), was also partly the doing of the enemies of France, who were inspired by the less exalted hope of weakening France imperially and materially. Again on the Church question, Acton's fine sense of mixed motives frustrated his will for moral indignation. He liked to speak of the dismemberment of the Church as the mortal sin against liberty, and of the abolition of the tithes as the primitive cause of the Reign of Terror. At the same time, however, he demonstrated how the Church, by tying its fortunes so closely to the monarchy, had precipitated its own ruin. The odium of religious persecution was associated with both the Church and the monarchy, so that even with the best intentions, the revolutionists would have had to abolish the power and privileges of both institutions.[2]

The *Lectures on the French Revolution* is generally consigned, in the factional spirit that characterizes the literature on the Revolution, to the party of the anti-revolutionists. To take Acton at face value, there is warrant enough for this. But if the lectures are read carefully, and particularly if they are confronted with the notes, it becomes less certain that he belongs with Burke, Carlyle, Taine, and the other uncompromisingly hostile critics of the Revolution. He judged the Revolution to be immoral because it violated the fundamental precept of morality, the injunction against murder, but he approved the

[1] Add. MSS., 4922.   [2] Add. MSS., 4992 and 4926.

act of revolution itself, which was an implicit—for Acton sometimes even an explicit—condonation of murder. He inveighed against the virus of democracy that contaminated the ideal of liberty, but he agreed that liberty without some measure of democracy would have been illusory, and that not all of the excesses of democracy were the fault of the Democrats. Like Tocqueville before him, he saw that democracy was a cultural product of the Old Régime, and that the old and the new had more in common than either cared to think. Unlike most other critics of the Revolution, he cannot be identified with any counter-revolutionary party; the group around Mounier and Malouet, who wanted the Revolution to terminate with the establishment of a constitutional monarchy, came nearest to his position, but even they received harsh treatment at his hands.

A close examination of Acton's notes, correspondence and lectures suggests the thought that there was an exoteric and an esoteric side to him: the exoteric, displayed mainly in the lectures (for he may have sensed that the good pedagogue, like the practical moralist, must deliver unambiguous judgments), bitterly condemning the Revolution; the esoteric, evident in his correspondence and notes and sometimes hinted at in the lectures, sympathizing with it as an historical tragedy of great nobility and inexorability. It was the esoteric Acton who boldly affirmed: 'A world has perished, a generation of men has been mown down so that the king might be Louis XVIII in place of Louis XVI, and the minister Fouché in place of Necker. According to the new doctrine of conscience it was not too dearly bought.'[1] Kant had earlier said that whatever success or failure, good or evil, might attend the Revolution, the philosopher could only give his benediction to it, for it proved the existence in human nature of an inclination or disposition to the better which no politician could have been able to predict. As a philosopher, Acton could not permit himself to be distracted by those details of violence or unfortunate political arrangements that were the concern of the historian and politician. 'We contemplate our ideas in the sunlight of heaven,' Acton observed, 'and apply them in the darkness of

[1] Acton to Lady Blennerhassett, undated, *Correspondence*, p. 279.

earth':[1] it was as a philosopher, an esoteric thinker, that he basked in the sun of an ideal world, as an historian, an exoteric teacher, that he inhabited the darkness of the real one. He himself, to be sure, would have been unhappy with this distinction. He sincerely believed that the truth was one, whether in heaven or on earth, and that it must be revealed in its entirety at all times. But his good intentions may have been outwitted by an instinct of a higher, more subtle and more intricate truth, a truth which gave sanctuary to contradictory, conflicting insights.

Between the philosopher and the historian there was no real meeting ground. Acton thought he had found such a meeting ground in the American experience, for, as he interpreted it, America had been providentially favoured with an idea revolutionary enough to satisfy the proudest philosophy and a set of institutions practical enough to secure liberty. But even as he described it there was no kinship between the two, the idea and the institutions being only fortuitously related. In America the transition from the revolutionary spirit of 1776 to the Conservative spirit of 1787 was smooth and tranquil; having cast off the dominion of England, the nation was able to proceed, with clear conscience and without significant opposition, to construct within the framework of a republic the Liberal institutions of England. But the French were less fortunately situated. The adoption of the English mode of Liberalism was precluded both by the nature of their ideal and the practical circumstances attending their revolution. The French Revolution was directed not only against a tyrannical ruler, as was the American, but against a social and political system embracing every aspect of life and having the sanction of the Law, the Church, and all the governments of the world. It was easy for English Liberals to advise that 'political forces are not to be destroyed, but domesticated and transformed and stripped of the power of doing harm'.[2] The French revolutionists could not afford that luxury. Had they not destroyed the forces ranged against them—the monarchy, aristocracy and Church —those forces would have destroyed them together with their ideal, an ideal which Acton himself described as 'the higher law [that] signified Revolution'.[3]

[1] Add. MSS., 4950.   [2] Add. MSS., 5409.   [3] *French Revolution*, p. 2.

There is more, however, to the opposition between a revolutionary ideal and a practical system of Liberalism than the exigencies of a special historical situation. The conflict is inherent in the nature of the ideal and in the nature of Liberal institutions. If the ideal is an absolute liberty to be achieved without compromise, concession, or delay—so that the threepence tax is as serious a provocation as the tyranny of a Nero— it is necessarily incompatible with the kind of Liberal spirit that governs English institutions. Liberty in the English sense is a modest conception. It is tolerant of opposing philosophies, parties and interests. It welcomes diversity and pretends to no final truth. It takes expediency and practicability as its criteria. It is a philosophy of moderate means and limited ends, of slow progression, many halts, and occasional regression. It is, in short, Whiggism, 'a policy aiming at a philosophy', not 'a philosophy seeking a policy'.[1]

Acton was torn between the practical and the ideal. At one moment he would write: 'Liberty wrought by thinkers, not by law-givers. The practical statesman is the obstacle. It is the theorist that works for it.'[2] But he was also sensible of the dangers involved in a crusade for an idea, even for the idea of liberty, and the greater security of a government in which tradition and the normal social forces frustrated the overweening pretensions of any single idea:

'Government by idea tends to take in everything, to make the whole of society obedient to the idea. Spaces not so governed are unconquered, beyond the border, unconverted, unconvinced, a future danger.'[3]

'Government that is natural, habitual, works more easily. It remains in the hands of average men, that is of men who do not live by ideas. Therefore there is less strain by making government adapt itself to custom. An ideal government, much better, perhaps, would have to be maintained by effort, and imposed by force.'[4]

On the one hand he criticized Döllinger for looking upon the institutions and traditions of history as a 'protection against

[1] See above, p. 210.   [2] Add. MSS., 5670.
[3] Add. MSS., 4941.   [4] Add. MSS., 4953.

219

theories and abstraction',[1] and upon politics as the 'domain of force, interests, and passions'.[2] On the other, he stated it to be the law of the modern world that 'power tends to expand indefinitely, and will transcend all barriers, abroad and at home, until met by superior forces'[3]—forces, not ideas.

He once posed the issue between the English and the French conceptions of liberty in its most abstract form: 'Are politics an attempt to realize ideals, or an endeavour to get advantages within the limits of ethics? Are ethics a purpose or a limit?'[4] The answer came easily: the ultimate ethical principle, liberty, was as much the end of politics as ethics were its means. But this could not satisfy Acton for long. Morality was no single or simple thing, as he would have liked to think. It could aspire to the heights of liberty, conscience and justice, but in that case it could not also have murder as its zero-mark; for it was when the call of liberty, conscience and justice were most insistent that murder was most readily justified. In any concrete, historical problem, the tension between morality as an end and as a means was unmistakable. When the tension became too great to be suffered, Acton generally retreated to the safer, less heroic position in which ethics was a limit of politics and liberty was the time-tested system of checks and balances. This happened in his *Lectures on the French Revolution*, and it is this that makes the work so much more provocative than most of his abstract, philosophical speculations, in which the absolute ethical end, the revolutionary ideal, won out handily over the more modest, temporizing idea of a practical Liberalism. In these lectures, more than anywhere else, can be seen the profound ambivalence that was at the heart of Acton's philosophy.

The man who spoke confidently of a political science whose principles are clear and certain, who cultivated the reputation of a dogmatic moralist prepared to pass unambiguous judgment on the most controversial subjects, and who used the superlative with an abandon perhaps unmatched by any other serious historian, was the victim of contradictions which a less ambitious, less subtle and less complex thinker would never have suffered.

[1] Add. MSS., 4911. [2] Add. MSS., 5644.
[3] *Modern History*, p. 51. [4] Add. MSS., 4916.

IX

RESOLUTION

THE HISTORIAN

THE public recognition enjoyed by Acton in the last years of his life could have done little more than assuage his private sense of loneliness and despair. Belying the superficial tokens of success was the compelling evidence of failure. There was no slow, mellowing maturation of thought, no gradual realization of long cherished dreams, no exultation of triumph. Between youth and maturity there had been an almost complete revolution of spirit, and, oddly enough, it was the mature Acton who invited frustration by setting before himself and the world goals impossible of achievement. The gap between the actuality and the ideal grew rather than diminished in the course of time, until finally no amount of public esteem could bridge it. Yet there were few apparent expressions of bitterness. It is as if he had become reconciled to the moral isolation and futility of which he had complained in the 'eighties, so that the tragedy was shifted from a major to a minor key. The biographer who described his development as comprising three stages, of which 'the first period was the explanation of the second, and both prepared the way for the golden assurance of his final years',[1] could not have chosen a more inept formula. As an historian, as a Catholic, and as a Liberal, Acton was even more removed from the satisfaction of his ideals at the end of his life than at the beginning.

The History of Liberty that was to have been his monument

[1] Mathew, p. 1.

as an historian was never constructed. Only fragments of it can be pieced together from essays and lectures posthumously published and from notes bequeathed to future historians. And the History of Liberty was only one of a score of projects and commitments that went unwritten, ranging from a history of the Popes of the Reformation (in German), to a documentary article on the Inquisition, an essay on the papal conclave of 1550 (both intended for the *English Historical Review*), and an article on the Jesuits solicited by the editors of the *Encyclopaedia Britannica*.[1] A biography of Newman, for which Acton collected a mass of notes,[2] was stillborn, in spite of the change of plans from a volume (or several volumes) to an essay and finally to a modest account for the *Dictionary of National Biography*. On the other hand, the biography of Döllinger fared somewhat better. And it is not generally known that the two-volume *Life and Times of Cardinal Wiseman* by Wilfrid Ward, one of the best sources of information about the Catholic community in Victorian England, owed a good deal of its historical background to information supplied by Acton.[3]

Acton's reticence seemed to govern the publication of his work as well as its initial composition. He yielded to the persistent urging of his friends sufficiently to consent to the publication by Macmillan of a selection of his essays, announced his intention to publish his lectures after he had delivered them two or three times, and agreed to a posthumous edition of his letters to Mary Gladstone. But after selecting the essays for Macmillan (he does not appear to have revised them at all), he soon abandoned the scheme, and although he had delivered his lectures on the French Revolution four times and those on modern history twice, they were not published in his lifetime. The few volumes he has to his credit were all issued posthumously. Without detracting from the intrinsic merit and

[1] Regarding the fate of earlier projects, see above, pp. 20 n., 129–31, 145.
[2] These notes include much valuable information and many insights unfamiliar even to-day. It is especially to be regretted that a collection of Newman's letters to Acton, or more probably excerpts from those letters, once contained among the notes (in Add. MSS., 4987) is now missing.
[3] Maisie Ward, *The Wilfrid Wards and the Transition* (London, 1934), p. 255.

interest of those volumes, it is nevertheless true that the correspondence, lectures and even the essays were the trivia that normally supplement a great historian's great work; they were not a substitute for that work. On this score, Acton did not deceive himself.

Nor was he deluded into believing that the project with which his name has become popularly identified, the *Cambridge Modern History*, was the *chef d'œuvre* worthy of a serious historian. Yet it is this work, in which he appears not as a writer but as an editor, and that only for a short time, by which his fame was established and his talents are customarily judged.

When the syndics of the University approached him, a year after his arrival at Cambridge, to serve as the editor of a co-operative historical enterprise, Acton must already have despaired of completing any of the more ambitious projects he had once entertained. For this reason among others—because he was genuinely convinced of the utility of such a work and because he took seriously the responsibilities of his office—he consented to edit the *Cambridge Modern History*.

In private he described it as the nineteenth-century historian's bequest to the twentieth century.[1] Some of his fondest ideas were brought into play: the idea of a universal history, of a scientific and objective history, and of a history of ideas. He was immoderately optimistic, for a while at any rate, about the combined effect of a 'judicious division of labour'[2] and the exploration of the recently opened archives of Europe: 'We approach the final stage in the conditions of historical learning'; 'all information is within reach, and every problem has become capable of solution'.[3] Man might not yet attain the goal of 'ultimate history', but he would at least have gone beyond 'conventional history'.[4]

[1] Add. MSS., 5699.

[2] Report to the Syndics, p. 4. A limited number of copies of this report (fourteen pages) were printed, one of which is now in the Cambridge University Library. The first page is headed, 'Strictly private and confidential'.

[3] Letter to the contributors, 12 March 1898, reprinted in *Modern History*, p. 315.   [4] Report to the Syndics, p. 4.

In the organization of the work, nations and even chronology were to be subservient to the leading ideas that gave meaning to universal history:

'By Universal History I understand that which is distinct from the combined history of all countries, which is not a rope of sand, but a continuous development, and is not a burden on the memory, but an illumination of the soul. It moves in a succession to which the nations are subsidiary. Their story will be told, not for their own sake, but in reference and subordination to a higher series, according to the time and the degree in which they contribute to the common fortunes of mankind.'[1]

The 'higher series' would include general topics: the Renaissance, the Reformation, the religious wars, absolute monarchy, and revolution. By emphasizing ideas rather than nations, an impartial, almost anonymous history might be achieved, a history revealing no trace of the country, religion or party to which the individual writers might belong. 'Contributors will understand', Acton admonished them, 'that we are established, not under the Meridian of Greenwich, but in Long. 30W; that our Waterloo must be one that satisfies French and English, Germans and Dutch alike; that nobody can tell, without examining the list of authors, where the Bishop of Oxford laid down the pen, and whether Fairbairn or Gasquet, Liebermann or Harrison took it up.'[2]

What Acton conspicuously omitted from his prospectus on the *History* was the question of judgment. Indeed his ideal of impartiality resembles nothing so much as that of Ranke which he had elsewhere so vigorously repudiated. It may be that he now felt it to be a necessary concession to harmony in an enterprise embracing so many men of different persuasions. Or perhaps, with the power of selecting authors, assigning subjects, and recommending methods of treatment, he felt secure in his ability to give unity and meaning to the *History*, to infuse it with a specific moral tone.

If he was relying on his discretionary powers as editor to

---

[1] *Modern History*, p. 317.   [2] ibid., p. 318.

mould the *History* to his fancy, he must have been quickly dis-
illusioned. It was his purpose, for example, to unite 'the moral
and intellectual realm with that of political force' in such a
way that about one-third of the contents would deal with the
history of ideas.[1] But few editors in his position, dependent
upon so many individuals for the execution of his ideas, could
have resisted the pull of conventional political history. He
could not always persuade men of his choosing to accept as-
signments on the *History*, or dictate to those who did accept
the exact terms of their engagement. Nor did he even have
complete initiative of choice with regard to contributors. For
the volume on the French Revolution he refrained from inviting John Morley because he suspected that the Bishop of
Oxford would object, and Henry Morse Stephens because the
syndics did in fact object.[2] Creighton had to retract his promise to contribute the important opening chapter on the
'Legacy of the Middle Ages', and the chapter was never written. In countless other respects, Acton's intentions were
thwarted.

From 1896 to 1901, Acton laboured on the *History*. In April
1901, when only the first volume was in type, he suffered the
paralytic stroke that brought his work to an end. The Romanes
Lecture at Oxford, which he had been invited to deliver, was
cancelled. His Cambridge lectures were withdrawn. The *Cambridge Modern History* passed to other hands. On 19 June 1902
Acton died.

In the *History*, as in so many of Acton's ventures, there was
a lamentable disparity of effort and result. For five years, he
had devoted to it all the time that could be spared from his
teaching duties. He wrote, in his own hand, hundreds of
letters to prospective contributors and to his principal con-
sultants, Creighton and R. L. Poole, mediated between the
syndics and the authors, ironed out difficulties with his own
staff, and read quantities of English and foreign publications
for bibliographical purposes and on the chance of finding the
obscure but perfect man for some difficult subject. Yet the

[1] Report to the Syndics, p. 12.
[2] Acton to Creighton, 26 November 1896, Add. MSS., 6871.

massiveness of the enterprise defied his attempts at organization. He had undertaken the work in the hope that it would compensate, at least partly, for his abortive History of Liberty, and in the illusion that it would represent his ideas. It did neither.

A more substantial contribution to his History of Liberty and a more certain means of promoting his ideas would have been the composition of an original work of much less ambitious dimensions. But the *Cambridge Modern History* itself precluded this, if nothing else did. In addition to his other roles, Acton had assumed those of bureaucrat and public relations man. Only the most indefatigable scholar or writer could have survived such a union. It is no wonder that the writer in Acton, a weak member at best, was completely swamped. He had originally intended to make more than an editorial contribution to the *History*: he was to have written the introduction to the series, the final chapter on contemporary England, and, upon Creighton's default, the opening chapter. When the first volume was set in type, however, before the onset of his illness, his chapters were missing. Added to the great pressure of editorial work was the familiar reluctance to write without having read everything remotely pertaining to the subject, or to say less than might be said about it. The *Cambridge Modern History*, which is sometimes seen as the highest attainment of Acton, can more significantly be taken as a deterrent to his real work. A later Regius Professor of Modern History, G. N. Clark (now Provost of Oriel College, Oxford), suspected that the *History* 'weighed him down'.[1] Not only did he fail to accomplish what he had set himself, but he even ceased writing for the *English Historical Review*, to which he had formerly been a regular contributor.

If the *History* was no satisfactory substitute for the more original work of which Acton was capable, it was a work of great merit in its own right. Among its contributors were some of England's best historians (the Continent and America were poorly represented): Lady Blennerhassett, J. B. Bury, M.

---

[1] G. N. Clark, 'Origin of the Cambridge Modern History', *Cambridge Historical Journal*, VIII (1945), 63.

Creighton, A. M. Fairbairn, J. Gairdner, G. P. Gooch, F. W. Maitland, C. W. Oman, W. A. Phillips, A. F. Pollard, G. W. Prothero, J. H. Rose and H. W. V. Temperley. It was certainly not the last word in history, as Acton knew it would not be, and in some respects it has been superseded. Generations of critics have delighted in cataloguing its faults: repetitiousness, errors of fact and eccentricities of interpretation, a pronounced English bias, an inadequate treatment of social and economic affairs, essays of disparate length, an over-abundance of details obscuring the general ideas, and no pervasive unity of theme. Yet it remains even to-day one of the best works of its kind ever attempted. Had Acton been more modest in his ambition, there would have been less temptation to carp. One critic expressed his resentment by dubbing it 'Lord Acton's Encyclical' and sneering at the idea of this sacred college of historical pundits from which there issued solemn decrees on all controversial subjects. That it was not truly 'Lord Acton's Encyclical', however, was perhaps its main fault, for each writer regarded himself as a pontiff in his own domain and extended to Acton only the courtesy title of Pope.

More serious was the criticism directed against the very idea of a co-operative historical work. Arnold J. Toynbee, himself a celebrant of universal history, has portrayed Acton as the victim of a sterile industrialism, a sacrifice to the modern idols of the division of labour and the exploitation of new materials. He has compared him with one of the finest of German historians, Theodor Mommsen, who similarly 'degenerated' into an editor of Latin inscriptions and an encyclopedist of Roman law. Mommsen had the advantage over Acton that at least one great work, *The History of the Roman Republic*, had been safely committed to paper by the time he was forty. Acton, 'one of the greatest minds among modern Western historians',[1] lacked that fortune or daring, and industrialism was permitted to paralyse his creative power at its source. Had he been a contemporary of Voltaire, Gibbon or Turgot, he would have written his History of Liberty, Toynbee was confident. In-

[1] Arnold J. Toynbee, *A Study of History* (6 vols.; London, 1934), I, 46.

stead it was Acton's tragic fate to become known only as the editor of the *Cambridge Modern History*.[1]

In an excess of sympathy, Toynbee tried to shift the burden of Acton's failure to the 'spirit of the times'.[2] In this, he was less than kind to Acton and quite unjust, for by making Acton a victim of a petty delusion, he robbed him of the grandeur of his ideal. Acton was not taken in by the idea of the division of labour any more than Toynbee himself was. The division of labour, for him, was only a second-best expedient when nothing else was feasible. He had as much contempt as Toynbee for the men of 'diligent mediocrity'[3] who never wandered outside the prescribed boundaries of some small, self-imposed task. His ideal historian possessed both knowledge and imagination in formidable quantities, and brought to the service of a grand philosophy a familiarity with masses of lowly monographs and documents. It is idle to bemoan the fact that Acton was not a Voltaire, a Gibbon, or a Turgot. He had hoped to be much more than any of them, to inaugurate a new era in history, where the techniques of a Ranke would be wedded to the vision of an Augustine, an Augustine with a new eschatology in which the plan of divine salvation would be identical with the history of human freedom. It was no spirit of the times that defeated Acton. It was his own restless, dissatisfied, ambitious mind, content with no small part of the whole, and for which no whole was quite good enough. To deplore the fact that he was not an eighteenth-century historian was to make of him not a tragic figure but a pathetic one.

THE CATHOLIC

The career of the Catholic, like that of the historian drew out to a quiet, anti-climactic end. The tensions and difficul-

[1] The most recent criticism of the *Cambridge Modern History* and Acton from this point of view came from the historian Max Beloff in a radio speech in England, in which he fixed the date of 'the decadence of English historical writing' as 12 March 1898—the date of Acton's letter to the contributors of the *History* ('A Challenge to Historians', *Listener*, IX [1949], 816).

[2] Toynbee, p. 46.

[3] 'German Schools of History', *Historical Essays*, p. 371.

ties of the previous years persisted, but remained below the surface of behaviour. It was thus, without apologies or complaints but also without enthusiasm, that Acton had permitted the History of Liberty to make way for the *Cambridge Modern History*. In the same rather weary spirit, he arrived at a *modus vivendi* with the Church.

It was with the Church and not with its dogmas *per se* that Acton had to come to terms. He was completely at ease with the dogmatic, sacramental religion of orthodox Catholicism. The dogmas, he recognized, were not the sufficient instrument of social salvation, of liberty and morality, but for himself, at least, he was certain that they were the necessary means of spiritual salvation. During the polemical days of the *Home and Foreign Review*, he once told his friend, Sir Mountstuart Grant Duff: 'I am not conscious that I ever in my life held the slightest shadow of a doubt about any dogma of the Catholic Church.'[1] Grant Duff, in his memoirs, expressed his astonishment that a man who was versed in all matters of theological controversy, history and philosophy could be so confident of the truth of dogmas. Of his absolute sincerity, however, he had no doubt. 'His mind', he concluded, 'worked in a way totally incomprehensible to me.'[2] Other friends marvelled at this strange union of intellectual scepticism and religious faith. Oscar Browning, a colleague at Cambridge, recalled Acton's claim that there was no doctrine of the Church which he had the 'slightest difficulty in believing'.[3] 'Believing,' of course, might carry a special connotation for Acton. To believe in the doctrine of papal Infallibility, for example, was to have faith that ultimately that doctrine would be reconciled with the true doctrines of antiquity, which meant in this case that it would fall into disuse. The harsh mind of the secularist might interpret this as a polite way of implying disbelief; the Liberal Catholic would see it as a legitimate exercise of the doctrine of development and as evidence of genuine religious piety. But it was seldom that a dogma required such strenuous theological cogitation. Most dogmas of the Church Acton could accept in much the same spirit as the untutored layman.

Because Acton was a Liberal Catholic (although privately

[1] Grant Duff, *Out of the Past*, II, 195.   [2] ibid.   [3] *Browning*, p. 16.

he distinguished himself from the French school of that name), it did not follow, as has sometimes been suggested, that he would have found himself in the ranks of the Modernists had he lived a few years longer. Modernism, a Catholic reform movement condemned by Pope Pius X in the encyclical *Pascendi* of 1907, attempted to do what Liberal Catholicism had never done: to reinterpret religion in a naturalistic sense. The error of the Modernists, Acton would have said, as he said of Renan, was that they tried to reduce history to science: 'History gives its due place to religion. Science moves in a world without it. That is why, on the whole, history is the refuge of religion in a scientific age.'[1] A good many miracles crumbled under the probing fingers of historians, Acton was ready to admit, but the idea of miracle did not, for each miracle was an historical fact to be judged like any other fact, not to be denied out of hand. Where Alfred Loisy, the great leader of the Modernists, thought that the logic of science required him to disbelieve the divinity of Christ, Acton objected to the intrusion of the arbitrary prejudices of scientific naturalism into a situation calling for historical objectivity and religious insight. He would have agreed with their critics that the Modernists, by reducing Christ to mythical or human dimensions and by converting dogmas into symbols and sacraments into signs, were not liberalizing religion so much as capitulating to irreligion. With the Modernists, Acton would have gone so far: like George Tyrrell, another leader of the movement, he would have said that Rome was at the cross-roads, that it was time to discard the excess baggage of antiquated philosophy, falsified history and immoral practices with which Catholicism was encumbered. But he would not have accompanied Tyrrell in his quest for a new philosophical interpretation of dogma, grace and the sacraments. For this reason, Tyrrell, in an article reviewing Acton's early career, regretfully concluded: 'With Acton history was irresistible, philosophy could be discounted.'[2]

The religious revival that seems to be taking shape to-day is also tempted to invoke the name and authority of Acton, but

[1] Add. MSS., 5689.
[2] M. D. Petre, *Life of George Tyrrell* (2 vols.; London, 1912), II, 359.

again without success. 'Principles make a strong man, maxims a wise man, doctrines a complete man,' Acton once noted;[1] like the Modernists of the early years of the century, many of the recent religious converts fall before the last qualification. The Modernists, come to emancipate religion, and the recent converts, come to revive it, share a common incapacity for belief. Acton would have said of them, as he said of the Biblical critics of his own time, that they were guilty of confusing religious feeling with religious belief.[2] He would have had no more in common with those of the recent converts who cling to religion for utilitarian reasons than with those Modernists who clung to it for sentimental reasons. Acton's religion was not the sociological contrivance of those for whom faith is the only cement capable of holding together a frail and tottering society, nor the refuge of unhappy aesthetes fleeing from the barren halls of science; nor was it even the rational act of will by which men, seeking to give depth to their spiritual experiences, resolve to act as if they believe in the truth of religious dogmas which, in another age, were implicitly and spontaneously believed. What so many ostensibly religious men to-day have to wrest from the intellect by violence, for the satisfaction of more urgent needs, Acton gave up naturally and effortlessly. The current religious revival can find in him rebuke more than sympathy.

For all of his piety—because of his piety, he would have said—Acton was less patient with the failings of the Church than most men who did not accept its dogmas as literal truths, or accepted them for the ulterior reasons of aesthetic gratification or social expediency. Others could find excuses for an Inquisition; Acton could not. It took Tyrrell many years to come to the point that Acton had occupied since his youth, to feel, as he confessed to Friedrich von Hügel, 'more and more, with Lord Acton, that the principle of Ultramontanism is profoundly immoral and unchristian and, in essence, pagan'.[3]

[1] Add. MSS., 5684. The epigram was repeated on another card in the same group with the word 'good' in place of 'strong'.
[2] Add. MSS., 5019.
[3] 2 April 1904, M. D. Petre, *Von Hügel and Tyrrell* (London, 1937), p. 151.

Other Modernists never arrived at this point. It was von Hügel who piously assured Wilfrid Ward that he had never held in his hands a number of 'that terrible *Home and Foreign Review*',[1] and who confessed to Mary Gladstone that he found Acton's 'direct and absorbing anti-Ultramontanism' to be no less disagreeable than Ultramontanism itself.[2]

If Hügel, himself touched with the suspicion of heresy, could be so little sympathetic to Acton, it is no wonder that others supposed him to be either fatuous in his piety or frivolous in his indignation. To those who could not understand how he could respect the principle of papal authority and at the same time revile the Popes, as he did at the Vatican Council, Acton explained that he meant to give the Popes whatever authority and credit was their due, but no more: 'Let everything be conceded to them that is compatible with their avowed character and traditions; but see that you do nothing that could shelter them from the scorn and execration of mankind.'[3] Acton had good reason for saying that there was nothing heretical in this attitude. Catholic theologians of whose orthodoxy there is no suspicion have applied to the Pope the teaching of Aquinas on kingship, arguing that it is legitimate to disobey a Pope who orders the commission of a sin or passes a decree subversive of the Church. Generally, to be sure, they hasten to add that this eventuality has never come to pass and that no Pope has ever forfeited his right to obedience. But the implication remains: if the authority of a Pope must be justified by some more ultimate principle, it can be controverted by that principle. It took Acton to transform into an urgent reality what had been conceded only as a remote theoretical possibility.

It was not the Inquisition alone, or the other scandalous episodes of persecution and intolerance, that provoked Acton's wrath. It was every effort of the Church, however subtle, to impose itself as an exclusive and absolute authority. So far was he from a utilitarian conception of religion that where others

[1] Wilfrid Ward, *W. G. Ward and the Catholic Revival*, p. 365.
[2] 4 June 1904, *Selected Letters of Von Hügel, 1896–1924*, ed. Bernard Holland (London, 1927), p. 127.
[3] Acton to Lady Blennerhassett, undated, *Correspondence*, p. 56.

welcomed the Church as an instrument of social stability, he distrusted it in that role. While some men, not themselves capable of a genuine submission of faith, would have liked to legislate such a submission for others, Acton, himself a devout believer, insisted upon the freedom of others to disbelieve. He had no sympathy with Protestantism as a religion, but he respected it as a community. His own membership in the Catholic Church, he said, was dearer to him than life, but he defended the right of others to separate themselves from it. During Döllinger's last illness, Acton urged Johann Friedrich to respect Döllinger's wish that the last rites be administered by an Old Catholic rather than a Roman priest.[1]

Without having to concede or conceal a single point in his indictment of the Church, Acton lived out his life at Cambridge undisturbed by quarrels with the hierarchy or threats of excommunication. Leo XIII had succeeded Pius IX at Rome, and Catholicism had settled down to a less turbulent existence. Acton had no exaggerated idea of the strength of Leo's Liberalism. If he found cause for praise in the opening of the Vatican library to Protestants, he found matter for blame in the papal condemnation of Victor Hugo's *Les Misérables*. As long as Roman institutions and canon law remained essentially unchanged, it was to be expected that Acton would be a very reserved admirer of the papacy, however gentle might be the hands of the reigning Pope.

The English hierarchy, taking its cue from the Pope, was eager to be conciliatory. Cardinal Vaughan was no less Ultramontane than his predecessor, Manning, but he was considerably more politic. Perhaps because Acton had demonstrated in his own person that Liberalism did not mean impiety, perhaps because his position made him too valuable an asset to trifle with, Vaughan took the initiative in bringing about a *rapprochement*. Congratulating Acton upon his Cambridge appointment, he made it a point to express confidence in his fidelity to the Church. At one of the great affairs presided over by the cardinal, the laying of the foundation stone of Westminster Cathedral, Acton was present at Vaughan's special invitation,

[1] Meyrick, p. 288.

and as an honoured guest he took the floor at the public luncheon following the ceremony.

The goodwill that seemed to surround Acton in the last years of his life was a triumph of good manners. A single discordant voice was enough to upset it. Between Acton and an unreformed Church there could be at most an uneasy truce, and the truce was broken, or so it seemed to some ardent churchmen, with the posthumous publication, in 1904, of his correspondence with Mary Gladstone. The letters (published with Acton's consent) included some of the harshest abuse he had ever levelled against the Church. With the appearance of the volume, it was no longer possible to take shelter, as many Catholics had, in the polite fiction that his conflicts with the Church were a forgotten episode of exuberant youth.

While some Catholics threatened to banish him posthumously from the Catholic communion, others took up the job of rehabilitating him. Of the latter, Dom Francis Gasquet, the historian of the English Reformation, was the most successful. In 1906 Gasquet published a collection of Acton's early letters, written in the years of the *Rambler* and *Home and Foreign Review*. How judiciously he chose and edited those letters (they were not printed in full) may be guessed by their inoffensiveness; what criticism of the Church remained was such as any Catholic might voice without imputation of bad faith.[1] The editors of the Catholic weekly, the *Tablet*, seized upon Gasquet's volume as a vindication of Acton's orthodoxy: 'The heady wine, as some thought it, of the *Rambler* would be but the lees of current polemics. . . . All Catholics now alive have the benefit of Lord Acton's having lived and learned before them. He goes to the general credit of Catholicism; he is a great asset.'[2] But not all were so easily won over. Father Herbert Thurston, a Jesuit, was indignant that the *Tablet* should so far betray its trust to the faithful as to ignore Acton's many

[1] Since this was written, the originals of these letters have been discovered and examined, and the supposition that Gasquet exercised considerably more than the customary editorial discretion has been amply confirmed. The re-publication of this correspondence, in full, is much to be desired. See A. Watkin and H. Butterfield, 'Gasquet and the Acton-Simpson Correspondence', *Cambridge Historical Journal*, X (1950), 75–105.

[2] *Tablet*, 22 September 1906.

public indiscretions, his repeated affronts to ecclesiastical authority, and his constant flirtations with heresy. For weeks the controversy between Thurston and Gasquet dragged on, snowballing until it involved personal friends of Acton and readers of the magazine only casually familiar with his name. A chaplain at Cambridge wrote testifying to his piety and contributing picturesque details of Acton carrying the pole of the canopy over the Blessed Sacrament in public procession, of his regular and punctual attendance at Mass every Sunday, of his final illness when, forbidden to move, he nevertheless sprang up and knelt to receive Holy Communion. Baron von Hügel added other pious touches, and insisted that although the correspondence with Mary Gladstone did not make edifying reading, neither did it contradict the fact of Acton's devoutness.

When Thurston carried the dispute into the *Catholic World*, Acton's son, the second Baron Acton, entered the lists with an open letter in *The Times*. The *Letters to Mary Gladstone*, young Acton explained, had appeared without the final approval of the family (he said nothing about the approval of his father), and the Gasquet volume had been intended to correct the unfortunate impression left by the earlier letters. Apparently to confirm the fact of his father's piety, he added: 'In the last years of his life, when he was stricken by illness, and during what was almost our last conversation, he solemnly adjured me not to rash-judge others as he had done, but to take care to make allowance for human weakness. And I was present at his farewell meeting with Cardinal Newman, the most moving scene I have ever witnessed.'[1]

It is difficult to know just what to make of these sentences. If Acton had meant to caution his son not only against rash judgments but against severe ones as well, it would have been a remarkable confession of retreat on his part. This was undoubtedly the way his son interpreted it. But the son's understanding of the father may have been faulty, as it evidently was in the episode of the farewell meeting with Newman. Whatever emotions the sight of the fragile, withered Cardinal, once a storm centre of history, may have aroused in Acton, they did

[1] London *Times*, 28 October 1906.

not signify respect, or sympathy, or even personal affection; Newman remained for him a Tory and Ultramontane who stood for religious persecution, political absolutism and intellectual sophistry. That his son apparently did not see it so makes his testimony on the first point suspect. Could Acton have meant not that one should make allowance for human weakness in the generally understood sense of making excuses for it, but rather that one should be prepared for weakness and always on guard against it? Since there is nothing, apart from this one casual report of a conversation held almost five years earlier, to suggest such a dramatic repudiation of his most cherished principle, it may be supposed that the son had misinterpreted the father. This is not to detract from the son's main point, the religious sincerity of Acton, but only to keep in mind the many shades and shadows in the picture. Acton is not easily cast as the subject of a study in black and white.

From the perspective of many years, it is possible to distinguish between what we owe to the memory of Acton's religious faith and what we owe to historical honesty and to the memory of his own honesty. In the course of the controversy in the *Tablet*, Acton's defenders sometimes overreached themselves in their effort not only to establish his orthodoxy but to pose him in an image of orthodoxy that would be agreeable to Ultramontanes. Thus it was falsely claimed that not Acton but some other editor had decided to assign the chapter on the Inquisition to Henry C. Lea, the American historian who was so critical of the Catholic Church. Lea had in his possession letters in which Acton had urged him, as the 'one indicated and predestined writer', to contribute the 'most critical and cardinal chapter' of the *History*.[1] When Acton's son released his communication to *The Times*, Lea decided not to publish those letters, because, he said, he did not want to jeopardize the son's 'little piece of filial piety'.[2] A later generation can afford to discriminate between filial piety and religious piety.

[1] 19 December 1896, Edward Potts Cheyney, 'On the Life and Works of Henry Charles Lea', *Proceedings of the American Philosophical Society*, L (1911).
[2] Edward Sculley Bradley, *Henry Charles Lea* (Philadelphia, 1931), p. 363.

THE LIBERAL

The poet William Butler Yeats once complained that few writers took their beliefs as seriously as he did, applying them to literature and politics and letting the chips fall where they might. 'Lord Acton', he illustrated, 'once said that he believed in a personal devil, but as there is nothing about it in the *Cambridge Universal History* which he planned he was a liar. My belief must go into what I write, even if I estrange friends.'[1]

It is a provocative idea to think of the devil in the *Cambridge Modern History*: instead of being instructed to throw off the shackles of nation, race and creed, contributors would have been exhorted to cast out the evil one from their midst. Acton would have liked nothing better. Unfortunately Cambridge was a conservative, phlegmatic institution, where the existence of the devil was perhaps secretly suspected but rarely discussed in public. Acton had to forgo the pleasure of solving, in such agreeable fashion, the problem of the dramatic unity of the *History*. It may have gratified Yeats to know, however, that he had already estranged his best friend and kept others at a distance the better to war upon the devil. His notes for the *History of Liberty* include an excerpt from Marlowe's 'Faustus':

> 'Hell hath no limits, nor is circumscribed
> In one self place; but where we are is hell,
> And where hell is, there must we ever be.'[2]

It was, in fact, Acton's obsession with the devil that establishes him in one political tradition and removes him from another. There is a kind of Liberal who is said to revere God but respect the devil. In that epigram Acton stands defined. 'Liberty', he noted, 'is so holy a thing that God was forced to permit Evil, that it might exist.'[3] Strangely enough, those of his contemporaries who were most notoriously sceptical of the reality of God were most firmly persuaded of the reality of evil. John Stuart Mill, who would have liked nothing better than to endow humanity with the attributes of a god, was

---

[1] Joseph Hone, *W. B. Yeats* (New York, 1943), p. 505.
[2] Add. MSS., 4938.   [3] Add. MSS., 5691.

frustrated by the knowledge that 'ordinary human nature is so poor a thing'.[1] And physical nature, the more thoughtful of the secular Liberals were ready to admit, was no more edifying a sight. Mill complained that the ordinary course of Nature was replete with all the characteristics that in human beings would be most abhorrent, and T. H. Huxley, in his famous Romanes lecture on 'Evolution and Ethics', put an end to the still prevalent illusion that naturalists look benignly upon Nature. Progress, Huxley said, meant not that men should imitate Nature but that they should liberate themselves from it by substituting for the cosmic process an ethical one.

On this score Acton had more in common with Mill and Huxley than with many a more sanguine religious thinker or more conventional Liberal. Where the Liberal born of the Enlightenment derived his philosophy of liberty from the perfectibility of man and the beneficence of Nature, Acton derived his from the corruptibility of man and the maleficence of Nature. Corruptibility, not corruption, Acton cautioned, for we should think well of any particular man until we are compelled to think ill of him. He hastened to add, however, that we must be prepared for that 'compulsion'.[2] This was particularly true of those who figured prominently in history, for few men exposed to history emerged untainted. 'Most assuredly, now as heretofore, the Men of the Time are, in most cases, unprincipled, and act from motives of interest, of passion, of prejudice, cherished and unchecked, of selfish hope or unworthy fear'.[3] The historian and the priest shared this bitter knowledge: 'No priest, accustomed to the Confessional, and a fortiori, no historian, thinks well of human nature.'[4]

The great temptation of history to which most men succumbed, it was apparent to many of Acton's contemporaries, was power. It had taken the shattering experiences of the French Revolution, the Napoleonic wars and the nationalist revolutions to explode the illusion of the Enlightenment that power itself was ethically neutral, that its potential for good

[1] Mill, 'The Claims of Labour', *Dissertations and Discussions* (5 vols.; New York, 1874), II, 288.
[2] 25 January 1882, *Letters to Mary Gladstone* (1st ed.), p. 228.
[3] ibid.   [4] Add. MSS., 4908.

was as great as for bad, that a benevolent despot was the best of all possible rulers. Henry Adams, Jacob Burckhardt, François Guizot, Alexis de Tocqueville, Thomas Carlyle, Henry Maine and Herbert Spencer are the more familiar names chosen from the roster of philosophers, historians and even statesmen who warned that the will to power is insensibly transformed into a will to evil. The one name to-day with whom this theme is invariably associated is Acton. His remark to Creighton, 'Power tends to corrupt, and absolute power corrupts absolutely,' generally quoted in its shop-worn form of 'All power corrupts and absolute power corrupts absolutely,' has become the tag by which both the idea and the man are identified.

By this maxim, Acton takes his place squarely in the tradition of political and philosophical pessimism. His pessimism worked its way into every corner of his thought, into his politics, religion and history, and it took on every emotional tone from passionate indignation through exasperation, despair, and what seemed to be a world-weary resignation. The spirit of moral indignation prevailed in his lectures, a subdued, quiescent, melancholy in his notes:

'Use of history—no surprises. He [the historian] has seen all this before. He knows what constant and invariable forces will resist the truth and the Higher Purpose. What weakness, division, excess, will damage the better cause. The splendid plausibility of error, the dazzling attractiveness of sin. And by what adjustment to inferior motives good causes succeed.'[1]

'History makes men understand that causes have very bad records and dark phases. They do not expect them to be practically what they are theoretically. They do not connect good ideas with good men. They do not believe that knowledge is virtue.'[2]

'History is not a web woven with innocent hands. Among all the causes which degrade and demoralize men, power is the most constant and the most active.'[3]

What saved Acton from the unredeemed bleakness of pessimism and gave meaning to his indignation was his refusal to

[1] Add. MSS., 4907.   [2] Add. MSS., 4908.   [3] Add. MSS., 5011.

succumb to philosophical or historical determinism. Man, he believed, for all his propensity to evil, was a free agent capable of choosing the good, and although original sin was always there to dog his steps, it did not always succeed in tripping him up. The forces of evil were 'constant and invariable', but so were 'the truth and the Higher Purpose' with which they had to contend. If the presumption of evil was in all good causes, the presumption of the good was in the very idea of evil. The Fall itself attested to the existence of God, and God attested to the source of goodness in man, his conscience. Power corrupted, conscience redeemed; history was a tug-of-war between the two, with tyranny and freedom as the stakes.[1] With one last twist, Acton took the idea of conscience out of the reign of metaphysics and placed it within the province of politics. While conscience itself was the metaphysical warrant for liberty, the conflict of consciences was its empirical security: 'Our conscience exists and acts for ourselves. It exists in each of us. It is limited by the consciences of others. . . . Therefore it tends to restrict authority and to enlarge liberty. It is the law of self-government.'[2]

Acton, then, was a pessimist with a difference. Santayana has said that of all systems an optimistic one is the most oppressive, for it would be a bitter mockery if everything in this best of all possible worlds was a necessary evil. But an unrelieved pessimism would be no less oppressive. To the religious thinker it would be surely just as much a mockery if this were the worst of all possible worlds and everything in it a necessary evil. Acton was a firm believer in a personal devil, but he was also a firm believer in a personal God.

Because he was a pessimist of this special order, he was also a Liberal with a difference. Political pessimism of the ordinary variety lends itself to a philosophy of *Realpolitik*. If man was created in the image of Hobbes, it is reasoned, he deserves to be ruled in the manner of Machiavelli. Or if not with the heavy hand of a tyrant, then with the hard heart of a *laissez-faire* state, in which beast is permitted to devour beast until there emerges out of the chaos some kind of expediential order, some provisional balance of forces. But Acton was a pessimist

[1] Add. MSS., 5552, 4929, 4901.   [2] Add. MSS., 4901.

who never broke faith with his own exalted vision of what man should be. Liberty was no mere social arrangement recommended by its convenience. It was no contrivance designed to accommodate the imperfections of man. On the contrary, it was the highest ideal of man, the reflection of his divinity. T. S. Eliot once said that the Catholic should have high ideals, indeed absolute ideals, and only moderate expectations. Acton had the highest of ideals and the most modest of expectations.

BIBLIOGRAPHY

GENERAL REMARKS

IT was not until 1935, thirty-three years after Acton's death that the first full-length study of Acton appeared. It was fitting that this mark of recognition should have come from Germany, for in his own life it was Germany rather than England that had originally stimulated his intellectual curiosity and had rewarded him with his first honours. It was unfortunate, however, that Ulrich Noack's *Geschichtswissenschaft und Wahrheit* and his *Katholizität und Geistesfreiheit* of the following year (both published in Frankfort) should have been so steeped in the special philosophical and sociological tradition represented by Dilthey, Weber, Troeltsch and Meinecke. Because Acton was primarily an historian and only secondarily a philosopher of history, his philosophy was rather a series of profound insights into historical truths than a steady, systematic and unified vision of a single truth. It is difficult enough to find in Acton's work of any one period a consistent scheme of thought; it is even more hazardous to try to reconstruct, as Noack does, a closed philosophy from the whole body of his work, from the early writings of the empirical Conservative to the later writings of the doctrinaire Liberal. Often it is not Acton who speaks through the pages of Noack so much as Noack's great masters, and there is sometimes a strange disparity of tone between the mass of quotations culled from Acton's essays and notes and the running commentary linking them together. Some of these defects are partly corrected in the more recent work of Noack, *Politik als Sicherung der Freiheit* (Frankfort, 1947). Here there is an occasional attempt to distinguish between the young and the mature Acton. Too often, however, Noack is still disposed to overlook contradictions and inconsistencies in his hero. Acton's first biographer proved to be guilty not of too little sympathy but of an excess of sympathy.

The next work to appear on Acton, F. E. Lally's *As Lord Acton Says* (Newport [R. I.], 1942), is a far less ambitious affair. It consists of a collection of essays on several phases of Acton's life, accompanied by lengthy excerpts from his writings. The work is useful for its straightforward, factual information and, more important, because it brings together passages, largely from his early journal contributions, which have not been reprinted and are not generally available in America. It does not, however, attempt a serious analysis of his ideas, a project which could not have been executed without consulting Acton's valuable manuscripts and notes on deposit at the Cambridge University Library.

A more interpretive but far less reliable study is that by Monsignor David Mathew, *Acton: The Formative Years* (London, 1945). Mathew set himself the interesting task of examining the background and early life of the historian. All too often, however, the background he examines is not that of Acton particularly but of nineteenth-century Catholicism and even nineteenth-century culture in general. Sections on Naples in the early part of the century, on the old Catholic squirearchy of England, or on the German Catholic world of the eighteenth century, feebly conclude with the comment that Acton did not, after all, inhabit these worlds. On the other hand, the significant events of his early life, his education and novitiate in journalism, are either quickly dismissed by the author or, which is worse, are distorted by numerous errors, misunderstandings and gaps of knowledge. Professor Döllinger, undoubtedly the most important single influence in Acton's early life, occupies less space than the architecture of the great houses of the eighteenth and nineteenth centuries and the physical impressions of the leading cities of Europe. What discussion there is of Döllinger is concerned with trivialities of his costume, eating habits and furnishings, but with few of the spiritual and intellectual qualities that first attracted and then repelled Acton. There are long, often pointless quotations from the memoirs of casual acquaintances, but not a single reference to the three-volume biography of Döllinger. There are citations from the manuscripts at Cambridge, but some of the crucial documents related to Acton's early years are not in evidence. The assertion that Acton remained throughout life a faithful disciple of Burke, a 'Conservative-believing Whig', is typical of Mathew's cavalier treatment of his subject.

For some reason, Acton has fared better at the hands of essayists than biographers. An excellent short study is that by G. P. Gooch in *History and Historians in the Nineteenth Century* (New York, 1913). Crane Brinton, in his *English Political Thought in the Nineteenth Century* (London, 1933), has a good summary of Acton's political ideas. A more perceptive and critical description of his intellectual evolution is Herbert Butterfield's *Lord Acton*, a pamphlet issued by the Historical Association (London, 1948). In my introduction to a collection of Acton's essays, *Freedom and Power* (Boston, 1948), I have tried to suggest some of the motifs of his thought.

SELECTED BIBLIOGRAPHY

A complete bibliography of Acton's writing has recently been compiled by Bert F. Hoselitz for the collection of Acton's essays, *Freedom and Power*. Only one addition need be made to that bibliography. The first item listed under 'The following articles appeared in the *Rambler, New Series*' should be: ' "Bossuet", X, part 54 (June 1858).'

The volumes of Acton's essays, lectures and correspondence are listed here only for convenience in referring back to the text. For all of Acton's other writings, the reader is referred to the bibliography in *Freedom and Power*.

This bibliography includes only those books and articles referred to in the text and footnotes, with the addition of several others which have been particularly useful. Of greatest value is an item which is worthy of its own catalogue: the mass of notes and manuscripts comprising the Acton Collection and housed in the Anderson Room of the Cambridge University Library.

ACTON JOHN EMERICH EDWARD DALBERG, 1st Baron. *Essays on Freedom and Power*. Edited by Gertrude Himmelfarb. Boston, 1948.

Historical Essays and Studies. Edited by J. N. Figgis and R. V. Laurence. London, 1908.

History of Freedom. Edited by Figgis and Laurence. London, 1907.

Lectures on the French Revolution. Edited by Figgis and Laurence. London, 1910.

Lectures on Modern History. Edited by Figgis and Laurence. London, 1906.

Letters to Mary, Daughter of the Rt. Hon. W. E. Gladstone. Edited by Herbert Paul. London, 1904. (2d ed. revised. London, 1913).

Lord Acton and His Circle. Edited by Francis A. Gasquet. London, 1906.

Selections from the Correspondence of the First Lord Acton. Edited by Figgis and Laurence. London, 1917.

ACTON, RICHARD MAXIMILIAN DALBERG, 2d Baron. Letter to the editor, *Nation and Athenaeum*, XXXII (1922), 194.

Letter to the editor, *The Times* (London), 28 October 1906.

ARNOLD, MATTHEW. *Essays Literary and Critical*. Everyman ed. London, 1938.

AUCHMUTY, JAMES J. 'Acton's Election as an Irish Member of Parliament', *English Historical Review*, LXI (1946), 394–405.

BELOFF, MAX. 'A Challenge to Historians', *Listener* (London), IX (1949), 816–18.

BLENNERHASSETT, CHARLOTTE. 'Acton', *Biographisches Jahrbuch und deutscher Nekrolog*, VII (1902), 16–22.
'The Late Lord Acton', *Edinburgh Review*, CXCVII (1903), 501–34.
'Lord Acton', *Deutsche Rundschau*, CXXII (1905), 64–92.
BLENNERHASSETT, W. L. 'Acton: 1834–1902', *Dublin Review*, CXCIV (1934), 169–88.
BRADLEY, EDWARD SCULLEY. *Henry Charles Lea*. Oxford, 1932.
BRINTON, CRANE. *English Political Thought in the Nineteenth Century*. London, 1933.
'Lord Acton's Philosophy of History', *Harvard Theological Review*, XII (1919), 84–112.
BROWNING, OSCAR. *Memories of Later Years*. London, 1923.
Memories of Sixty Years. London, 1910.
'Personal Recollections of Sir John Seeley and Lord Acton', *Albany Review*, II (1908), 548–56.
BROWNSON, HENRY A. *Orestes A. Brownson's Middle Life*. Detroit, 1899.
BRYCE, JAMES. 'The Letters of Lord Acton', *North American Review*, CLXXVIII (1904), 698–710.
'Lord Acton', *Proceedings of the British Academy*, I (1903–4), 277–82.
Studies in Contemporary Biography. London, 1903.
BURKE, EDMUND. *Works and Correspondence*. 8 vols. London, 1852. Acton's annotated copies.
Works. 2 vols. London, 1842. Acton's annotated copies.
BURY, J. B. *History of the Papacy in the Nineteenth Century*. London, 1930.
BUTLER, EDWARD CUTHBERT. *Life and Times of Bishop Ullathorne*. 2 vols. London, 1926.
Vatican Council. 2 vols. London, 1930.
BUTTERFIELD, HERBERT. 'Journal of Lord Acton: Rome, 1857', *Cambridge Historical Journal*, VIII (1946), 186–204.
Lord Acton. ('Pamphlets of the English Historical Association', No. G9). London, 1948.
Review of David Mathew's *Acton: the Formative Years*, in *English Historical Review*, LXI (1946), 414.
Whig Interpretation of History. London, 1931.

Cambridge Modern History: an Account of its Origin, Authorship and Production. Cambridge, 1907.
CHEYNEY, EDWARD POTTS. 'On the Life and Works of Henry Charles Lea', *Proceedings of the American Philosophical Society*, L (1911), v–xxiv.
CLARK, G. N. 'Origin of the Cambridge Modern History', *Cambridge Historical Journal*, VIII (1945), 57–64.
COULTON, G. G. 'Mistaken Ascription to Acton?' *English Historical Review*, XLVI (1931), 460.
Papal Infallibility. London, 1932.
CRAVEN, AUGUSTUS. *Life of Lady Georgiana Fullerton*. Translated by H. J. Coleridge. London, 1888.
Récit d'une soeur. 2 vols. Paris, 1892.

CREIGHTON, LOUISE. *Life and Letters of Mandell Creighton*. 2 vols. London, 1904.

DÖLLINGER, JOHANN IGNAZ VON. *Declarations and Letters on the Vatican Decrees*. Edited by F. H. Reusch. Edinburgh, 1891.
'Döllinger', *Catholic Encyclopedia*. Vol. V.
'Döllinger and the Temporal Power of the Popes', *Dublin Review*, L (1861), 195–234.
'Döllinger on the Temporal Power', *Edinburgh Review*, CXVI (1862), 261–93.

DREW, MRS. MARY (GLADSTONE). *Acton, Gladstone and Others*. London, 1924.
Her Diaries and Letters. Edited by Lucy Masterman. London, 1930.
Lord Acton's Legacy to Liberals', *Optimist*, III (1908), 34–9.

ELLIOT, ARTHUR D. *Life of George Joachim Goschen, 1st Viscount Goschen*. 2 vols. London, 1911.

ENGEL-JANOSI, FREDERIC. 'The Correspondence Between Lord Acton and Bishop Creighton', *Cambridge Historical Journal*, VI (1940), 307–21.
'Reflections of Lord Acton on Historical Principles', *Catholic Historical Review* (Lancaster), XXVII (1941), 166–85.
'Some Notes on Lord Acton Suggested by a Recent Book', ibid., XXIX (1943), 357–61.

FALLOUX, FRÉDÉRIC ALFRED PIERRE, COMTE DE. *Memoirs*. Edited by C. B. Pitman. 2 vols. London, 1888.

FIGGIS, J. N. 'Acton', *Dictionary of National Biography*. 2d supplement.
Churches in the Modern State. London, 1914.

FINER, HERMAN. 'Acton as Historian and Political Scientist', *Journal of Politics*, X (1948), 603–35.

FISHER, H. A. L. *James Bryce*. 2 vols. London, 1927.
'Lord Acton's Lectures', *Independent Review*, XI (1906), 224–8.
Studies in History and Politics. Oxford, 1920.

FITZGERALD, PERCY H. *Fifty Years of Catholic Life and Progress*. 2 vols. London, 1901.

FITZMAURICE, EDMOND. *Life of Granville George Leveson Gower, 2nd Earl Granville*. 2 vols. London, 1905.

FREEMAN, D. S. *Robert E. Lee*. 4 vols. New York, 1935.

FRIEDRICH, JOHANN. *Geschichte des vatikanischen Konzils*. 3 vols. Bonn, 1877.
Ignaz von Döllinger. 3 vols. Munich, 1901.
'Römische Briefe über das Konzil', *Revue internationale de théologie*, XI (1903), 621–8.

GIBBON, EDWARD. *Memoirs of My Life and Writings*. Edited by Lord Sheffield. London, 1907.

GILLOW, JOSEPH (ED.). *Bibliographical Dictionary of the English Catholics*. 5 vols. London, 1885–95.

GLADSTONE, WILLIAM EWART. 'Robert Elsmere: the Battle of Belief', *Nineteenth Century*, XXIII (1888), 766–88.

GLADSTONE, WILLIAM EWART, AND SCHAFF, PHILIP. *The Vatican Decrees in Their Bearing on Civil Allegiance; a Political Expostulation*. London, 1874.

GOOCH, G. P. *History and Historians in the Nineteenth Century*. London, 1913.

GOWER, F. LEVESON. *Bygone Years*. London, 1905.

GOWER, GEORGE LEVESON. *Years of Endeavour*. London, 1942.

GOYAU, GEORGES. *L'Allemagne religieuse; le Catholicisme*. 4 vols. Paris, 1905–9.

GRANT DUFF, MOUNTSTUART E. 'Lord Acton's Letters', *Nineteenth Century and After*, LV (1904), 765–75.
Notes from a Diary. 14 vols. London, 1851–1901.
Out of the Past. 2 vols. London, 1903.

GRANVILLE, HARRIET. *The Letters of Harriet, Countess Granville*. Edited by F. Leveson Gower. 2 vols. London, 1894.

GREGOROVIUS, FERDINAND. *Roman Journals, 1852–74*. Edited by F. Althaus. Translated by G. W. Hamilton. London, 1911.

Greville Memoirs. Edited by Lytton Strachey and Roger Fulford. 8 vols. London, 1938.

GWYNN, DENIS. *A Hundred Years of Catholic Emancipation*. London, 1929.
Lord Shrewsbury, Pugin and the Catholic Revival. London, 1946.

GWYNN, STEPHEN, AND TUCKWELL, GERTRUDE M. *Life of the Right Hon. Sir Charles W. Dilke*. 2 vols. London, 1917.

HANSARD. *Parliamentary Debates* (3rd series). Vols. CLVIII–CLXVI (1860–2).

HASHAGEN, JUSTUS. 'Leo', *Encyclopaedia Britannica*.

HENDRICK, BURTON J. *Life of Andrew Carnegie*. 2 vols. London, 1933.

HERGENRÖTHER, JOSEPH VON. *Anti-Janus*. Translated by J. B. Robertson. Dublin, 1870.

HIMMELFARB, GERTRUDE. 'The American Revolution in the Political Theory of Lord Acton', *Journal of Modern History*, XXI (1949), 293–312.

Historisch-politische Blätter für das katholische Deutschland. Munich, 1838–1923.

HONE, JOSEPH. *W. B. Yeats*. London, 1943.

HÜGEL, FRIEDRICH VON. *Selected Letters, 1896–1924*. Edited by Bernard Holland. London, 1927.

HUTTON, ARTHUR W. 'Personal Reminiscences of Cardinal Newman', *Expositor* (4th series), II (1890), 223–40, 304–20, 336–48.

HUXLEY, LEONARD. *Life and Letters of Thomas Huxley*. 3 vols. London, 1903.

HUXLEY, THOMAS H. *Evolution and Ethics*. London, 1894.

JANUS (pseud.). *The Pope and the Council*. London, 1869.

JÖRG, EDMUND. 'Döllinger', *Historisch-politische Blätter*, CV (1890), 237–48, 248–62.

KENRICK, PETER RICHARD. *An Inside View of the Vatican Council*. Edited by Leonard W. Bacon. New York, 1872.

KIRK, JOHN. *Biographies of English Catholics in the Eighteenth Century.* Edited by J. H. Pollen and E. Burton. London, 1909.

KNAPLUND, PAUL. *Letters from the Berlin Embassy, 1871–4, 1880–5.* Annual Report of the American Historical Association, Vol. II, Washington, 1942.

KOBELL, LOUISE VON. *Conversations of Dr. Döllinger.* London, 1892.

LALLY, FRANK EDWARD. *As Lord Acton Says.* Newport (Rhode Island), 1942.

LAVELEYE, EMILE DE. *Le Gouvernement dans la démocratie.* 2 vols. Paris, 1891.

LEA, HENRY CHARLES. *Minor Historical Writings and Other Essays.* Edited by A. C. Howland. Oxford, 1943.

LECKY, ELIZABETH. *A Memoir of the Right Hon. William Edward Hartpole Lecky.* London, 1909.

LESLIE, SHANE. *Henry Edward Manning.* London, 1921.

Letters of the Empress Frederick. Edited by Frederick Ponsonby. London, 1908.

LOW, D. M. *Edward Gibbon.* London, 1937.

MACCAFFREY, JAMES. *History of the Catholic Church in the Nineteenth Century.* 2 vols. Dublin, 1910.

MAINE, HENRY SUMNER. *Popular Government.* London, 1918.

MAITLAND, FREDERIC WILLIAM. *Collected Papers.* Edited by H. A. L. Fisher. 3 vols. Cambridge, 1911.

MANNING, HENRY EDWARD. *Caesarism and Ultramontanism.* London, 1874. 'The True Story of the Vatican Council', *Nineteenth Century,* I (1877), 122–40, 177–97, 479–503, 596–610, 790–808.

MATHEW, DAVID. *Acton: the Formative Years.* London, 1946. *Catholicism in England, 1535–1935.* London, 1936.

MEYER, BERNHARD von. *Erlebnisse.* 2 vols. Vienna, 1875.

MEYRICK, Frederick. *Memoirs of Life at Oxford, and Experiences in Italy, Greece, Turkey, Germany, Spain and Elsewhere.* London, 1905.

MILL, JOHN STUART. *Dissertations and Discussions.* 5 vols. London, 1875. *Three Essays on Religion.* London, 1874. *Utilitarianism, Liberty and Representative Government.* London, 1871.

MONKSWELL, MARY. *A Victorian Diarist.* Edited by E. C. F. Collier. London, 1944.

MORGAN, JOHN H. *John Viscount Morley.* London, 1924.

MORLEY, JOHN. *Critical Miscellanies.* 4 vols. London, 1904. *Life of William Ewart Gladstone.* 3 vols. London, 1903. *Recollections.* 2 vols. London, 1917.

MOZLEY, THOMAS. *Letters from Rome on the Occasion of the Oecumenical Council.* 2 vols. London, 1891.

MURRAY, ROBERT H. *Studies in the English Social and Political Thinkers of the Nineteenth Century.* 2 vols. Cambridge, 1929.

NEWMAN, JOHN HENRY. *Essay on the Development of Christian Doctrine.* Edited by Charles F. Harrold. New York, 1949.
Letter to the Duke of Norfolk. London, 1875.
Letters and Correspondence. Edited by Anne Mozley. 2 vols. London, 1891.
NIELSEN, FREDERICK. *History of the Papacy in the Nineteenth Century.* 2 vols. London, 1906.
NOACK, ULRICH. *Geschichtswissenschaft und Wahrheit.* Frankfort, 1935.
Katholizität und Geistesfreiheit. Frankfort, 1936.
Politik als Sicherung der Freiheit. Frankfort, 1947.
PAGET, JAMES. *Memoirs and Letters.* Edited by Stephen Paget. London, 1901.
PETRE, M. D. *Life of George Tyrrell.* 2 vols. London, 1912.
Von Hügel and Tyrrell. London, 1937.
PHILLIPPS, L. M. *Europe Unbound.* London, 1916.
PLUMMER, ALFRED. 'Recollections of Dr. Döllinger', *Expositor* (4th series), I (1890), 212–25, 270–84, 422–35.
POLLOCK, JOHN. 'Lord Acton at Cambridge', *Independent Review,* II (1904), 360–78.
POOLE, R. L. 'John Emerich, Lord Acton', *English Historical Review,* XVII (1902), 692–9.
PURCELL, E. S. *Life of Cardinal Manning.* 2 vols. London, 1896.
QUIRINUS (pseud.). *Letters from Rome on the Council.* London, 1870.
RENAN, ERNEST. *Recollections of My Youth.* Edited by G. G. COULTON. London, 1929.
RENDEL, STUART. *Personal Papers.* London, 1931.
ROSKELL, M. F. *Memoirs of Francis Kerril Amherst.* London, 1903.
RUSKIN, JOHN *Modern Painters.* London, 1867.
RUSSELL, GEORGE W. E. *Portraits of the Seventies.* London, 1916.
Saturday Review (London). Vols. XII–XV (1861–3), LXXIX (1895).
SCHAFF, PHILIP. *Creeds of Christendom.* 3 vols. New York, 1919.
SCHULTE, JOHANN FRIEDRICH VON. *Der Altkatholicismus.* Giessen, 1887.
Lebenserinnerungen. Giessen, 1908.
SHAW, W. A. *A Bibliography of the Historical Works of Dr. Creighton. . . . Dr. Stubbs, Dr. S. R. Gardiner and the late Lord Acton.* London, 1903.
SHORTER, CLEMENT. 'Lord Acton's Hundred Best Books', *Pall Mall Magazine,* XXXVI (1905), 3–10.
SMITH, R. A. L. *Collected Papers.* London, 1947.
SNEAD-COX, J. G. *Life of Cardinal Vaughan.* 2 vols. London, 1910.
Somers Tracts (2nd series). 4 vols. London, 1750.
Spectator, LXXIV (1895).
STRACHEY, LYTTON. *Eminent Victorians.* London, 1929.
SULLIVAN, WILLIAM K. *University Education in Ireland; a Letter to Sir John Dalberg Acton.* Dublin, 1866.
Tablet. Vol. CVII (1906).
TEDDER, H. L. 'Lord Acton as a Book Collector', *Proceedings of the British Academy,* I (1903–4), 285–8.

TEMPERLEY, HAROLD. 'Lord Acton on the Origins of the War of 1870, with Some Unpublished Letters from the British and Viennese Archives', *Cambridge Historical Journal*, II (1926), 68–82.

THEODORUS (pseud.). *New Reformation*. London, 1875.

THORNELY, THOMAS. *Cambridge Memories*. London, 1936.

THUREAU-DANGIN, PAUL. *English Catholic Revival in the Nineteenth Century*. Translated by Wilfrid Wilberforce. 2 vols. London, 1914.

THURSTON, HERBERT. 'The Late Lord Acton', *Catholic World*, LXXXIV (1906), 357–72.

Times (London). Obituary of Acton. 20 June 1902.

TOYNBEE, ARNOLD J. *A Study of History*. 6 vols. London, 1934.

TREVELYAN, G. M. *An Autobiography and Other Essays*. London, 1949.
    The Present Position of History. Cambridge (England), 1927.

ULLATHORNE, WILLIAM BERNARD. *A Letter on the 'Rambler' and the 'Home and Foreign Review'*. London, 1862.

WALLACE, LILLIAN PARKER. *The Papacy and European Diplomacy*. Chapel Hill (N. C.), 1948.

WARD, BERNARD. *The Sequel to Catholic Emancipation*. 2 vols. London, 1915.

WARD, MAISIE. *The Wilfrid Wards and the Transition*. London, 1934.

WARD, WILFRID. *Life of John Henry Cardinal Newman*. 2 vols. London, 1912.
    Life and Times of Cardinal Wiseman. 2 vols. London, 1897.
    William George Ward and the Catholic Revival. London, 1893.

WHITE, ANDREW DICKSON. *Autobiography*. 2 vols. London, 1905.

WISEMAN, NICHOLAS. *Reply of his Eminence Cardinal Wiseman to an Address Presented by the Clergy Secular and Regular of the Archdiocese of Westminster*. London, 1862.

WOODWARD, E. L. 'The Place of Lord Acton in the Liberal Movement of the Nineteenth Century', *Politica*, IV (1939), 248–65.

YOUNG, URBAN. *Life of Father Ignatius Spencer*. London, 1933.

ZIRNGIEBL, EBERHARD. *Johannes Huber*. Gotha, 1881.

INDEX

INDEX